Reverend Joseph Tarkington,
Methodist Circuit Rider

&

Reverend Joseph Tarkington, Methodist Circuit Rider

FROM FRONTIER EVANGELISM TO REFINED RELIGION

David L. Kimbrough

With a Foreword by
Wilma Dykeman

THE UNIVERSITY OF TENNESSEE PRESS / KNOXVILLE

Library of Congress Cataloging-in-Publication Data

Kimbrough, David L., 1951–
Reverend Joseph Tarkington : Methodist circuit rider : from
frontier evangelism to refined religion / David L. Kimbrough; with
a foreword by Wilma Dykeman. —1st ed.
p. cm.
Includes bibliographical references and index.
ISBN 0-87049-979-3 (cloth: alk. paper)
1. Tarkington, Joseph, 1800–1891. 2. Methodist Church—Indiana—
Clergy—Biography. 3. Tarkington family. I. Title.
BX8495.T23K56 1997
287'.6'092—dc21
[B]   96-51234
                                              CIP

To Mom and Dad
Bill and Jane Kimbrough

Contents

Illustrations

Foreword

Sometimes the life of an individual or a family is so joined with the history of a place, a movement, or an era that their stories are inseparable. This symbiotic relationship is central to David Kimbrough's account of the Tarkingtons of Indiana.

In the summer of 1977, Kimbrough discovered in the woods near his home a graveyard. On stones shaded by tall old trees, he found the name "Tarkington," familiar in the cultural, religious, and economic past and present of his state. Prompted by memories of Booth Tarkington's literary renown and his own curiosity as a historian, Kimbrough began extensive research that resulted in this valuable book.

Its story centers around the life of Joseph Tarkington, whose work and influence as a Methodist minister spanned the nineteenth century and whose ancestors traveled the long route from England to Maryland (where a son, now nameless, was "stolen by Indians" and "never heard of again"), to North Carolina (where the Episcopalian church to which the Tarkington family belonged was looked on with suspicion immediately after the Revolutionary War), to Tennessee (where an earthquake literally shook the earth even as the Great Revival shook frontier religion to its roots), and finally, while Joseph was a youth, to Indiana (after the family had refused moving to economically booming Alabama, because it chose to "go where there were no slaves").

Against this background, the author follows Joseph's rise as a Methodist minister, a man of influence and affluence who "represents a collective character" of Indiana's early Methodist circuit riders. Kimbrough believes that much of the history of Methodism has been neglected. Exploration of these areas brings a necessary scholarly dimension to Joseph Tarkington's biography.

Issues of national concern posed challenges he did not avoid. Among these were slavery, women's rights, temperance, political leadership, education, church simplicity versus elaborate surroundings and rituals.

Fortunately, scholarly matters do not overwhelm Joseph's individuality. His character emerges in details of daily life set forth in an inimitable resource Kimbrough had at hand. Joseph Tarkington's autobiography was published in 1899, eight years after his death. Descriptions of his family's laborious move to Indiana, of his harrowing wedding journey with his remarkable bride, Maria Slawson, and a full measure of illness and grief sustained by irrepressible hope and faith, are sharp and vivid.

Here, then, is a unique story firmly placed in a universal context of religious history during a century of America's great social change. It is an important work.

Wilma Dykeman

Preface

I became interested in the Rev. Joseph Tarkington and the Methodists by accident. In August of 1977, I settled on a small farm near Stanford, Indiana. Stanford is located approximately eight miles from Bloomington, the site of Indiana University. Shortly after the move to my new home, I found an old graveyard situated in the woods within three hundred yards of my house. It could hardly be seen because of the huge trees that surrounded it. The burial ground is known as the Keller Cemetery. The names found there include Harmon, Gardner, Freese, Meredith, Whaley, Smith, Reeves, Trabue, and Tarkington.

When I showed my father the cemetery he remarked, "I bet those Tarkingtons are some of ol' Booth's people." My father's comment aroused my curiosity, and I found that the Tarkingtons buried in Keller Cemetery are in fact Hoosier author Booth Tarkington's great-grandparents. In 1817 Jesse and Mary ("Polly") Tarkington were the first white people to settle on my farm. Indiana had become a state the year before.

Other than the fact that he had lived on my farm, what attracted me to Joseph Tarkington was that he had been a Methodist circuit rider who traveled throughout most of southern Indiana during the nineteenth century. Tarkington joined the Methodists when the church was virtually a sect. During Tarkington's lifetime the Methodists passed from being a sect to becoming a denomination.

As Methodist scholar Russell E. Ritchey claims, early Methodism had an "Edenic quality" about it, but as the nineteenth century progressed the movement lost its innocence.[1] As the Methodists became denominational they became more liturgical, implementing rituals and practices and displaying characteristics that were unheard of in earlier years. Methodism lost its communal and spiritual character as cultural alienation gave way to a pilgrimage toward respectability.[2] By the mid-nineteenth century, the emotional preaching found in the camp meetings had passed to refined sermons delivered by educated preachers. Ornate and elaborate churches replaced the old meeting houses where preachers such as Joseph Tarkington were so successful in gaining converts.

I must agree with Nathan O. Hatch that little attention has been given to the Methodists in historical scholarship. Few people know anything about this faith. Hatch states that "perhaps historians ignore Methodists because Wesleyans are too quintessentially American." However, Methodism has been the most powerful religious movement in American history, "and it appeared at the most crucial juncture in our history." Other than England's E. P. Thompson, scholars of Methodism have not reached the stature of scholars of Puritanism, like Perry Miller, Edmund Morgan, or David Hall. Nevertheless, Hatch adds that if "American religion is anything writ large, it springs from a Methodist rather than a Puritan kernel."[3]

Methodism boomed in the United States following the American Revolution because of its simplicity and appeal to the common man. As Donald Matthews found, the Methodists "gained sufficient momentum to become a major force in shaping the antebellum United States." In 1776 the Methodist Church claimed 2.5 percent of all religious adherents in the nation, and by 1850 the number had risen to 34.2 percent, a total that represented the largest denomination in the United States.[4] To explain the Methodists' triumph over the other churches in gaining members, Elizabeth K. Nottingham stated that "its salient characteristics were the itinerancy with its circuit riders, the class meeting, and a strongly centralized administration which functioned through annual conferences of the preachers."[5]

Early Methodism was a pietistic movement that rebelled against the highly liturgical and ritualistic churches found among Anglicans and other highly formalized churches of the East. American pietism was grounded in the "protest of Protestantism against the ecclesiastical corruptions of the Christian church in the sixteenth century."[6] The Methodists, as Richard Jensen found among the pietistic groups in general, "had little respect for elaborated ceremonies, vestments, saints, devotions, and frequently opposed organ music in church. Theologically the key to pietism was the conviction (called Arminianism) that all men can be saved by direct confrontation with Christ (not with the Church) through the conversion experience."[7]

In the southern Indiana pioneer period, class boundaries were not easily recognizable. If families enjoyed wealth they were generally found among the ranks of the Presbyterian Church. However, by the mid-nineteenth century a socially and politically elite group had emerged that was identified in the Methodist Church. In many respects the Methodist Church fostered social mobility; preachers used the ministry as a means of social uplifting. Joseph Tarkington was very successful in using the ministry as a way to gain affluence.

Tarkington was not a unique preacher on the Indiana frontier; many preachers experienced the trials and tribulations that Tarkington did. However, he represents the collective character of the Indiana Methodist itinerants. Allen Wiley, Tarkington's longtime friend, supervisor, and the preacher that married him to his wife, Maria, praised the circuit rider:

> Look here, boys, and see a young man who received sixty-two and a half cents at the first quarterly meeting, and only fourteen dollars in the whole year partly money and partly clothing, and who had to stop in the woods among the brush to mend his own clothes. . . Tarkington is still in the work, and with medium preaching talents has been able to sustain himself well in all the charges where he had labored, whether circuits, or stations, or district. The secret of his great acceptability and usefulness is to be found in his faithful pastoral work, in which he greatly delights; and he must have a very sluggish and lukewarm helper, if he does not make him a good pastor. His colleague this year on Rushville was William Evans, mentioned before in connection with Wayne and Connersville circuits. These brethren were young and vigorous, and travelled this heavy, muddy circuit with industry and the Head of the Church gave them favor in the eyes of the people, and success in their work; and the circuit increased one hundred and fourteen. The last quarterly meeting was an excellent camp meeting, at which many souls were converted and reclaimed.[8]

The only record of Joseph Tarkington's early life is his autobiography, which was published in 1899, eight years after his death. There is no reason to doubt the accuracy of the narrative, because of Tarkington's apparent modesty and because, in any case, we have no other or better source than Joseph himself. Joseph kept a diary of his final four years of life (1888–91). However, the 1890 diary is missing. Letters and records of Maria Slawson Tarkington's family survive in the Indiana Historical Society at Indianapolis. James Welch of Vevay,

Indiana, and Russell Manuel of Colorado also provided Slawson family letters and other forms of public history. The Firestone Library at Princeton University houses the Booth Tarkington Collection, which contains some early Tarkington family history and DePauw University is rich with materials on early Indiana Methodism.

The nineteenth-century Protestant worldview as represented by the Methodists penetrated virtually every area of American culture.[9] It is through the life of Joseph Tarkington that I tell the story of Methodism in Indiana. Tarkington's story is unique in that his lifetime spanned the entire nineteenth century, and most studies of Methodism do not cover the entire period. The introduction traces the rise of Methodism following the American Revolution and illustrates how the church capitalized on a "free market" religious economy. Chapter 1 introduces Joseph Tarkington and analyzes his birth and childhood. Many of Tarkington's religious convictions were developed during this period. Chapter 2 charts the development of Methodism in pioneer Indiana and shows how the church withstood calamities such as Indian attacks. Chapter 3 covers the Tarkington family's move to the Indiana frontier and to the farm at Stanford, Indiana, where Joseph grew into manhood and where his religious beliefs crystallized. While living in Tennessee, he developed a hatred of drinking, dancing, and "frivolity of all sorts." Joseph was exposed to the highly emotional religious style of the Methodists in Tennessee when a Reverend Pope preached in the area where he was living. At a multidenominational camp meeting near Bloomington, Indiana, in 1820, Joseph experience conversion. After wrestling with various denominational doctrines, Joseph finally joined the Methodists on June 10, 1821, at a church meeting being conducted at the home of a neighbor. Tarkington then played the roles of class leader and exhorter before joining the ministry in the fall of 1824.

Chapter 4 begins with Tarkington launching his preaching career in the old Missouri Conference on the Boonville Circuit by assisting the Rev. Orcenath Fisher. His first year's pay was nine dollars and a pair of trousers. In many places Joseph actually formed classes after preaching in private homes. Virtually nothing could stop Joseph from making his appointments. Throughout his preaching career, Tarkington only missed one conference meeting.

Chapter 5 describes Joseph's marriage to Maria Slawson at her father's home near Vevay, Indiana. Thereafter, Joseph and Maria became "people on the rise." Throughout his life, Joseph was an avid reader and was demanding of his children. Joseph used the ministry to raise himself above the modest means of farming that generations of his ancestors had repeated over and over.

The next three chapters illustrate Joseph's rise from a simple circuit rider to a respectable preacher and covers the Methodists' move from old-time religion to a more affluent condition. In chapter 9 the effect of the Civil War and issues such as slavery are presented. The final chapter covers Joseph and Maria's final years. Tarkington's rise in position during his life had a profound impact on his family. A two-time Pulitzer Prize winner and the Indiana state flag are only two of the gifts that Tarkington's line has given to the Hoosier state. There is little that the Tarkingtons have not influenced in Indiana, and few other states have had a family that compares to them. They are affluent, but their prosperity is of recent origin. Their fame and fortune was gained during the latter part of the nineteenth century as the Hoosier state reached maturity.

This work is an attempt to explain and reveal the history of this remarkable family and its contributions to an important movement in nineteenth-century America, providing a window into the cultural, social, and religious history of the period. This work is not the final word on Methodism, as there are still mountains to be uncovered. I hope that it fosters historical scholarship and additional research into a highly neglected chapter of United States history.

Acknowledgments

I received valuable assistance from many people and in many ways. My mentor
and close friend, Prof. Paul Lucas, read the manuscript and made many valuable suggestions. Even though I long ago departed graduate school, he makes
himself available for help any time I need him. I cannot express how valuable
he has been to me. I also would like to thank Professors George Juergens, Larry
Friedman, and Jim Madison for their encouragement. Bill Leonard of Wake
Forest made many valuable suggestions, as did Deborah Vansau McCauley, who
is perhaps the best young scholar of religion in the country. Even though they
were often strongly critical, both Leonard and McCauley's friendships are price-
less to me.

Numerous librarians and libraries deserve thanks. The staffs at Princeton
University and the Cincinnati Historical Society were very helpful. Assistance
from county libraries, such as those in Monroe, Decatur, and Switzerland Counties, is appreciated. My good friend Clay Housholder always comes through for
me when I am producing a manuscript; this work was no exception. In looking
for reference materials that I requested, I am confident that he completely exhausted every source in helping me. I have never seen a reference librarian
who is comparable.

Of course, my alma mater, the University of Mary Hardin-Baylor, with
Professors William Harlow and P. K. Anderson, is my favorite college, but
DePauw University runs a close second. Wes Wilson and his staff, Joan Stevens,

John Riggs, and Beth Goodman, are simply fantastic people who provided a great service for this work. The Indiana Historical society was also helpful, and I would like to give special thanks to Susan Sutton, Bruce Johnson, Alexandra Gressitt, and my good buddy Wilma Gibbs.

There are many other individuals to thank, including Jackie Mendenhall, who helped me in various ways in Decatur County, Indiana, where the Tarkington spent the last forty years of their lives. Diana Davis of the Decatur County Clerk's Office helped me find Joseph and Maria Tarkington's wills. Likewise, there are many people in Bloomington, Indiana, to thank. My good friend Robert Royer, C.P.A, came through again in helping me reproduce some of the pictures used in the text. I appreciated F. G. Summitt's interest in the project and all of the people at Kalina's Korner, the newest, best coffee shop in town.

R. W. Manuel was very kind and trusting to send me his valuable Slawson Family Papers from Colorado. I cannot express the gratitude I feel toward Jim Welch and his family of Vevay, Indiana, for sharing their Welch family collection along with feeding me every time I was in Switzerland County. Mrs. Johanna Welch is one of the kindest people that I have ever met. R. D. and Cathy Slawson of Vevay were also very helpful and generous people who have become close friends.

The Tarkington family of Indianapolis is too large, unfortunately, to thank everyone individually. All of them have given me some form of aid for this project. A special thanks is given to Mr. Brent Moore. He never leaves me out of any family event, including the family's large Christmas Eve party. He is also a walking Tarkington family historian. The three people whom I want to thank most for their many contributions to this work are direct descendants of Joseph and Maria Tarkington: Patricia Cochran, Barbara Werbe, and Jeanette Stokely have given me time and help that I cherish. The four of us have traveled to many historic places together. Patricia Cochran (a descendant of John Tarkington) has simply given me more than I could ever repay. She has invited me into her home many times and has honored me in various other ways. I certainly appreciate the photos and other materials that she has given me. Barbara Werbe (a descendant of Martha Stewart) has also given much to this project. She has also become one of my best friends.

Jeanette Tarkington Stokely (a descendant of Joseph Asbury Tarkington), the wife of Alfred Stokely of Stokely Van Camp fame, has become one of my best friends. We have spent many hours going over Tarkington family history and Indiana history. The Stokelys are among the most impressive families that I have ever met. Tarkington family members continue to excel at everything they do. Louise Tarkington Smith (a descendant of Joseph Asbury Tarkington) of Morrow, Ohio, is a walking history book and the mother of the famous David Tarkington Smith, one of the most noted furniture builders in the world.

I would also like to thank Jennifer Siler, Kim Scarbrough, Scot Danforth, and Kay Jursik at the University of Tennessee Press and Jean Tyrone for making this work possible. However, there is no one at the press I appreciate more than Meredith Morris-Babb. I have never worked with anyone like her.

Finally, there is no one that I would like to thank more than my wife, Elizabeth Kay Kimbrough. It would be impossible for me to tell all of the ways she helps me on my projects and the tremendous sacrifices she constantly makes. In my eyes, Kay is the greatest.

On November 18, 1996, a tragedy struck that hurt worse than anything that I had suffered in the past. Professor Paul Lucas died from a heart-attack at the age of fifty-six. I will never be able to replace him. He was one of the few people in this world that gave me a chance. I hope I did one little thing to make him proud, because he is totally responsible for anything that I have accomplished. Professor Lucas was one of the brightest and best teachers that I have ever encountered. One wonders how someone like him could be taken from this world when he had done so much good and had so much left to do. Regardless, out of love and appreciation for Paul R. Lucas I dedicate the rest of my scholarly life to his memory.

Introduction

In his famous work *The Circuit Rider: A Tale of the Heroic Age,* Hoosier author Edward Eggleston commented that "Methodism was to the West all that Puritanism was to New England."[1] At the close of the eighteenth century and the opening of the nineteenth, Methodism was gaining a stronghold in America as one of the paramount faiths of the time. By 1830, Nathan O. Hatch claims that Methodism held five hundred thousand members nationally.[2] Sociologists Roger Finke and Rodney Stark state that in "1776 the Methodists were a tiny religious society nominally connected to the Church of England and had only 65 churches scattered through the colonies. Seven decades later they towered over the nation. With 13,302 congregations enrolling more than 2.6 million members, Methodism was the largest single denomination, accounting for more than a third of all American church members."[3] The primary cause for the boom in Methodism was that, in America, there was no single established church; in contrast, for example, in England civil government and Anglicans working together were successful in suppressing dissenting rival sects. Nathan O. Hatch adds:

> America's nonrestrictive environment permitted an unexpected and often explosive conjunction of evangelical fervor and popular sovereignty. It was this engine that accelerated the process of Christianization within American popular culture, allowing indigenous expressions of faith to take hold among ordinary people, white

and black. . . . The rise of evangelical Christianity in the early republic is, in some measure, a story of the success of common people in shaping the culture after their own priorities rather than the priorities outlined by gentlemen such as the framers of the Constitution. . . . These groups also shared with the Jeffersonian Republicans an overt rejection of the past as a repository of wisdom.[4]

Finally, Hatch sees the boom in evangelical sects as a cultural shift or class struggle, not as a "clash of intellectual and theological differences" but as a "passionate social struggle with power and authority." The evangelicals "assumed that the leveling of aristocracy, root and branch, would naturally draw people together in harmony and equality. In this way, religious movements eager to preserve the supernatural in everyday life had the ironic effect of accelerating the break-up of traditional society and advent of a social order of competition, self-expression, and free-enterprise."[5]

Following the American Revolution came the rise of a free market religious economy, or the conception of free market competition between churches. The Methodist Church in pioneer Indiana was one of the first and most successful evangelical denominations in gaining converts to its creed. R. Carlyle Buley comments that "this feature came about through the system of itinerancy."[6] As the frontier border thrust westward, Methodism was but one stride behind the settlers. Ministers of most denominations waited for the people to call them to their areas to preach. However, the Methodist circuit riders preached *ad populum*: they took their message to the people. Many of the preachers were lay members who had risen from the ranks of certain congregations.[7] Most of the "early itinerants literally lived with the people to whom they preached."[8] The Methodists made their greatest gains where clergy were in short supply, as opposed to denominations such as the Congregationalists, who "retained their greatest strength in the most settled areas where the highest proportion of the residents had been born in-state."[9] The Methodist circuit riders were truly the traveling salesmen of the eighteenth century.

The Methodist power structure divided the settled regions of America into conferences. Within each conference there were generally five to ten districts. Each district had a presiding elder "appointed to it on a yearly basis." Charles C. Cole Jr. describes the duties of the presiding elder as "traveling the circuits, preaching, counseling the circuit riders and local preachers, conducting quarterly meetings, and attending other events to advance the cause of the church."[10] The districts were separated into circuits. Circuits comprised local societies, which were made up of classes. According to John H. Wigger, all members of a local church were "required to attend a weekly 'class meeting' where their spiritual lives and temporal dealings were open to examination by the class leader and the preacher."[11]

The successive ranks, or order, of the ministry consisted of bishops, elders, and deacons. Bishops were elected by the General Conference, which met every four years. The General Conference "was the supreme governing body," which received elected delegates from the annual conferences.[12] This hierarchical organization was one of the primary reasons the Methodists were so successful in gaining converts on the frontier. However, the hierarchy must be understood from the bottom up. Control of the church rested solely in the hands of the laity. The Congregationalists and several other churches were hierarchical, but their hierarchies tended to concentrate control at the top of the hierarchy and their influence waned. The Methodists, on the other hand, were bound by local regulation. For example, the classes, those on the lowest rung of the ladder, chose their class leaders and exhorters and eventually the circuit rider.[13]

Of all the religious workers in early Indiana, the circuit riders were the best known. Buley adds that their scriptures were learned from "Brush College" rather than "eastern colleges and theological seminaries."[14] What these men had grasped from experience on the frontier and from the Bible was supplemented by the *Discipline* and *Wesley's Sermons*.[15] Very few of the circuit riders had a formal education, but, as Finke and Stark found, "Genteel social origins, combined with advanced levels of education, often increased the social distance between the minister and many of his congregants. . . . The highly educated minister might have enhanced the 'respectability' of religion, but he did little to gather the flock."[16] The famous Methodist itinerant Peter Cartwright "estimated that at the General Conference of 1844 fewer than 50 (of approximately 4,282 travelling ministers) 'had more than a common english education [grade school], and scores of them not that.'"[17] Instruction "in the duties of a pastor" were also included in the *Minutes* and various *Rules*.[18] Cole states that Peter Cartwright's attitude toward educated ministers was typical of his generation. Cartwright wrote: "A Methodist preacher in those days, when he felt that God had called him to preach, instead of hunting up a college or Biblical institute, hunted up a hard pony of a horse, and some traveling apparatus, and with his library always at hand, namely Bible, Hymn Book, and Discipline, he started." Ohio circuit rider James B. Finley expressed a similar opinion: "larnin isn't religion, and eddication don't give a man the power of the spirit. . . . St. Peter was a fisherman—do you think he ever went to Yale College?"[19]

On the Indiana frontier God was experienced as well as taught, and the Methodist itinerants were ordinary men who could relate their "trials, experiences, travels, persecutions, sorrows, and joys" to a people who had similar lifestyles.[20] A preacher relied on divine inspiration to preach, and his delivery style was "entirely extemporaneous very loud and animated."[21] Written sermons were not acceptable.

The Methodists did not have the largest religious body among the first settlers in nineteenth-century Indiana. Their numbers were probably exceeded by both the Baptists and New Lights (a Presbyterian group).[22] Other Presbyterians were also present, but L. C. Rudolph claims that their progress was "disappointingly slow." Small congregations met at "Vincennes (1806), Charlestown (1807 and again in 1812), Washington (1814), and Madison (1815)."[23] The Synod of Indiana was not erected by the Presbyterian General Assembly until 1826.[24]

The Baptists were by no means a unified movement. They had splintered into Separates and Regulars. Some rejoined and became "United Baptists." There were also various "Free-Will" groups.[25] These groups were constantly splitting over various issues. R. Carlyle Buley comments:

> Although revivalism and the question of freedom of the will precipitated sectarian difference, there were really dozens of matters of dogma and church organization and government which caused fission. Denominations split along one line on one issue, along another line on another. So numerous and complex were the schisms and crossings over and so illogical were many of them, that groups and sects not infrequently found themselves back in the fold whence they had started. So confusing did the history of the Protestant sects become that no historian, church or lay, has been able to make a clear and organized presentation of its course.[26]

Around 1800, a series of revivals were launched, known as the "Great Revival." These revivals were not "spontaneous outbreaks," as many scholars contend. They were well-planned events used to gain large numbers of converts. Often, signs were posted along roads advertising upcoming camp meetings. Camp meeting grounds were well prepared "with tents in regular street order."[27]

These revivals doubled the membership of the Methodists' Western Conference and increased the "number of both local and traveling preachers."[28] The leader of the revival movement across the Ohio River in Kentucky was a Presbyterian minister named James McGready, who had come from North

Carolina. During this period McGready was serving three churches jointly: the Gasper River Church, Muddy River Church, and Red River Church. Walter Brownlow Posey states: "McGready's diligent effort to revive the spiritual temper of his people began to produce striking results. An actual movement of awakening was distinctly noticeable by the spring of 1799." In July of 1800, McGready conducted a four-day camp meeting on the Gasper River. Large crowds of people gathered from Tennessee and other neighboring states. Since there were few accommodations for the huge assembly of people, it was suggested that they camp at the site. Thus, the idea of camp meetings was born in Kentucky.[29]

Large displays of emotion accompanied the camp meetings. Hundreds who attended the gatherings "fell out under the power," or went into a trance, and would lie prostrate for hours and sometimes for days. To prevent them from being walked on or trampled by others who were in a highly emotional state, they were "collected in one place and laid out in order, where they were cared for and prayed over by anxious friends."[30] Elizabeth K. Nottingham asserts that "hymns would be sung for the mourners as they groaned and cried and fell about in the altar enclosure":

> Sinners through the camp are falling
> Deep distress their souls pervade
> Wondering why they are not rolling
> In the dark infernal shade.[31]

When they came out of this state of insensibility, they would start praising God and beg for his mercy and "redeeming love." Massive numbers of men and women would jerk "backward and forward with great rapidity and violence, so much so that their bodies would bend so as to bring their heads near to the floor, and the hair of the women would crack like the lash of a driver's whip."[32] This display was not confined to one particular class. All were subject to this phenomenon.[33] At a camp meeting near Maysville, Kentucky, itinerant preacher Maxwell P. Gaddis described the preaching as "attended by the power of the Holy Ghost, and hundreds were awakened and converted."[34]

The most famous of the revivals was conducted by another Presbyterian congregation in August of 1801, at Cane Ridge, Kentucky, under the leadership of Barton W. Stone. However, the gathering was interdenominational.[35] Dozens of preachers—Presbyterian, Baptist, and Methodist—"preached simultaneously from platforms, wagons, stumps, logs, and other vantage points."[36] Rev. James B. Finley of Ohio reported seeing seven ministers preaching at one time. The Rev. William Burke was "standing on a tree which had, in falling, lodged against another." Between ten and twenty thousand people gathered for the meeting. Finley, who attended the meeting, reported "twenty-five thousand." Thousands fell or were "brought to the ground" in a sea of emotionalism. Many went into ecstatic trances and began barking, jerking, screaming, or crying. Other physical exercises were also reported as God's power moved the gathering. The noise "was like the roar of Niagara."

Finley described the scene: "The scene that then presented itself to my mind was indescribable. At one time I saw at least five hundred swept down in a moment, as if a battery of a thousand guns had been opened on them, and then immediately followed shrieks and shouts that rent the very heavens. My hair rose up on my head, my whole frame trembled, the blood ran cold in my veins, . . . A sense of suffocation and blindness seemed to come over me, and I thought I was going to die."[37]

Even the most hardened drunkards, thieves, harlots, killers, and other rogues were "slain," or converted, at the revival. Scores of camp meetings followed Cane Ridge, and Methodist itinerant preachers became more involved in organizing the meetings. In most cases the meetings lasted from three to five days.

Opposition to the camp meetings was common, and the Presbyterians abandoned them because they rejected the emotionalism that the participants displayed. Loyal Calvinists within the Presbyterian Church ranks also feared that "the revivals would open the minds of Presbyterians to the doctrine of grace [Arminianism] as held by the Methodists."[38] The Methodists favored the camp meetings, and their denominations thrived as a result of them. Methodist circuit riders took their doctrines wherever they could. Circuit riders were found in revivals, taverns, and the most profane places. They did not wait for the coarser elements to come to them. When educated clergyman such as Lyman Beecher attacked common preachers, Methodist itinerants would respond as Lorenzo Dow did: "I see no gospel law that authorizes any man, or set of men, to forbid, or put up bars to hinder or stop any man from preaching the gospel."[39]

The "soberminded and judicious men of religion" claimed that the emotional displays conducted at the revivals were performed by impostors "designed to attract the giddier and rowdier elements of the population."[40] Some believed that the gatherings were the "work of the devil, who had been unchained for a season."[41] Critics also claimed that the revivals had no lasting effects. Much condemnation was found in the newspapers. In 1831, editor John R. St. John of the *Cleaveland Herald* wrote: "We have only to remark that the mind is as susceptible of disease as the body." He agreed with the eastern newspapers that an "intellectual, or rather religious *cholera morbus* was roaring among the people."[42] With regard to St. John, Buley adds: "He spoke of religious demagogues who took their followers 'to some wild woody place . . . and there, by platoons, pray and preach, and tear and astonish, and excite themselves and others into the wildest frenzies.' He minced no words in analyzing the technique of revivalism, called it a system of chicanery, and said that preachers could be as ambitious, as fallible, and as dangerous as other men."[43]

One writer at the Ravenna *Western Courier* gave an account of a man that "got delirium" at a meeting and became a "raving maniac." He added that others had died of the same.[44] The defenders of the camp meetings admitted that the revivals attracted the bad elements of society, but used this very fact as a basis for a counterargument: "Strong diseases required strong remedies; men of learning, books, and logic alone could not be relied upon to reach the roarers, snorters, and hardened blasphemers of the frontier."[45] In the year 1813, at White Brown's, on Deer Creek in Ohio, thousands gathered at one of the largest camp meetings ever held in the West. Circuit rider James B. Finley commented that many came to the camp meetings out of "idle curiosity," while others came to "curse and oppose the cause of God." Several of the skeptics and agitators ended up uniting with the faithful before the meeting closed.[46]

Camp meetings became common in pioneer Indiana in the decades following Cane Ridge and the Kentucky meetings. Camp meetings provided the opportunity for social intercourse. Most camp meetings were held in the autumn months following the harvest period. Families traveled great distances to participate in the event. People deserted their homes, "settlements were temporarily abandoned, and fields were left unworked." As travelers approached the camp meeting grounds, the entire woods seemed alive with their brothers and sisters. For late arrivals, the "road to the clearing was marked by blazing pine knots."[47] The camp's grounds were normally located close to a thoroughfare, near a river or stream, and the camp meeting was conducted deep in the woods in the shade.[48] People camped in small cotton or cloth tents and sometimes in crude, temporary cabins. Others dwelled in the wagons that they had ridden to the meeting in. Generally, a stand or platform was constructed in order that the preachers could be elevated above the crowd so they could be seen. At night the camp was lit by lanterns or blazing logs, which also provided heat on cool evenings. When a preacher arrived at the meeting, he was frequently exhausted from his journey. The night before, if he had not slept on the ground, he probably had spent the evening "in a cabin infested with bed bugs, fleas and itchy children."[49]

On the morning of a camp meeting, a trumpet was sounded, which called the meeting together. The principal event of the gathering was the sermon. In the afternoon less formal sermons were delivered by other preachers and exhorters, sometimes continuing well into the night. Some services continued until dawn.[50] Many informal and unplanned prayer meetings were also conducted. At the large camp meetings there were so many people that it was necessary to divide into groups; each group had its own preacher or exhorter. On occasion women were separated from the men.[51]

Frontier evangelical religion, especially Methodism, was a perfect example of Manichean dualism. The world was viewed as being black or white with few gray areas. A conflict between good and evil was dramatized while God and the Devil were seen as waging eternal warfare for the souls of human beings. Even those who did not attend evangelical church meetings "were the products of a Protestant upbringing or children of an evangelical culture," so this dual struggle between good and evil was a broadly disseminated cultural idea throughout the frontier.[52]

Near the end of the service the preacher would make the call for the unsaved to approach the mourner's bench. The early Methodists held that there was no hope of salvation except through conversion and regeneration. Throughout the nineteenth century the Methodists emphasized the importance of experiencing conversion by citing Matthew 18:3 to their congregations: "Verily I say unto you, Except ye be converted, and become as little children, ye shall not enter into the kingdom of heaven." The conversion experience was a vibrant and immediate transformation or reorientaion of self where a person "changed from a life of sin to one of salvation."[53] Conversion was a symbolic means of rejecting sin and being elevated into the glorified state of the saved. Insistence on an open confession of sins in the form of public testimonials was a means of breaking down personal pride and self-possession. It also reinforced egalitarian bonds of kinship, community, and social solidarity.[54] In sermons preachers would often recount their own conversion experiences to a congregation as resanctioning of the preacher's position within the community.

In some cases sinners were forcibly converted. During an 1820 camp meeting, an "unregenerate husband" dragged his newly converted wife away from the altar and threatened to confront any person who interfered. The minister first tried to reason with the man but to no avail. He then wrestled the man to the ground, "flat on his face." The pastor then sat on the back of the husband and said that he would not let him up until he prayed. The wife and others prayed ardently, and the preacher joined in. "As he prayed he felt the man's muscles relax," and the cruel and harsh husband began to weep and cry out, "God be merciful to me a sinner." Finally, the shout of victory arrived.[55]

Some refused to be converted or accept evangelical religion, even on their deathbed. The following is a tale of Greensburg's first lawyer when he was near death:

> The *Cincinnati Enquirer* several years ago told a story of James T. Brown, the first lawyer of Greensburg, who came here in the year 1822 and remained until 1838. Brown was a bachelor and humorist of the final water. The story relates that when he was about to die at Lawrenceburg a preacher was called, and knelt in prayer by his bedside. The prayer had not proceeded far until Brown reached for his trousers and got a ten-dollar bill and shook it close to the parson's ear. The minister stopped, looked up and remarked that he did not make any charge for his services. "Don't you?" gasped Brown. "Well, I'll be d——d if I'd make such a plea as you've made for less than ten dollars."[56]

Frontier Indiana's first preaching circuits were so large that it usually took the circuit rider six to eight weeks to "make the round"; therefore, meetings were rare. Circuits were sometimes a hundred miles or more. On occasion members conducted prayer meeting in their homes without a preacher. Four times yearly, quarterly meetings were held on every circuit, and the presiding elder would attend. These gatherings usually lasted for two or three days. "These were the times when the two and three day meetings were held, the usual way being, the meeting beginning on Saturday afternoon and lasting through, with little intermission until Monday morning."[57]

On many occasions the circuit riders preached not only to Methodists but also to many other denominations that gathered. When the itinerant preachers met their preaching appointments, the benches of the early, coarse churches were usually full. Even in small settlements where only a few people lived, Methodist preachers regularly paid a visit.

The circuit riders lived under extreme hardship to spread the Methodist faith on the frontier. In conjunction with ministering to dispersed congregations, many circuit riders cleared their own farms and grew crops to provide for their families. Their families also suffered. While the preachers were away, families might be forced to defend themselves from Indians and wild animals, and they agonized over other catastrophes that arose. It should be noted that conditions were no better for most other settlers. Indiana Methodist itinerant George K. Hester comments in his diary that in 1829 most settlers near the

The circuit rider arrives. DePauw University Archives and Special Collections.

Ohio River were hunters "living on congress land."[58] Hester's diary graphically portrays their hardships:

> In 1820 I was appointed to Mt. Sterling circuit in Crawford county, which was then one of the most gloomy regions in the State. This circuit embraced a very poor and broken part of the State. Many of the people were destitute of the necessaries of life, and, of course, I had to share with them in this matter. On one occasion I recollect to have visited a family, preached, and remained twenty-four hours, and left without breaking my fast. They had nothing, the man having gone a distance to get breadstuff, and failing to return while I remained. This was a four-weeks circuit. The number of attempts to preach must have averaged with the number of days in the year, and I must have travelled 3,000 miles, and this without any quarterage, except a few dollars' worth of sugar for my family.[59]

In addition to being exposed to the elements, hunger, and disease, the early ministers preached every day of the week and usually twice at what Buley called the "Saturday-Sunday 'two-day' meeting." Sometimes they did not preach on Mondays; it was ordinarily the day of rest, or "preachers day."[60] When they presented a sermon, it was usually extended for hours. If a second preacher was in the crowd, he would follow with another long message, often filled with energy and fire. Many preached until they were exhausted and hoarse from screaming. On occasion several preachers delivered nonstop preaching "a form of worship referred to as 'muscular.' "[61]

Recurrently, "religious debates were held where such questions as election (calvinism) vs free grace (arminianism), immersion vs sprinkling, and many others were hotly disputed."[62] In order to argue about these issues, a good preacher was full of facts and anecdotes and employed them effectively in his preaching. Peter Cartwright, for example, used his wit to battle with an adversary, Mr. Roads, a New Light preacher, on the subject of baptism. On the morning following a rain, Cartwright met Roads and said:

> "Good morning, sir." Roads responded, "Good morning." Cartwright then said, "We have had a tremendous rain" and Roads replied, "Yes sir . . . the Lord sent the rain to convince you of your error." Cartwright inquired, "Ah! What error?" Roads answered, "Why, about baptism. The Lord sent his flood to convince you that much water was necessary." "Very good, sir," said Cartwright; "and He in a like manner sent this flood to convince you of your error." "What error?" questioned Roads. Cartwright replied "Why, to show you that water comes by pouring, and not by immersion."[63]

The early clergymen were often dressed in buckskin or coarse, homespun clothes.[64] However, their garb was diverse. Buley describes them in the following manner: "Though not uniformly dressed, the circuit-riders were usually recognizable—perhaps by the straight-breasted coat, high collar, long waist-coat, sometimes short breeches and stockings, long hair, often a wide-brimmed fur hat of a light shade."[65] They traveled on horseback and frequently lived out of their saddlebags. One saddlebag usually carried the preacher's clothing and the other contained his food. The itinerant preachers also typically carried a blanket. Many times when night overtook them and there was no nearby cabin in close proximity, the blanket could provide shelter, or they simply wrapped themselves in it and slept on the ground. It was common for Indiana's frontier preachers to swim swollen streams, wade through snow and ice during the winter, and stride through quagmires of mud in the spring and autumn to reach their preaching assignments. There was no excuse for failure to meet an appointment. The presiding elders also kept close watch on the circuit riders, which further pressured the itinerants to reach their ministerial engagements.

The congregations viewed the Methodist preachers as being "imbued with all knowledge of both Heaven and Hell—especially of the latter." Walter

Brownlow Posey elaborates: "The very looks of a Methodist preacher would strike terror into a sinners heart." He usually spoke in a thunderous voice to the gatherings of people that had come to listen to him, "hurling at them warning of the judgement; he accused, convicted, and consigned them to the hottest hells." They preached in the style of fire and brimstone, and their messages were punctuated by the crowd with cries of "Amen!" "Yes, I know it!" "Praise God!" "Tell it Brother," and "Come to the Lord!"[66] Rev. Henry Baker's sermon on death gives some of the flavor of this style of preaching:

> There shall be a resurrection of the dead, both of the just and of the unjust. For the hour is coming in the [sic] which all that are in their graves shall hear his voice, and come forth; they have done good to the resurrection of life, and they have done evil to the resurrection of damnation. Behold, I show you a mystery: we shall not all sleep; but we shall be changed in a moment, in the twinkling of an eye, at the last trump; for the trumpet shall sound, and the dead shall be raised incorruptible, and we shall be changed; for this corruption must put on incorruption, and this mortal must put on immortality.[67]

The preacher's voice usually "rose to tumultuous volume, then dropped to a hissing whisper to run the range again. The crowd swayed to the rhythm of his voice; some rose to their feet to continue the tempo in a loose dance."[68] Sermons were frequently punctuated with anecdotes and homely incidents as their "rough and tumble" style was forceful. Buley comments that less effective preachers "tried to compensate for their lack of understanding with bluster, brimstone, and the 'holy whine'; some blubbered others bellowed."[69]

Frontier preachers entered their careers on a calling from God. Conversion usually preceded the calling, but there was "nothing to prevent the call from descending upon the ignorant and crude as well as upon erudite and qualified persons." The calling had to be powerful, though, because pay was scant for the circuit riders. The 1816 *Discipline* awarded a single preacher one hundred dollars for his year-long labor. A married preacher was usually paid double that amount. If a minister had children, collections were taken, but little money was forthcoming from the generally impoverished congregations. Generally, it was difficult to collect from the conference if full pay had not been received. Payment in currency only was also unusual.[70]

The circuit riders continually rode from "settlement to settlement" spreading the "gospel and good cheer." It is believed that Francis Asbury rode a distance throughout his ministry that would have taken him around the world twelve times.[71] Indiana historian William Frederick Vogel gives us a picture of an early Indiana itinerant preacher in a document he located:

> Lest you might think there was a danger of us becoming semi-barbarous in this wild region, I will state we have circuit preaching every four weeks, by old father Emmett, a veteran minister of the Methodist denomination, who had been a faithful watchman on the walls of Zion for more than forty years. He is beloved by all who know him—old and young, saint and sinner. His preaching is of the plain, practical, but effective kind that reaches the hearts of his hearers. He has three preaching places within reach of us, viz: at John Simpson's, Kempner's Schoolhouse above the forks of Coal creek, and in White's neighborhood in the direction of Covington.[72]

When a meeting house did not exist for church service, members met in each other's homes. The preacher usually took his place in the middle of the entryway and frequently stood on a chair in order that he might be seen by everyone. The women and men did not sit together in the service; women sat on one side of the room and men on the opposite.

The Methodists constantly battled rival denominations in pioneer Indiana. Rev. Aaron Wood claimed that the Methodists' "churches and preachers grew and were multiplied; we began to be puffed up at our prosperity."[73] However, Methodist pride was soon humbled. Within the Methodist Vincennes circuit was a Shaker settlement, known as "Busroe" or "Bushrun."[74]

Three missionary Shakers from the East named Bates, Mitchum, and Young moved to the area and began drawing members from the Methodists, Baptists, and Cumberland Presbyterians who had settled in the area. Wood said that the missionaries "were eminently qualified for their mission. Their appearance was prepossessing—their dress was plain and neat—they were grave and unassuming at first in their manners—very intelligent and ready in the Scriptures, and of great boldness in their faith."[75] The Shakers informed the Methodists that they had heard of them back East and rejoiced in their work for God, but argued that the Methodists had not progressed far enough in their work. Wood reported that the Shakers claimed:

> they were sent by their brethren to teach the way of God more perfectly, by obedience to which we should be led into perfect holiness. They seemed to understand all the springs and avenues of the human heart. They delivered their testimony; and labored to confirm it by the Scriptures—promised the greatest blessings to the

obedient, but certain damnation to the disobedient. They urged the people to confess their sins to them, especially the sin of matrimony, and to forsake them all immediately—husbands must forsake their wives, and wives their husbands. This was the burden of their testimony. They said they could perform miracles, and related many as done among them, but we never could persuade them to try to work miracles among us.[76]

Many confessed their sins to the Shakers "and forsook the marriage state," among them three preachers, Matthew Houston, Richard McNemar, and John Dunlavy.[77] Other preachers and church members also left the Methodist and joined different "sects."[78] Methodist preachers worked hard to compete against the Shakers. Aaron Wood "labored so hard and constantly that a profuse spitting of blood ensued." As a result the Shakers and Methodist became bitter enemies. Wood listed the basic tenets of the Shakers:

They denied the literal resurrection of the body from the grave; they said the resurrection meant the resurrection of Christ's body, meaning the church. They the elders had constant communication with angels and all the departed saints. They looked for no other or better heaven than that on earth. Their worship, if worthy of name, consisted of voluntary dancing together. They lived together, and had all things in common, entirely under the direction and control of the elders. . . . Their doctrine was, that the Christ appeared first in a male, and through life was preparing the way of salvation, which he could not accomplish till his second appearance in a woman. Ann Lees, who was now the Christ, and had full power to save. They had new revelations, superior to the Scriptures, which they called the old record, which were true, but superseded by the new.[79]

During the year 1808, Peter Cartwright went to the area around Vincennes to "stem the tide" of Shakers. Cartwright commented that there were no Methodist circuit riders in the area at the time other than "old brother, Collins, a local preacher, who withstood the Shakers, and in private combat was a full match for any of them; but he was not eloquent in debate, and hence the Shaker priests overcame my old brother, and by scores swept members of different churches away from their steadfastness into the muddy pools of Shakerism."[80]

Upon arriving at Busroe, Cartwright sent out an invitation to meet any of the "Shaker priests in public debate." The Shakers did not meet with Cartwright but warned the believers to keep away from his meeting. Many disregarded the warning and went to hear Cartwright. The Shakers then asked him to attend their meeting. Cartwright went, and there was a "great crowd." At the meeting, he again proposed to have a debate. The Shakers agreed to the discussion, and Cartwright described the event: "A local preacher I had with me was to open the debate; then one or all their preachers, if they chose, were to follow, and I was to bring up the rear. My preacher opened the debate by merely stating the points of difference. Mr Brayelton followed, and, instead of argument, he turned everything into abuse and insulting slander. Then he closed, and Mr Gill rose, but instead of argument, he uttered a few words of personal abuse, and then called on all the Shakers to meet him a few minutes in the yard, talk a little, and then disperse."[81]

Cartwright then stood and stated that he would "bring up the rear, or close the argument." He then said that it was cowardly to run and that if he were the devil himself, and they were right, he could not hurt them. Most of the Shakers returned to their seats. Gill did get some of them to leave with him. The Shaker preachers then told the congregants that if Cartwright continued to oppose them, God would make an example of him, and send fire from heaven and consume him. In response, Cartwright remarked: "When I rose to reply, I felt a Divine sense of the approbation of God, and that he would give me success."[82]

Cartwright preached to the congregation for three hours, and he invited all who would renounce Shakerism "to come and give me their hand." Forty-seven came forward and renounced the "dreadful delusion." The following day, Cartwright went from cabin to cabin, taking the names of those who had "returned to the solid foundation of truth." The number of converts rose to eighty-seven. He organized this group into a regular society, and the next fall he had a preacher sent to them.[83]

By 1812 several additional circuits had been added to the conference. Two of them were "the Lawrenceburg circuit in the southeastern corner of the territory, between the Whitewater and the Silver Creek circuits, and the Patoka circuit in the southwestern corner, south of the Vincennes circuit and to the west of the Silver Creek."[84] The year that Indiana achieved statehood, 1816, the settled portion was divided into two conferences, the Ohio and Tennessee. There were only seven circuits that made up the conferences. The "Ohio Conference, Miami District, with two circuits, the Whitewater and the Lawrenceburg, and the Salt River District, with only one circuit, Silver Creek in Indiana. Tennessee Conference, Illinois District, with four circuits, the Wabash, Patoka, Blue River, and Vincennes."[85] At the time Indiana was admitted to statehood, there were approximately two thousand Methodist Church members. At the state constitutional convention, the Methodists were represented by Hugh Cull of the Whitewater Circuit and Dennis Pennington of Harrison County.[86]

Peter Cartwright. DePauw University Archives and Special Collections.

Pennington was not a preacher. He was a lay member and later served several years in the state legislature. Other denominations were also represented at the constitutional convention. Ezra Ferris, a Baptist preacher from Dearborn County, was present, and Judge James Scott, a Presbyterian, also attended.[87]

After Indiana became a state, several more circuits—Madison, Bloomington, Mount Sterling, Corydon, and Charlestown, which had previously been known as the Blue River circuit—were added. In 1818 a reorganization was conducted, and some parts of Indiana were encompassed by the Missouri Conference. Also included in this conference along with the sections of Indiana were Illinois, Missouri, and Arkansas. In 1824, the General Conference divided the Missouri Conference, and placed the states of Illinois and Indiana in "what they termed the Illinois Conference."[88] The conference of Indiana was divided into two districts, Madison and Indiana, which were then divided into the following circuits and preachers:

Madison District—John Strange, Presiding Elder
Madison Circuit—Allen Wiley and Aaron Wood

Lawrenceburg Circuit—James Jones and Thomas Hitt
Whitewater Circuit—Peter Stevens and Nehemiah B. Griffith
Connersville Circuit—James Havens
Rushville Circuit—Thomas Rice
Indianapolis Circuit—John Miller
Flat Rock Circuit—Thomas Hewson and James Garner
Eel River Circuit—John Fish

Indiana District—James Armstrong, Presiding Elder
Charlestown Circuit—James L. Thompson and Jacob Varner
Corydon Circuit—George K. Hester and Dennis Willey
Salem Circuit—Samuel Low and Richard Hargrave
Paoli Circuit—Edward Smith
Boonville Circuit—Orsenith Fisher
Patoka Circuit—W. H. Smith and George Randle
Vincennes Circuit—Edwin Ray
Honey Creek Circuit—Samuel Hull
Bloomington Circuit—Daniel Anderson and John Cord
Vermilion Circuit—Hackaliah Vredenburg and Robert Delap[89]

The schedules the preachers were supposed to maintain on these circuits were impossible. F. C. Holliday listed the appointments on the Madison circuit that Allen Wiley and Aaron Wood were expected to meet: "Rising Sun, Buell's Mill, Green's, Davis's, Spoon's, Campbell's, Vevay, Mount Sterling, Slawson's, Alfray's, Bellamy's, Brooks, Crooked-Creek, Meeting-house, Simper's, Hyatt's, Overturf's, Brown's, Herkul's, Versailles, Wiley's, Allensville, Downey's, Dexter's, including all of Switzerland and Ohio Counties, and the larger portions of Jefferson and Ripley Counties."[90]

In 1810 the population of Indiana was 24,875, and the Methodists claimed 755 members. By 1830 the state's population had grown to 147,178, and Methodism claimed 4,410 within its ranks. The work of the itinerant preachers enabled the Methodists to keep pace with the expanding population. Their success in gaining converts is attributable to their ability to preach in open fields, barrooms, barns, forts, as well as in the cabins of the first settlers.[91] The circuit riders were men who endured extreme hardships, gained little gratitude for their sacrifices, and frequently found an early grave due to their exposure to a difficult climate and to their travails. The Methodism that had surfaced on the Indiana frontier during the first decade of the nineteenth century was a simplistic and highly emotional religion that appealed to the common pioneer. The Methodists capitalized on the free market religious economy in making tremendous gains in membership. These were the conditions of the faith on the Indiana frontier when Joseph Tarkington launched his preaching career with the Methodists in 1824.

Chapter One

Joseph Tarkington's Birth and Early Life

Joseph Tarkington was born near Nashville, Tennessee, on October 30, 1800.[1] Tarkington's ideas about religion and life were developed on the Tennessee frontier. He developed a hatred of any form of alcoholic beverage. He also acquired a compassion toward African Americans and a hatred of slavery.

At the time of Joseph's birth, John Adams was president of the United States, and it was a time of great uncertainty. The economy was suffering, and the possibility of war with both France and England lurked in the background. From the start the new nation was in a state of chaos and appeared to be doomed to failure. However, many evangelical religious groups made immense gains during this period. Following the American Revolution and the Christmas Conference of 1784, Methodism began to spread rapidly to the frontier and the West. In 1812, Bishop Francis Asbury traveled four thousand miles in eight months preaching the gospel.[2] Dickson D. Bruce Jr. describes the attractions of this new faith:

> Religion on the Southern frontier, particularly Methodist and Baptist religion, developed within a context of tension and instability and offered the plain-folk an alternative way of life. Institutionally, the sects provided a disciplined community in which proper relationships between individuals were spelled out and rules rigidly enforced, just as the internal affairs of the sects provided an alternative sphere of action where people could assert themselves in ways other than those denied

them by secular Southern society. The sect provided a different society in which the contradictions of frontier life no longer occurred.[3]

Most settlers who had moved to the interior had done so to acquire land for farming. Families like the Tarkingtons were not aimless drifters. Bruce holds that they were "people who thought by leaving their old farms and starting afresh in a new territory they could achieve a measure of success and security." The Tarkingtons were among the small farmers referred to as "the Southern 'plain-folk,' who owned no slaves, or at most a few."[4] People were moving to the West and the South in such large numbers that, by the end of the eighteenth century, "twenty-five of every one hundred acres had been stripped of forests" in the state of Virginia.[5] "Crowded off the best lands, plain-folk tended to be congregated in particular neighborhoods, even though they lived throughout the South."[6] Evangelical missionaries moved to the new lands with the settlers, and it was in these frontier communities—places like where the Tarkingtons lived—that Bishop Asbury and the Methodists made their greatest gains.

The first Tarkington to immigrate to America from England was John Tarkington, who settled in Maryland with his wife, Prudence, around 1668. John and Prudence Tarkington were Joseph Tarkington's great-great-grandparents. They had three sons upon arriving in America: John Jr., William, and Samuel. The Tarkingtons secured 1,050 acres of land from Lord Baltimore on September 7, 1675, in Cecil County on the Sassafras River.[7] In the early 1690s the Tarkingtons moved to North Carolina. On March 1, 1694, the North Carolina colonial records reveal that John Tarkington had secured 180 acres of land referred to as "Tarkington's quarter." The land was on Albemarle Sound in present-day Tyrrell County. However, John was convicted of an unnamed felony and forfeited the land.[8] In spite of losing their land, the Tarkingtons remained in Tyrrell County.

Just before moving to North Carolina, John and Prudence had two more sons; one was named Joshua and the other son's name is unknown. The unknown boy was kidnapped by Indians shortly after the move as the two boys were hunting strayed cows. He was never heard from again.[9] Joshua Tarkington Sr. (Joseph's great-grandfather) married early in the eighteenth century and fathered three sons, William, Joshua Jr., and Zebulon. Joshua Jr. was Joseph Tarkington's grandfather. Joshua Tarkington Jr. and his wife, Zelphia Alexander, lived their entire lives in Tyrrell County, North Carolina, and were the parents of six sons, Richard, Joseph, Isaac, John, William, and Jesse (Joseph's father), and one daughter, Elizabeth.

The Tarkingtons were Episcopalians. Joseph claims that his early religious training also "was in accordance with Episcopal usage" since his parents were "reared in that order of faith."[10] However, the Revolution had left the Episcopalian church as "a church in ruins."[11] Many of the church members had been Tories and left the new country during and after the Revolution. The remainder found a clergy that was few in number and that made almost no effort to sustain membership and gain new converts. As outlined in the introduction, churches such as the Episcopalians "limited their range to established markets."[12] They were also "lax in their duties, and uninspired in their preaching."[13] William W. Sweet claimed that "just to belong to the old established church in the years immediately following the Revolution was enough in itself to mark one as a suspicious character."[14] As a result families such as the Tarkingtons lost much of their religious enthusiasm.

On August 28, 1792, Jesse Tarkington married his first cousin Mary, or "Polly" as she was known. Mary was the daughter of Jesse's uncle Zebulon. Around 1800, Jesse and his uncles, Zebulon and William, decided to leave North Carolina and moved to Tennessee with their families. The churches that they found, which included most of the southern church membership, were the evangelical Methodists, Baptists, and Presbyterians. The Tarkingtons showed little interest in joining these churches when they first settled in Tennessee.

Jesse Tarkington purchased a small farm from a man named David Beatty and lived a subsistence lifestyle for three or four years. Hardship struck when Indians stole "all his horses." As a result, Tarkington sold his land lease back to Beatty and, with a small sum of capital, moved to the area where Franklin, Tennessee, is now located. He purchased land from two men named Tatum and Murray who had acquired the property with Revolutionary War land grants. Jesse immediately cleared land, built a house and barn, "and soon had a very good orchard."[15] Jesse Tarkington became popular among his neighbors during this time for his ability to distill peaches into brandy. Joseph described his father's enterprise:

> So abundant was the fruit that he and his neighbors got a still, and made peach brandy, worth one dollar a gallon. The purest spring water which bubbled up from among the rocks was ruined in making it. The success in making brandy in peach-

time encouraged them to make whiskey; so they went at it. My father was engaged to run the still. My mother protested strongly against the enterprise, but it was of no avail. The neighbors brought meal for him to distill. In that day no house or cabin could be raised or logs rolled without whiskey to boost it, nor could a child be born in cabin or camp without its coming being celebrated with a dram. . . . The still-house was a great trouble to my mother . . . she said she wished the still and all were burned up. . . . If the church members had not had their liquor made there, it would have been better; but they did and would have it at all their gatherings. Even preachers would patronize the thing. Neighbors would sometimes come to the house drunk, and mother would have to take them in the house, or they would lie outdoors all night. Her wish came true. The still burned up. How it was fired, or by whom, no one knew.[16]

Shortly after the still burned, Joseph's mother, Mary, persuaded her husband to "invite the Rev. John Pope" to preach in the Tarkington household. Pope, a Methodist, was described as a "heavy set man with a good voice." He baptized six of Jesse and Mary's children, including Joseph, at one meeting in Johnson's Grove, located three miles west of Franklin. Joseph remembered that at the baptism he heard someone shout "Glory to God" for the first time while the minister was preaching. He added that during Pope's visits the drinking habits of his neighbors diminished, and people began attending church services on Sunday mornings and nights at various homes in the community.[17] The sermons that Pope and his counterparts gave were "grim in tone and often stressed the fury of God directed at the unrepentant. Sermons with titles such as 'Knowing the Terror of the Lord,' and 'The time is Short,' which were preached by Francis Asbury in Ohio and Kentucky in 1815, were commonly heard by the populace."[18] These sermons were often repeated by other circuit riders throughout the settlements.

John Pope and other circuit-riding Methodist preachers, along with Calvinist Baptists, practiced a religion that was highly emotional and very physical. Pope and his fellow itinerants made the woods ring with hymns, including those composed by Watts or the following one by John Wesley:

> O sun of righteousness arise
>   With healing in thy wing;
> To my diseased, my fainting soul,
>   Life and salvation bring.
> These clouds of pride and sin dispel,
>   By the all-piercing beam;

Lighten my eyes with faith; my heart
With holy hopes inflame.

In the summer of 1800, the Great Revival surfaced around Nashville. It began in this country in Logan County, Kentucky, which adjoins Tennessee.[19] But it had serious obstacles to overcome. Jeremy Rifkin and Ted Howard point out that "[t]his desolate Godforsaken area was a little hellhole in the year 1800. Nicknamed 'Rogues Harbor' because it was often used as a sanctuary for outlaws and runaway slaves."[20] Rogues Harbor was very similar to the area where Joseph Tarkington lived. Often preachers and church gatherings were badgered by these hostile denizens that were not hospitable to religion. On occasion, preachers were physically attacked and church meetings were broken up. To make matters worse, these outlaws were immensely popular. Even Congressman David Crockett and President Andrew Jackson identified with these rogues. Catherine Albanese reports on Crockett: "After Crockett was fifteen, he tells us he went into the 'eye business.' He boasted a thumbnail, 'hard as a buck's horn,' which worked as well as a rifle. . . . A[t] death, Crockett was mourned as 'an ornament to the forest,' 'When he war alive, it war most beautiful to hear his screams comin' through the forest.'"[21] In 1806, while serving as a Tennessee Supreme Court judge, Andrew Jackson killed fellow Tennessean Charles Dickinson in a duel after Jackson took offense to remarks that Dickinson made about his wife. Jackson also received a near fatal gunshot wound from Thomas Hart Benton, just prior to the famous battle of Horseshoe Bend in 1814.[22] Outlaws and murderers such as Micajah and Wiley Harpe were a threat to settlers in Tennessee and Kentucky.[23] The Kentucky historian Collins referred to the Harpes as the "most brutal monsters of the human race."[24] The Harpes left dead bodies throughout Tennessee and Kentucky. In one memorable event, they represented themselves as Methodist preachers before they slaughtered their victims.[25]

Joseph Tarkington was also witness to the high levels of sexual promiscuity on the frontier. Sexual ill-conduct reflected the "general structure of Southern ethics." Male sexuality was encouraged. To repress "natural impulse was to defy nature itself, leading to prissiness and effeminacy."[26] Bertram Wyatt-Brown claims that "[y]oung males made sexual experience a point of honor and boasting among themselves. Older men found that a masculine odor of mild indiscretion enhanced their respectability."[27]

Bishop Asbury was constantly depressed because of the evils that he saw in the frontier communities like the one the Tarkingtons inhabited. While in

Tennessee on April 25, 1796, he told a Baptist preacher that he feared "that the ministers in Kentucky will be a curse to each other, and the people too. Good religion and good land are not so easily matched together."[28] As a result of the "sin" that the God-fearing sects viewed, their religion became more ingrained into their society and religious practice. Joseph commented on their religious zeal:

> In those times the exercise of religion was very vigorous. I have seen the women shouting, and, in bending backwards, their hair would stream down, touching the floor. It seemed that they would break their backs. Some would have the jerks. No two men could hold them still. The holders would be thrown down. The best way to treat them was to get out of their way when they had the jerks, and only see that they did not hurt themselves. There is something in the jerks that is unexplainable. I asked Mrs. John Givens, who at times had them, to explain what they were. She said that, when she felt like shouting praises to God, if she did it willingly, she did not have them; but when she resisted shouting, which she said she had done until the blood had ran out of her nose, then the jerks came, and were very hard with her. She was a pure, good woman, a Presbyterian, and a great help to young Christians.[29]

Twelve years after the Tarkingtons settled at Franklin, tragedy struck again. Jesse lost his land to another overlapping claim to the land conveyed by Murray and Tatum. Murray and Tatum were insolvent, and Jesse lost his investment completely. Tarkington then leased land for two years from William Hadley, a neighbor. To make matters worse, Creek Indians stole Jesse's horses for a second time.

It was during this period of despair that a series of earth tremors known as the New Madrid Earthquakes struck, beginning in December of 1811. The tremors were felt from "New York to the Floridas, from the Atlantic Ocean to the Mississippi River."[30] The earthquakes left a lifelong impression on Joseph Tarkington.[31] Years after the event, he recalled: "The incidents connected with this 'stirring time' are fresh in my memory to-day. Sixty years 'are as a few days' in this connection."[32]

It was a common belief among "western settlers" that God could be expected to punish them for their sins by intervening in natural affairs. Even though rationalism and a confidence in the ability of the human mind to decipher natural phenomena had penetrated learned circles, most evangelicals believed that earthquakes, tornadoes, famines, and other disasters were signs of God's wrath. Puritan John Winthrop's great-great grandson, who was professor of mathematics and natural philosophy at Harvard in the 1730s, took the position that earthquakes had natural causes, resulting from the shifting of the earth's surface. But his position was rejected by most frontier pioneers and by many other clergymen. In 1750, John Wesley published a sermon entitled "The Cause and Cure of Earthquakes" that declared: "Of all the judgements which the righteous God inflicts on sinners here, the most dreadful and destructive is an earthquake. . . . Earthquakes are set forth by the inspired writers as God's proper judicial act, or the punishment of sin: sin is the cause, earthquakes the effect of his anger."[33]

As a result of the earthquakes, many houses and countless chimneys fell in Tennessee and adjoining states. The chimney in Jesse Tarkington's house, which was "built of stone, two stories high, was split eight or ten feet in the breast." At a church meeting that the Baptist Reverend McConica was preaching, "the cry was made that the house was sinking, and, such was the chronic terror of the people, the whole congregation was in confusion; some running away, shouting, 'He is coming! He is coming!' some screaming for mercy; some fell out of the gallery of the meeting-house; others lay down groaning and crying."[34] In Kentucky, Valentine Cook, a former circuit rider and Cokesbury College graduate ran from his house after the tremors started, shouting, "My Jesus is coming." His wife, Tabitha, chased him, begging, "Don't leave me!" But he continued running, replying: "My Jesus is coming and I can't wait for you." A ten-year-old boy in Arkansas was gathering hazelnuts on Sunday, "and when the earthquakes began he was certain that his errant ways must be the cause. Accordingly, he carried the nuts back into the woods and scattered them behind a stump."[35]

As might be expected, Marshall Legan points out that "[p]erhaps the most significant reactions to the tremors were the religious revivals that ascribed them to the power of God."[36] Joseph described the earthquake's impression on his family:

On a pleasant Sabbath evening, the children, having retired early, were called down-stairs, with the announcement that the house was falling down; and in great fear and trepidation we sat up the entire night, my father going out frequently to ascertain whether evil-disposed persons might have shaken the house, by some means, in order to terrify the family. The dusty old prayer-book was brought forth from its place, its pages scanned eagerly to find something pertaining to earthquakes; but as we could find nothing, we felt that the interests of a large and flourishing family were in jeopardy for lack of the much needed prayer. After a night of watching and fear, it was agreed that we should say nothing about our fears and their cause, lest we be ridiculed by our neighbors. But with the morning came the neighbors, with startling accounts of this strange visitation; and while they yet talked of this night of terrors, a sound like loud, distant thunder startled them. Rushing out of the house, they found the earth trembling violently and the trees vibrating hither and thither. 'Surely,' thought they, 'the end has come;' and the promises made to God by the terrified people were not few nor far between.[37]

After the tremors began, church attendance increased.[38] Many who had never frequented the gatherings before started attending the meetings. James B. Finley recalled that John Crowe, a Tennessee circuit rider on the Duck River Circuit, drew thousands to his services in 1812. Some circuits increased their membership by 69 percent during this period.[39] Memberships in the "Western Conference of the Methodist church jumped some fifty percent in 1812."[40]

Prior to the earthquake, Joseph Tarkington's mother was what Richard J. Carwardine describes as a "Laodicean," or a nominal or lukewarm Christian "of superficial piety." Her evangelicalism was certainly not the organizing principle of her secular life.[41] Following the earthquake, Mary Tarkington was convinced that she must work to "clean the world" in order to usher the thousand years of peace prior to Christ's second coming.[42] As a result she experienced conversion, but failed to continue with her convictions. She did not join the Methodist Church and later backslid. Mary later told Joseph that she failed to make a profession of her beliefs and "put her light under a bushel."[43] Mary may have claimed that she did not make a profession of her beliefs, but her life was influenced by the evangelical culture. She fully absorbed the oral traditions of her environment, which were largely based on the language of the Bible. She generally spoke in a Biblical style, drew upon its content, and used its syntax, all of which had an influence on Joseph. Joseph carried on his life in the same oral style while developing few writing skills.

Some women were not as fortunate as Mary. Jesse allowed her to practice—or not practice—her religious beliefs without interference. The fascination with the Methodist Church that many women experienced was dampened by their husbands' intervention. Bill Cecil-Fronsman reports a man that "went so far as to apply a blister plaster on his wife to cure her of Methodism."[44]

Just as Mary's enthusiasm for evangelism flagged, many other people's interest in religion also diminished when the earthquakes were no longer a threat.[45] Fifty years later, itinerant preacher Jesse J. Ellis complained that between the camp meetings and protracted meetings, he found a "general lack of religious fervor in the rural settlements." He complained about the populace's drunkenness; Ellis expelled several members from various churches because of intoxication. A young boy was found in one church, drunk.[46]

If some aspects of the social life of the frontier seem hopelessly backward, others were not, at least by the standards of the time. Joseph, for example, was exposed to a biracial culture as a child. During the earthquake he claimed that "[a]n old colored woman came up to father and asked, 'Massa, did you try to shake my house down last night?' Another said, 'I thought the horses were rubbing my cabin down.'"[47] Blacks also attended local church gatherings with whites. Joseph commented that "[t]he white folks were not so particular then in keeping their darkies at a distance. Some of Mr. Reese's slaves were often called in to pray for the whites. One of them who had power with God, was a leader in many revivals of religion."[48] In fact, blacks and whites worshipping together was common. As Larry James points out, "Individual church records, associational minutes, ministerial diaries, and tombstone inscriptions in old cemeteries all document the biracial nature of antebellum worship."[49] Bishop Asbury made a journal entry on a black man's religious practice in Delaware on April 1, 1779: "A black man, who had been liberated by Mr. Blades, gave such an extraordinary account of the work of God in his soul, and withal displayed such gifts in public exercises, that it appears as if the Lord was preparing him for peculiar usefulness to the people of his own colour. Let the Lord choose his own instruments, and sent by whom he will."[50] However, it should be noted that Asbury "while remaining a trenchant critic of slavery in private, decided that antislavery activity must be abandoned if Methodism was to flourish in South Carolina" and other southern states.[51] Asbury was far from alone in holding this opinion.

In 1812, America entered its second war with England. Joseph claimed that "animosities of the War of Independence lasted in the hearts of good people." Amos Adkins, a Revolutionary War soldier, told Joseph stories of the war, "of suffering for food and clothing" at places like Bunker Hill and Valley Forge. Adkins's wife, a strict "oldstyle Methodist," said that "she wished she had some boys to send into the army."[52] During the war, Jesse Tarkington's oldest son, Sylvanus, volunteered to fight, and his next oldest, Burton, was "pressed into the service" with Jesse's team of fine horses to haul provisions "in Southern Alabama, where the army was fighting the Indians."[53] When Sylvanus and Burton returned to Tennessee they learned that their father had planned to move to "Indiana Territory."

Originally Jesse had planned to move to Alabama. His brothers tried to persuade him to move farther south, but he refused, claiming that he wanted to "go where there were no slaves."[54] Moreover, land prices in Alabama were soaring at the time due to technological improvements in the manufacturing industry that caused increased demands for raw cotton. The "Alabama Fever" was stripping many southern states of their populations. A North Carolina planter wrote in 1817 that the great migration to Alabama "has carried off vast numbers of our Citizens."[55] Ambitious planters and speculators drove the price of land in Alabama "high above the official minimum price of $2.00 per acre, to $4.00 or as much as $25.00 an acre."[56]

The "New Purchase" lands in Indiana offered cheap land for farming, but slavery did exist in some areas of the state even though the Northwest Ordinance of 1787 proclaimed that "[t]here shall be slavery nor involuntary servitude in the said territory."[57] Slavery had been introduced in the Northwest Territory by French colonists. In 1746, at Vincennes, there "dwelt a group of forty white men and five Negroes." These blacks were slaves of the French settlers. One Jesuit priest at Vincennes owned slaves.[58]

When the British acquired Vincennes in 1763, black slaves were brought from Jamaica. George Rogers Clark captured Vincennes in 1779, and the area came under the jurisdiction of Virginia. Virginia gave up its claims to territory in 1783. In 1787 the Continental Congress "adopted the Northwest Ordinance for the government of the territory." Article VI of the Ordinance stated: "There shall be neither slavery nor involuntary servitude in the said territory, otherwise than in punishment of crimes, whereof the party shall have been duly convicted." Regardless of the Northwest Ordinance, "slavery and involuntary servitude persisted for many years in Indiana." There are legal records of numerous cases in which the "judges clearly assumed the legality of slavery."[59]

At the time that the Tarkingtons began their move, the population of Indiana was growing rapidly. In 1810, it was estimated that there were approximately 4,875 inhabitants. By 1820, after the Illinois Territory had been "separated from it, Indiana had a population of 24,520; by 1830 the population was 147,178."[60] Population growth west of the Appalachians was booming. In 1810 only one American in seven lived west of the mountains; by 1820, it was one in four.

Chapter Two

Religion in Early Indiana

The first Protestant church in Indiana was a Baptist church that was organized on November 22, 1798, in Clark County, near Owens Creek. The church later became known as the Silver Creek Church. In 1829 the church split into other churches over differences in belief. On July 1, 1837, the remaining Baptists organized the Charlestown Baptist Church. In 1799 Methodists began to settle in Clark's Grant "near Springville and above Charlestown." Nathan Robertson, a Kentuckian, was one of the first Methodists to arrive with a large family. Other settlers carried the names Prather, Jacobs, Gazaway, Mitchell, and Robinett.[1] Eva Elizabeth Luke of the *Western Christian Advocate* states that the "first preaching in the grant was in 1801, when Samuel Parker, not yet licensed to preach, and Edward Talbott spent two days at Springville, preaching and exhorting, sowing the first seeds for Christ in the wilderness."[2] In the summer of 1802, Andrew Mitchell, a Methodist stone mason and carpenter, took William McKendree, the presiding elder of the Kentucky district, "across the Ohio river in a canoe."[3] McKendree formed two classes in Clark County,[4] one at present-day Charlestown and the other at a place referred to as New Chapple.[5]

In the spring of 1803, Benjamin Lakin of the Salt River circuit in Kentucky crossed the river and preached "in the woods, near the present town of Charlestown." Lakin made that neighborhood and Robertson's, located five miles north of the town, part of his "regular preaching places."[6] There were no

A circuit rider preaching. DePauw University Archives and Special Collections.

roads other than old Indian paths, or "blazed bridle trails," no clearings, other than a few acres around the occasional log cabins that existed, and only two settlements, Springfield and Clarksville, located at the falls of the Ohio. During the first year of his ministry, Lakin was assisted by Ralph Lotspeich and, later in 1803, by Adjet McGuire. However, these men did not preach at regular intervals, and it was difficult to spread the news when a preacher was planning to hold a meeting. It was common for a settler across the river in Kentucky to "ride down to the water's edge, and halloo across, stating that the circuit rider was coming to them on such a day. Word would then be quickly passed through the settlement, and when the preacher came he found a crowd awaiting him."[7]

The following year, in 1804, Rev. F. C. Holliday states that Peter Cartwright preached "in the territory of Indiana."[8] In his autobiography, Cartwright commented: "In the fall of 1804, Clark's Grant or the Illinois Grant, as it was called, was opposite and north of Louisville, was then included in the Salt River and Shelbyville Circuits, and Brother Benjamin Lakin and myself crossed the Ohio River, and preached at Brother Robertson's and Prather's."[9] In 1805, A. C. Shinn and D. Young were the preachers, while Frederick Hood became the regular pastor in 1806.[10] At the time that Methodism was being introduced at Clark's Grant in the first few years of the nineteenth century, it also surfaced in another section of Indiana. In 1805 Hugh Cull began preaching in the southeastern section of the Whitewater country. Soon after, the area became included in the Whitewater circuit, which was mainly situated in Ohio. The circuit appeared for the first time in the annual "minutes" in 1808. Joseph Williams was listed as the preacher, with 165 members and "one colored."[11] Blacks were not excluded from participation in religious services in early Indiana. A black man named Benjamin Lankford was a member of the quarterly conference and traveled to various sites preaching to other blacks in southern Indiana.[12]

The minutes of the quarterly conference reflect general business concerns, such as providing welfare for the elderly. On occasion "subscription papers" were sold to church members in an attempt to provide for people who could not maintain themselves. Other matters were also discussed, including the building of a meeting house or setting the date and place for the next quarterly conference. It was also decided whether prospective exhorters and preachers would be assigned to their desired positions in the church. On September 14, 1811, Jacob House was denied "to be received as a traveling preacher," and Robert Monroe's license as an exhorter "was taken from him." Quarrels and disagreements among church members were also settled at the quarterly conference. On April 9, 1809, a complaint was received by Stephen Beman in response to a charge "laid against him" by John Lemaster's for "having Deceived him in the Sail of a mare." Charges were brought against Jeremiah Stilwell for using "immoral language to Sally Brown" on September 10, 1809, and on August 6, 1810, Brother Paine accused Susanna Prather of using immoral language. Not only were allegations of "reproachfull language" common in the quarterly conference, threats of using a "rifle, pistol, or sword, against a brother" frequently surfaced, as did charges of failure to pay tavern accounts, unlawful matrimony, and Sabbath breaking. Often the members were expelled from the church but were generally allowed to reenter after the matters were fully mediated.[13]

Prior to 1800 the Methodist Conference in the west was part of the Kentucky Conference. During 1800, the name "was changed to the Western Conference." The Western Conference remained until 1812, "when it was divided into the Ohio and Tennessee Conferences." In 1800 the Kentucky district was divided into nine circuits within Kentucky and the settled parts of Ohio and a section of Tennessee. None of these circuits extended into Indiana. The first Kentucky circuits that included parts of Indiana were the Salt River and Shelby circuits.[14]

In 1807, the first circuit that was formed in Indiana was the "Silver-creek Circuit, in Clark's Grant, now Clark County, under the ministry of Rev. Moses Ashworth." At the end of the year Ashworth reported that he had gained 188 members within the circuit.[15] The following year, on August 5–8, the first quarterly conference was held at Nathan Robertson's home. Members present were "Deacons, Jeremiah Stillwell, James Garner, Thomas Allen, and John Ervin; licensed preacher, Jake Rowland; exhorters, Amos Chitwood, Nathanial Parker; stewards, William Bullock, William Lockheart, Evin Thomas, Salathial Newman, Edward Jacobs, David Floyd, and George Crutchings." Josiah Crawford was pastor; William Burke, presiding elder, and Jesse Rowland was secretary, a position he held for twenty years.[16] According to Rev. F. C. Holliday, an early itinerant preacher and Methodist historian, three log meeting houses were con-

Bethel Church as it appeared in 1955. DePauw University Archives and Special Collections.

A camp meeting. DePauw University Archives and Special Collections.

structed on the circuit during the first year. Before the meeting houses were completed, church was conducted in members' homes.[17]

Generally, home meetings were held in the winter months, and when spring arrived members worshipped outside "under the trees."[18] Several meetings were conducted in the home of Andrew Mitchell, who lived in "Robertson's neighborhood." Mitchell built a log meeting house on the farm of Nathan Robertson in late 1807 or early 1808.[19] The meeting house was the first Methodist church in Indiana. The small, primitive church was named the Bethel Meeting House. The building was located on a knoll near a blockhouse that protected settlers from Indians.[20] William Warren Sweet describes the construction of the first churches in Indiana: "The roofs were made of clapboards held on by weight poles, the floors were made of puncheons, the chimneys of sticks and clay, and the seats were split logs, hewn smoothly with an ax, while the pulpits were made of clapboard smoothed nicely with a drawing knife."[21]

In 1808, it was at the Bethel Meeting House that the first Christmas service was conducted in the state. James Garner preached the sermon from the text "we have seen his star in the East, and have come to worship him" (Matt. 2:2). Many funerals, weddings, and revivals were held in the building.[22] The next church was constructed in 1809 with buckeye logs and became known as the "Buckeye Church."[23] Shortly after construction of the first two meeting houses, a third church was built in the area. Churches were built at New Chapel in 1809, "Chitwood in Jefferson County, in 1810, and Ebenezer, two miles southwest of the town of Memphis in 1811."[24] The first churches built in pioneer Indiana were simple and had no belfries or bells.

In many of the pioneer communities, the settlers were not able to construct a church for each denomination, thus multidimensional churches were

Reverend James Havens in the mid-1840s. Note the camp meeting in the background. From F. C. Holliday, Indiana Methodist, *1878.*

built, and different congregations held services on alternate Sundays. Many members of different denominations attended all of the services. Pioneers longed for social intercourse and companionship and turned out in large numbers. Some settlers came a distance of ten miles in ox carts to a service, "some came in wagons drawn by horse, and others on foot."[25] Indiana historian William Frederick Vogel describes an early service:

> There were no musical instruments, and usually there was no choir, the singing being entirely congregational. More than one church was divided later by the introduction of an organ. As there were few hymn books, the preacher "lined off" the hymn which all sang with loud enthusiasm. The sexes were seated on opposite sides of the house. Services began by reading a chapter from the Bible, followed by prayer. The hymn was then "lined off" by the minister, and a person somewhat acquainted with music led the singing, in which all the congregation joined. In later days the parts, bass and treble, were carried in the song, for that time the singing school had become an established institution and the singing master was a well-known character. Then came the reading of the text.[26]

Ashworth closed his first year with a camp meeting held at Nathan Robertson's place.[27] In 1808 the Indiana district was organized, with Samuel Parker as presiding elder. The district extended from "the western border of the state of Ohio to Mexico."[28] The new district had six circuits, "namely Illinois, which included all the settlements at that time in that great territory; Missouri, another state-wide circuit; Maramack (sometimes spelled Merrimack), Cold Water, Whitewater, and Silver Creek, the last two being the only circuits in Indiana."[29] The first settlements were along the creeks and rivers, "as these were the natural highways of the country; and hence the early circuits derived their names from some river or creek upon which they were located."[30] Later, the circuits were named after the small cities and tiny towns that had sprung up on the frontier. Holliday listed the circuit riders in 1808 as follows:

INDIANA DISTRICT—SAMUEL PARKER, Presiding Elder

Illinois—Jessee Walker
Missouri—Abraham Amos
Merrimack—Joseph Oglesby
Coldwater—John Crane
Whitewater—Hector Sanford and Moses Crume
Silver-Creek—Josiah Crawford[31]

After the establishment of the first circuits and churches, institutions, such as the Sabbath Schools, began to surface on the Silver Creek circuit. George Knight Hester recounted:

> Such a thing as a Sabbath-school was not heard of for many years by the first settlers of the country; and where the subject was first agitated about one, it was opposed by different persons, and by some who were official members of the church, as being a reflection on the citizens of the place as not being to school their children at common schools. The catechetical instruction of children by the ministers of our Church, according to its discipline, was not entirely over looked at the first introduction of Methodism here. I recollect that the minister who was the regular pastor on the Silver Creek Circuit in 1810 purchased a number of catechisms at his own expense and bestowed them to the children of the members of the Church, who were advanced sufficiently to read, and then formed regular classes round the circuit, and met them for [the] purpose of prayer, recitation, and advice. In one of those classes I was placed and learned to recite the whole of our church catechism. This I have found to be beneficial to me through the whole course of my life.[32]

The Methodists continued to gain new adherents and build more churches until 1811 when Indian problems surfaced. Only intermittent fighting between whites and the Indians had occurred until that time. By 1811, relations between the United States and England were at a point of war, and these tensions escalated to actual warfare the following year in the War of 1812. A Shawnee chief and British ally, Tecumseh, went South in 1811 to build up an Indian Confederacy in order to crush the frontier settlements. British agents in Canada and the Northwest were also active in stirring up Indian hostilities on the frontier.

On September 4, 1812, the Indians attacked Fort Harrison, located north of General Harrison's post at Vincennes. The Indians launched an almost simultaneous assault on the people in Clark's Grant, on September 3, at a place known as Pigeon Roost.[33] Throughout the War of 1812, settlers were under constant threat from Indians. It was not until 1819 that Methodism fully recovered.

But even though the growth of Methodism on the Silver Creek circuit had been bridled due to the War of 1812 and Indian problems, the faith's reach did progress somewhat. The Methodists continued to hold revivals, quarterly meetings, weddings, funerals, along with regular preaching and camp meetings. New churches were also built. In 1814 a church was erected at

Jeffersonville. By 1815 the circuit had grown to an "eight weeks circuit, and a division was now made so that preaching could be held every fortnight."[34] A "second revival of religion" commenced in the fall of 1819. It was held at Jacob's Campground. George Knight Hester stated: "Never did I witness such a season of awakening and converting power. Many, very many on that occasion made a profession of experimental religion. This blessed work continued to spread this conference year, until the whole of the circuit shared in its saving results."[35]

Chapter Three

The Tarkington Family Moves to Indiana

In October 1815, the Tarkingtons set out for Indiana with a five-horse wagon "tightly packed" with their household goods. Joseph provided an account of their journey:

> My mother rode on horseback, carrying the youngest child. The three children next older rode in the front part of the wagon; the rest walked and drove the cattle and hogs. The first night we all slept in a barn; the next day we passed Nashville, and forded the Cumberland below that place. We intended to reach the Ohio River at Diamond Island. By and by we came to White's Creek, and on a high hill we stopped at a hotel styled "paradise." Before reaching the Ohio, I sold my Indian pony—"Tackey," as he was called, which I had got in exchange for a calf before starting—because I did not want to pay his ferriage over the river and winter him afterwards. I sold him to some darkies, who came into our camp, for a skillet. It took the ferry boat all day to ferry us over the Ohio, just above Diamond Island. Some of the cattle and hogs jumped off the boat, the sides of which were not over a foot high, with nothing at the ends, and swam over. At dark we were all over, and glad of it. We camped for the night a mile or two from the landing. As soon as the meat began to fry for supper, the wolves commenced howling. From the sound, there seemed to be fifty of them. Our dogs would not go twenty feet from the camp. We could see the wolves by the firelight, and shot amongst them, but it did

no good. They howled around all night. This was down in the neck between the Ohio and Wabash, in Posey County.[1]

Crossing the Ohio River was a rough experience, and many lost their household possessions and livestock in the river. One man reported losing an entire team of mules that fell off a ferry. On occasion, human lives were lost crossing the river. Allen Wiley reported that a Methodist presiding elder named Learner Blackman drowned while crossing the Ohio at Cincinnati.[2]

After crossing the Ohio and spending the first night in Posey County, Indiana, the Tarkingtons moved on until they came to a farm owned by a man named Tweedle at Patoka, located in Gibson County. Jesse left his boys with Tweedle to help him gather his corn while he looked for a place to house his family for the winter. He returned and moved them to "Bushroe or Bushrun."[3] The Tarkingtons then helped people in the small community gather their corn. Jesse went farther into Indian country looking for a "winter home" for his family. A man named Hackett told Jesse that he could move his family to General Harrison's blockhouse on White River (now Edwardsport). Tarkington returned and moved his family to the blockhouse after finding that hunters had carelessly burned it down.[4] Jesse and his sons built a log house at the site of the blockhouse. There was an abundance of deer and wild game, and there were several sugar camps in the area. William Polk had a sugar camp of "eight hundred trees, and a Mr. Chambers had a large one."[5] They processed thousands of pounds of maple sugar.

During the winter of 1815–16, Joseph Tarkington said that they cleared twenty acres of land and lived on a "school section" of land that had not been put on sale by the government. On the other side of the White River, no one lived within ten miles of the settlement. Joseph rode a horse ten miles to Emerson's Mill, located between Vincennes and Shakertown, in order to get cornmeal ground. Indians would bring "turkeys and venison hams to exchange for meal."[6] Tarkington was always "obliged to keep a good lookout" anytime he left home because of the threat of Indians. The Delaware and Miami Indians living in the area were friendly, but Indiana was still in a state of war.[7] Shawnee Chief Tecumseh had only been killed two years earlier at the Battle of Thames.[8] Several people had been killed near the area where the Tarkingtons were living during the War of 1812.

In 1811, William Boggs and his family were killed by Indians in Martin County. The following year, John McGowan was also killed in Martin County.[9]

In 1815, at Lawrence County just north of the present town of Leesburg, a group of Potawatomis attacked the blockhouse where an inhabitant, John Guthrie, was tomahawked and scalped.[10] One year prior to the "Leesville Massacre" a trapper known as Pierre was killed by Indians in Bono Township, also located in Lawrence County.[11] It was not until 1818 that the United States government obtained a treaty concerning Indiana, known as the "New Purchase," with several Indian tribes.[12] The land was bought from the Potawatomi, Miami, Delaware, and other tribes for an upfront price of thirteen thousand dollars and over eight thousand dollars annually in silver. Due to the shortage of currency on the frontier, the silver spent by the Indians at Indian posts boosted the Indiana economy.[13]

On one occasion during the winter of 1815–16, Indians who had camped near White River were caught in deep snow from a blizzard. Joseph claimed that "the bucks came and begged us to let their squaws and papooses into our cabin to save their lives. All of one end of the cabin was chimney, eighteen feet wide. We could haul logs in with a horse, and pass him out by an opposite door. Father let the Indians in, gave them a corner, and hung blankets up for a partition."[14]

In the summer of 1816, Joseph comments that people in the country were very sickly. His eighteen-year-old brother Jesse, who was two years older than Joseph, died.[15] Five additional members of the family became sick, and the Tarkingtons decided to move yet again. Joseph's father and a Mr. Shields attended a land sale at Vincennes in the fall of 1816. Tarkington, with only meager cash, bought one quarter section of land at two dollars per acre, west of what is now Stanford, Indiana, located in Monroe County.[16] The land had to be paid for in four installments, which caused hardship for many pioneers. Many of the initial settlers to Monroe County could not pay for their land outright, so the government allowed them to take less land than they bid for at the land sale. The land office required payment to be made in gold, silver, or United States Bank notes. Other forms of money were accepted, but were usually devalued from twenty-five to seventy-five cents on the dollar. The Tarkingtons paid for their land by making fence rails at twenty-five cents a hundred. Hoosier historian Benjamin S. Parker comments on the scarcity of money and claims that the backwoods were "cleared and improved" on credit freely given by merchants and the "great eastern houses."[17]

The shortage of money caused pioneers to use a barter system of exchange. Settlers traded among one another and with the early stores, which had staples such as "powder, lead, salt, iron, leather and whiskey." Pioneers obtained these goods by exchanging products like "beeswax, tallow, feathers, ginseng, furs, deerskins, and wild hops."[18] Coffee, tea, sugar, and tobacco were luxuries most pioneers could not afford. On the other hand, farm produce was almost worthless. "It took eighty bushels of corn to buy a yard of silk, eight bushels to buy a yard of calico, and one hundred bushels to buy a yard of broad cloth" during the pioneer period.[19] Credit was advanced toward purchasing everything but powder, shot, whiskey, and salt. These items were too rare and in too much demand for advances to be made. One store owner stated that he would receive "pay for subscriptions in corn, ginseng, honey, flour, pork, or almost anything but promises."[20]

The few stores that existed "quickly became the heartbeat and pulse of a good portion of American business." Virtually no banks existed, so the stores circulated the small amounts of cash that were available. In their own communities, these stores were the center of neighborhood activities and were the source of information. Everything of importance that happened was reported at the local stores.[21]

Religion also had "hard beginnings" in southern Indiana at the time the Tarkingtons arrived. Nevertheless, there were many kinds of "Churches and preaching." Joseph indicated that he wanted to attend all of the meetings. The family did not belong to any church, and Joseph stated that the first time he heard any preaching in the territory "was at the funeral of his brother Jesse, who died at Edwardsport."[22] The funeral service was conducted by Mr. McCoy, who was a missionary to the Indians.[23]

En route to Monroe County, the Tarkingtons paddled a pirogue, borrowed from a Mr. Buckles and loaded with what goods they could carry, up the White River.[24] The river was high and swift, which made travel difficult. After a week of traveling, Jesse and Mary, along with Eli and George, made camp at the mouth of Richland Creek, while Joseph, Burton, and a hired hand took the pirogue back to Mr. Buckles at Edwardsport. Harden, John, Berry, and Joseph's sister, Mary, had remained at Edwardsport to care for the stock. After Joseph returned they loaded their remaining household goods in a wagon and drove the cattle and hogs across the river at Edwardsport.[25] The first day of travel, the Tarkingtons came to the log cabin of Zeb Hogue. The hogs were penned, and the cattle were allowed to graze freely with a "bell leader." Joseph recalled the journey:

> With a cold breakfast of bread and meat the next morning, we were off before
> daylight on the Indian trail. We had often to cut the way for the wagon through

the brush. We went through Owl Prairie, and got over Richland Creek the second day. The smaller children slept in the wagon, the rest of the family on the ground. Those on the ground were blanketed with snow in the night. The next morning repeated the starting of the day before, and leaving the trail we went up on the ridge. Father had blazed the trees for three miles from the deposit to the trail in the direction he thought we would come. The snow was ten inches deep.[26]

From Richland Creek there was a distance of thirty miles to their destination on Indian Creek. Judge Joseph Berry and Eli Lill had gone on to their new home on Indian Creek to put up cabins. Along the way, Berry and Lill were "hacking the bushes, marking a 'B' or an 'L' on the trees."[27] The Tarkingtons' livestock did well on the "march through the great woods"; there was acorns, nuts, and grass under the snow. After the first day of travel from Zeb Hogue's cabin, the Tarkingtons came to a large hill and were forced to unload their wagon and carry supplies on their shoulders. At night the party piled brush on the snow and placed deer and bear skins on top for a place to sleep.

On the second day, Joseph claims to have seen more wild turkeys than he had ever observed. He adds that "a half-mile square appeared covered with them." As travel commenced on the second day, the briars grew thick and strong, which cut the legs of horses and people alike. They wrapped the horses' legs with deerskins for protection. Joseph points out that "the boy with the buckskin trousers had to do the running in driving the stock. He had to run or give up his trousers, and he chose the former alternative all the time."[28] The second night of the journey, the Tarkingtons stopped at what they called the "Johnny-cake Camp." The party had cut a large chip out of a hickory tree and baked bread on it by the "log heap fire." By the third night, the weather had turned warmer and it rained. Mary and the smaller children got into the wagon. The remainder of the party got under the wagon or sat by the fire, covering themselves with skins as protection from the rain.[29] On the fourth day, the Tarkingtons arrived at their new home. Joseph described the final leg of his family's move to Monroe County.

The fourth day we struck the blazed trees which led to the Indian Springs. (The Indian or Blue Springs in Monroe County were a resort for Indians going back and forth from Vincennes to Fort Wayne.) When we came to a certain blazed tree, we turned off the ridge and came to the Twins Springs, which come out of the bank a few feet apart and run into Indian Creek. We then followed up the creek until we came to a branch of it, which we followed to the land father had purchased, and in the middle of this land we stopped, and built a camp on the banks of the branch.

The camp was a clapboard tent, the clapboards put up endwise, one end open to a large log-heap fire. We then built a cabin on the north end of the land, near a running-out spring; but having discovered the "cave spring," which was of pure water, welling up among large rocks, the next fall we moved down near it, and built a good house, which became the home of father and mother until their death.[30]

Most of the early pioneers in Monroe County lived in what was called the "half-faced camp" for the first few months.[31] This type of dwelling was also known as a "lean-to." It was built by cutting two forks from saplings and driving them into the ground only a few feet apart and close to a fallen tree. A cross pole was then placed in the forks, with one end on the cross pole and the other on the fallen tree. Poles were then placed horizontally across the structure to form the roof. The roof was completed by piling brush upon the poles.[32] The Tarkingtons' neighbor, John Sadler, lived in this type of home for twelve months or more.[33] These shelters were hastily constructed for temporary use in order that the ground could be cleared and the first crop (Indian corn) planted.[34] Some families lived in a covered wagon until their homes were built. After the crops were planted, a permanent cabin was constructed. Most pioneers who settled in southern Indiana were not able to construct large or elaborate homes. Most early dwellings were a "box-like" one-room structure. Settlers' homes were usually placed in an area with good drainage and an abundant water supply.[35]

Jesse Tarkington built a two-story house of "hewed" poplar logs. Cracks between the logs were filled with bits of wedged wood and then daubed with mud to "keep out the weather." The lower level of the Tarkingtons' home had two rooms and the upper part had two large rooms.

Upon arriving at their new home on March 10, 1817, the Tarkingtons immediately began clearing ground to raise corn. Joseph claimed that they worked early and late to get the ground ready to plow. As they were engaged in clearing land, Indians stole all of the horses but two. These two were used to pack provisions. When five acres had been cleared, Joseph began to plow, and Jesse obtained a three-year-old colt to aid in the plowing. The plow was "all wooden but the share," so Joseph was required to go over the ground two or three times in order to make one furrow. The Tarkingtons had nothing to feed the colt but grass. The horse was turned loose over night to graze, and he would "wander two or three miles."[36] Joseph placed a bell around the colt's neck, but was required to get up in the night to catch him. He claims the locusts were so bad that year that they were capable of drowning out the sound of the bell. While Joseph was plowing, Jesse and his other sons worked to clear five additional acres. In order to obtain seed corn, they had to travel a distance of "sixty-five to seventy-five miles." In spite of all the obstacles associated with farming, the Tarkingtons raised ten acres of corn the first year.

L. C. Rudolph comments that "[i]n the woods of Indiana these southern settlers became specialists in subsistence living."[37] It is true that self-sufficiency was born out of necessity and isolation. Pioneers like the Tarkingtons were forced to produce their own tools, furniture, medicines, and clothing. They grew most of their food, but items that were not homemade, such as coffee and salt, had to be procured from a great distance initially. Meal also could not be purchased locally. The closest hand mill was ten miles away. After traveling to the distant mills, many times Joseph had to sleep on a bearskin, eat parched corn, and wait a couple of days for the corn to be ground.[38] On occasion, the Tarkingtons beat corn into a mortar by hand and used it for bread. The remaining portion was too coarse for bread and was used for hominy. Flour was bought by the barrelful. It usually molded and made them sick. However, as Joseph remembered, "[W]henever the nausea from eating passed off, we would go at it again with tears in our eyes."[39] In 1818, Col. John Ketcham built a water mill on Clear Creek between Bloomington and Stanford.[40] Tarkington added, "There were good times, indeed, when Colonel John Ketcham built a water mill on Clear Creek."[41] Usually the mills were efficient in providing meal for the pioneers. Twice a year, during the autumn drought and the spring floods, the streams were either too high or low for the mills to function. During bad times, pioneers borrowed meal from one another until "the last sack was gone."[42]

When returning from one of the trips to get corn ground, Joseph and one of his brothers met a neighbor who informed them that their brother George had died two days earlier. With "grief stricken and heavy hearts," the brothers hurried home and arrived in time for the burial. Jesse made his son a coffin, which Joseph described: "Our father had made a coffin by splitting a piece of timber, scooping out a trough from the lower, and a corresponding excavation from the upper piece, and then fastened them together with wooden pins."[43] After the coffin was made, George was placed in it, and then lowered into the ground with the assistance of neighbors. Joseph indicated that the burial was the first on "Indian Creek, Monroe County."[44]

Just as his neighbors had helped bury his brother, Joseph was quick to assist them when labor was needed. He claimed that the "only profane word" he ever uttered was when he was helping build the Hamilton mill, located five miles from Bloomington.[45] As he was using a whipsaw with Campbell Berry, Berry jerked the saw into a knot and sent the opposite end into Tarkington's forehead, "raising a great welt" and causing him to cry out. In his *Autobiography*, Joseph commented that he had regretted his vulgar expression for nearly seventy years.[46] Berry was described by Joseph as a "stubborn sinner" who reproved him for his cursing, which made the young Tarkington feel "the more awful."[47] According to historian Benjamin S. Parker, Campbell Berry was typical of many Indiana pioneers. They were "unlettered, careless of apparel, uncouth of speech, and, when intoxicated, abusive, profane, and obscene."[48]

However, many of Indiana's settlers were not like Berry. Pioneers enjoyed recreation, especially recreation that took place alongside work; "house raisings, log-rollings, wood choppings, sawings, corn-huskings, hog-killings, wool-pickings, quiltings, apple-parings, rag-cuttings, carpet-tackings, and even chicken-pickings were often converted into festive occasions by social cooperation."[49] Dancing was also a joyous frolic in southern Indiana, along with games that ended with kissing or, in graphic frontier terms, "gum sucking."

> *Down on this carpet you must kneel,*
> *And kiss your true love in the field;*
> *Kiss her now and kiss her then*
> *And kiss her when you meet again.*[50]

The frontier frolics often aroused a sense of Wesleyan guilt in men like Joseph Tarkington or Peter Cartwright. From these men's childhood, good times equated with sin and turning away from God. As mentioned, churches were rare in the early days of settlement. It was also difficult to supply enough clergymen to keep up with the expanding population of the West.[51] The first church meetings in Monroe County generally held by the Methodists, Baptists, and Presbyterians were conducted in private cabins.[52] Often the home would be "crowded with strangers."[53] After the large immigration of the 1830s had commenced, other denominations such as the Campbellites began to emerge. Soon after the Tarkingtons settled in Monroe County, they attended a church meeting eight miles from their home. Joseph claimed that they were "all anxious to go; so the larger children of the neighborhood, boys and girls, walked this little distance barefooted, with shoes in hand, until near the house, where a halt was called for putting on shoes before going into meeting."[54]

The preacher at the gathering was "the Rev. Morgan." Morgan's sermon was on the "Songs of Solomon ii, 3: 'As the apple-tree among the trees of the wood, so is my beloved among the sons. I sat down under his shadow with great delight, and his fruit was sweet to my taste.'" Morgan compared evil to the "tree of the woods, very knotty and exceedingly crooked—with the righteous as the healthy apple-tree, very smooth and comely, and abounding in much good fruit." Not only did Morgan's sermon around the gathering's spiritual desires, it also made them crave apples, which were nonexistent in Monroe County at the time. Joseph stated, "His description of the large, ripe, luscious apples caused many of the young people, as well as old, to yearn after the good apples they had enjoyed in the years gone by."[55] As a result of the sermon, Joseph rode a horse seventy miles to Knox County and procured twenty-four apple trees. When he returned to Stanford, he planted the trees, which produced fruit for several years.[56]

The first Methodist preachers in Monroe County were Daniel Anderson and his brother George. Tarkington described Daniel as a man who was "six feet four inches tall. He had a lion's voice, was a good preacher, and better, he was a good man."[57] Anderson was sent to the Bloomington circuit by Elder Samuel Hamilton in 1818.[58]

Shortly after the people started settling in Monroe County, various religious groups began to conduct camp meetings. William W. Sweet states that camp meetings were usually conducted "on each circuit at some time during the summer months."[59] Religious camp meetings in the proximity of Bloomington were usually conducted twice a year.[60] The camp was located around five miles west of the city where the Crossroads Methodist Church now stands.[61] The meetings were festive occasions, when families left their homes for two weeks to live in tents, regular churches were closed, and children were taken out of the few primitive schools that existed.[62] Baynard Rush Hall described a camp meeting at the Bloomington site:

And so all Woodville [Bloomington] and its vicinities were in the ferment of departure for a camp-meeting! Now as this was to be a big meeting of the biggest size, and all the *crack* preachers within a circle of three hundred miles were to be present, and also a celebrated African exhorter from Kentucky, and as much was said about 'these heaven-directed, and heaven-blessed, and heaven-approved campings.' . . . The camp proper was a parallelogramic clearing, and was most of the day shaded by the superb forest trees, which admitted here and there, a little mellow sunshine to gleam through the dense foliage upon their own dark forms, quivering in a kind of living shadow over the earth. All night the camp was illuminated by lines of fires, kindled and duly sustained on the tops of many altars and columns of stone and log-masonry—a truly noble and grand idea, peculiar to the West.[63]

Camp meetings did not always contain only members of the same faith; Joseph reported many denominations at the gatherings in Monroe County. The denominations also intermarried. At one camp meeting Campbell Berry, whose father was a New Light preacher, called on his sister-in-law, Betsy Burton, a Methodist, to pray for him. Then they sang, "O, that my load of sin were gone!" Berry's mother-in-law then prayed, and they sang, "Of Him who did salvation bring."[64] Berry's wife, who could "pray like a saint," led in prayer. Then Berry started crying, as Joseph described it: "[f]rom a low murmur, his voice grew louder and louder, higher and higher, till he could be heard a mile. His grief seemed unutterable, and he found no relief. He seemed to lack faith in Christ to save."[65] At one of the interdenominational camp meetings conducted at the "Crossroads," Joseph experienced conversion. He recounted the event:

My conversion took place at a camp-meeting four miles west of Bloomington, on August 27, 1820, at eleven P.M., with a Methodist class-leader, Daniel Rollins, on one side, and a Presbyterian elder, Samuel Dodds, on the other. I praised God, and commenced to look after my comrades. It appeared to me that God at that time called me to look for the lost. The next morning, Monday, the meeting closed, and I went home. None of our family made any profession of being religious. In the afternoon of that day my mother proposed going to my brother's, half a mile from our house. As we walked we talked of the camp-meeting. Mother said, "We hear you were converted last night." I answered, "Yes." She said, "Hold fast to your profession." I saw tears falling on her cheeks as she spoke. She said she was converted the time the earth shook in Tennessee, in 1811; that she had backslidden from not joining Church and making profession of it, and so had put her light under a bushel. We encouraged each other as we walked. I had not then joined any Church, but intended to do so after I should study the doctrines of the Churches. I joined the Methodist Episcopal Church on June 10, 1821, at a meeting held in Benjamin Freeland's house by Rev. David Chamberlain, who the folks called the "Wild Yankee."[66]

Prior to Joseph's conversion, Methodist preacher Daniel Anderson was preaching in the area around the Tarkingtons' home at Stanford. Joseph was plowing a field when the Freeland, Rollins, and other families passed en route to a meeting Anderson was conducting. Joseph remembered that there was bread, venison, and bedding packed on their horses. Benjamin Freeland had four children who experienced conversion at the meeting, and on their return Joseph claimed one of them stopped "and exhorted me to turn to the Lord and seek the new peace in which he now rejoiced; and as he talked with an earnestness irresistible, I promised to attend the approaching camp-meeting near Bloomington, and endeavor to seek the Lord; and I kept my promise faithfully. I went to the meeting intending to avail myself of all its privileges and benefits; and on Sabbath evening, under the preaching of John Shrader, I was caused to cry for mercy."[67]

After Joseph had experienced conversion, it took him ten months before he decided what church he would join. He first read the *Confession of Faith of the Presbyterian Church*, which he borrowed from Samuel Dobbs, who lived on Clear Creek. His friend David Rollins gave him a copy of Fletcher's *Checks on Calvinism*, which turned him away from the Presbyterians. Joseph's neighbor John Saddler gave him the *Philadelphia Confession of the Baptist Church*, which did not win him over.[68] Finally, Rollins gave him the *Methodist Discipline*, and he said "the doctrine of that suited me, as it has so many thousands, to guide the way to Christ."[69]

The immigrants from the South who moved into southern Indiana all brought with them different forms of belief. In his autobiography, Tarkington claimed that in Monroe County alone there were "two kinds of Baptists, three kinds of Presbyterians, with New Lights, Christians, Disciples," and others. Most preached a modified version of Calvinism, except the Old Side Baptists, "who took it straight, infant damnation and all."[70]

Examining a few examples of new churches on the frontier should convey some idea of the diversity of religious experience there. The Vernal Baptist Church was formed on August 14, 1817. The first service was conduced September 7, 1817, at the home of Benjamin Parkes. On January 12, 1822, a site was selected for a church on James Parkes's property. People who had moved into Monroe County and wished to join the church had to present a letter of good standing from the church "from whence they Came." Elizabeth Basker of North Carolina claimed that "[s]he had been a baptist in N. Carolina and had moved with out Requesting a letter the Church a Gree to write to the Church

She Came from in her behalf for a letter." Church membership could be revoked for several reasons. Not paying creditors, "too much spirits," assault and battery, being quarrelsome, or long absences from church were common grounds for expulsion. William and Polly Rawlins were excluded from the Vernal Baptists after "joining a people cal'd Christians of another faith."[71]

The followers of Barton W. Stone also began having church meetings around 1818. Because they had no church, meetings were conducted in private homes. John Henderson was their preacher. Henderson was described as a "large man, had a strong voice and was a great singer."[72] Henderson could be heard singing "old-time hymns" a mile away. Assisting Henderson was "an ex-slave brought from Kentucky." He was known as "Black Aaron" Wallace. Wallace was known for preaching and acting out his sermons at the same time. "When he took David and Goliath as his text he would fold his handkerchief into a sling, put in the stone, whirl it and let it fly, then turning quickly he would personate Goliath, receive the stone in his forehead and fall down dead on the platform."[73]

In 1816, the Presbyterian Societies in New England sent several missionaries to Indiana. Two of the most noted were Isaac Reed and William W. Martin. These missionaries played a role similar to that of the Methodist circuit riders. They rode from settlement to settlement, preaching the gospel. The first organized church in the county was a Presbyterian Church. It was established on September 26, 1819, by Rev. Isaac Reed. The church service was conducted at the log courthouse.[74] In his correspondence, Reed later confirmed that he had established the Bloomington church: "At Bloomington I spent the Sabbath with the little church, which I had formed in the year 1819, and preached twice. They were still vacant, and but little increased. The Lord's supper had been twice dispensed to them since its constitution."[75] The first regular minister was David C. Proctor, who took the position in 1822. Proctor preached three-fourths of his time in Indianapolis and the remainder in Bloomington.[76] The Christians also began to conduct church meetings around 1820. The Methodists built a permanent church in Bloomington around 1826.[77] Joseph Tarkington's friends Benjamin Freeland and Daniel Rollins were in the congregation.[78]

Ruffians constantly mocked preachers and their congregations in early Indiana. Most who did the harassing were usually inflamed by drink. These episodes only reinforced Joseph's hatred for spirits, which he had developed in Tennessee. Many early Hoosier preachers consumed whiskey along with the ruffians. To refuse a drink when offered, frequently resulted in an insult that might lead to a fight.[79] Most preachers simply ignored the agitators or they responded in a gentleman's style.

After Joseph joined the Methodists, he spent little time with the coarse and crude friends he had associated with before. With his passive personality, intelligence, and other admirable qualities, he was a good candidate for becoming a circuit rider.

Chapter Four

Hearing the Calling

A short time after Joseph joined the Methodists, he was called on to lead a prayer during a church service. Joseph stated, "It was not long before I was found leading in prayer at our class-meetings, and occasionally exhorting my young friends to accept the overtures of mercy, and travel with me to the heavenly country. In my public efforts in prayer and exhortation, I found great difficulty on account of my limited education; but feeling that there was something for me to do for the Heavenly Father, I commenced the study of English Grammar under the direction of my class-leader (Daniel Rollins); and as I was in earnest, with a direct object in view, I made rapid progress."[1] Due to Joseph's rapid development in the faith and mastery of grammar, he was appointed class leader in 1821 by Rev. John Cord after Daniel Rollins (Rawlins) moved to Bloomington.[2] It was the duty of the class leader to meet with every member of the class once a week. If not everyone attended class, it was the class leader's duty to visit the absentee or sick person in their homes. The purpose of the visits was to give religious counsel, advice, encouragement, or administer shame if needed. The class leader also met with the preacher to turn over any money that was collected, along with reporting any member who needed aid. Classes were usually conducted in members' homes, since few churches existed in early Indiana, and they usually opened with hymn singing and then were followed with a prayer or reading of the Scriptures. The class leader then spoke to each member of the class, usually to discuss each other's divine experiences. On occasion, special topics and other pressing church matters were addressed. It was believed that these meetings cultivated a stronger, "more vigorous type of Christian piety."

In 1822 the Rev. James Armstrong was appointed to the Bloomington circuit.[3] Armstrong preached frequently at the Tarkington home and was popular among the people living around Stanford. Shortly after Armstrong's arrival, he made Joseph an exhorter. The exhorter was required to have a license signed by the preacher in charge and to attend the quarterly conference and district conference. Exhorters were licensed to speak and evangelize but not to serve as ordained ministers. They also "could not base their remarks on the Scriptures."[4] Exhorters were subject to annual examinations of their character and their licenses were renewed yearly.[5]

The people in Bloomington built a large meeting house shortly after Armstrong began preaching in the area. Joseph "hewed every log and hauled them to the place." Joseph continued in his role as exhorter throughout 1823. Armstrong was appointed as presiding elder of the Indiana district in 1824. Armstrong took Joseph with him on the district for five weeks. It was Armstrong's plan to make Joseph a minister and place him on the Boonville circuit. Tarkington refers to this process as "traveling the circuit under the presiding elder by one who had not been appointed by the Conference."[6] The Bloomington circuit at the time consisted of Lawrence, Monroe, Owen, and Greene Counties, along with parts of Morgan and Jackson Counties.

The early circuit-riding preachers had little money to live on, and on the "few spare days" at the end of their circuit they worked a variety of tasks to earn more. Rev. John Cord split rails for fifty cents a hundred. Joseph commented on Cord: "Once I took him some cornmeal, flour, bacon, and hay in a wagon, and found him near his house, coming out of the woods with ax, maul, and wedge, and as he saw what I had brought, he wept with grateful joy like a child. I had gathered the provisions from my class, here a little and there a little, what each could spare."[7]

In the fall of 1824, Joseph was licensed to preach when Armstrong took a recommendation to the district conference at Shiloh, in Lawrence County.[8] Armstrong sent Joseph to the Boonville circuit to assist Rev. Orsenath Fisher, who was in bad health. When Joseph received his instruction he stated, "During the year 1824, at a local conference. . . . I was licensed to preach the Gospel; and when Armstrong handed me the paper announcing the fact, he stated that there was immediate use for me, that one of the preachers on Boonville Circuit had failed on account of ill health, and that I must depart for my field of labor immediately. Excuses of every kind proved unavailing, and as it seemed to be the will of the Lord."[9]

Joseph pleaded, "I am not prepared; I have just begun to go to school here [Bloomington], and how can I leave school?"[10] Armstrong replied, "No, you must go." Joseph responded, "But I have no horse for such travel." Armstrong then asked a young man named Wilson if he would change horses with Tarkington. Wilson gave his consent. Tarkington then complained that he had no great coat. Armstrong then asked Daniel Rollins to give Joseph his coat, and Rollins complied. Armstrong then said to Joseph, "There, no more excuses. Meet me tomorrow at Judge Sedgewick's, or God will curse you."[11] Armstrong's declaration "fell heavily" on Joseph. He went home to Stanford and told his family about his decision to become a circuit rider. Tarkington was visited by his neighbors, who bid him farewell. He claims that his father's house was filled with members of his old class. They encouraged him to preach them a farewell sermon. Joseph preached his third sermon to the gathering, and he "talked as well as I could, urging them to hold fast to the faith, that we might all meet in heaven."[12] As he was coming to the end of his message, he asked "if there was anyone who wished to join the Church." Both of Joseph's parents came forward with two neighbors.[13] Tarkington described the scene: "At the close of the sermon I opened the doors of the church, and two or three came forward. A slight pause ensuing, my father and mother, hand in hand, presented themselves as candidates for membership in the Church. O, the joy of that hour! The long-prayed-for event had happened! To God be all the glory!"[14]

The next morning Joseph left to meet Armstrong at Judge Sedgewick's. As he was preparing to leave, he comments that his mother "fell on my neck and kissed me, and the family, in tears, said good-bye. I was starting on a life's journey." When Tarkington arrived at Sedgewick's, he found that Armstrong had already left. Joseph caught the preacher at a ferry that crossed White River. The two stayed at a Mr. Paine's house in Owen County that night. The next evening they reached Greencastle and stopped at Mr. Haresty's cabin. Tarkington commented that they were "very hungry, and cornbread never tasted better." On the third day Joseph and Armstrong halted at Sugar Creek without eating, and finally on the fourth day they "crossed the Wabash and went to Helt's Prairie, where the quarterly-meeting was held."[15] Joseph recalled what happened next:

When we got there Rev. John W. McReynolds was preaching. Armstrong exhorted after him. The meeting was at a private house. Rev. Hackeliah Vreedenburg was one of the preachers on that circuit, a very good man and poorly paid. Rev. Robert Delap was the other preacher. From there we went to Mayo's. Mayo was the clerk of Edgar County, Illinois, but lived on a farm; for the office would not support him. . . . I preached the first night from Amos iv, 12 'Prepare to meet thy God.' I was badly scared; but the wife of Rev. J. W. McReynolds shouted and helped me out.[16]

Usually when preachers were young and afraid, they related their own experiences, especially their conversion experiences. Eggleston commented that "[t]he early preacher's universal refuge was his own experience. It was the sure key to the sympathies of the audience."[17] Tarkington claimed that people came "six or eight miles" to attend the meetings. Joseph and Armstrong then left Illinois and went to Mr. Barnes's home, which was ten miles north of Terre Haute, Indiana. They attended the quarterly meeting of the Honey Creek circuit. From Honey Creek they went to Rev. Samuel Hull's place in Carlisle and then to the Vincennes circuit at the Rev. J. Posey's home at Bruceville. Armstrong preached, and then he and Joseph went to the quarterly meeting "at Mr. Hinckley's, on Black Creek." On Saturday Armstrong preached. Rev. Edwin Ray delivered the Sunday morning message, and Joseph gave a sermon, "Do not quench the Spirit," from 1 Thessalonians 5:19 during the evening service. Armstrong and Joseph then left the quarterly meeting and went to Vincennes. With a man named David Bonner they went to the courthouse and listened to a Presbyterian missionary, Mr. Martin, preach a sermon on the topic "the kingdom shall be taken away from thee."[18]

Conservative Presbyterian ministers on the frontier desperately attempted to stem the tide of revivalism. Many frontier Presbyterian preachers, like James Welsh, "shunned the emotional excesses that grew out of the camp meetings and opposed Arminian tendencies that grew out of popular revivalism." However, the Presbyterians were suffering from problems within their own ranks and suffered many schisms. Emil Pocock writes that during the late 1780s there was a dispute among Presbyterian churches in Lexington, Kentucky, because a "popular revivalist minister, Adam Rankin, had refused to adopt Isaac Watts's modern hymnal, claiming that only the literal versions of the Psalms were fit to sing in church." Presbyterians were also split between liberals, who supported Thomas Jefferson's political beliefs and religious deism, and those who were more conservative and identified with the Federalists.[19]

After attending the Presbyterian gathering, Tarkington and Armstrong passed through Princeton, Indiana, and on to Mr. Nesbit's residence. The next day they went to Jonathan Jacque's, where they met Rev. John Shrader. Shrader had preached the sermon the night Joseph was converted, near Bloomington.[20] Joseph and Armstrong next went to Evansville, "which at the time, 1824, was very sickly."[21] Joseph described Evansville:

> It appeared that half the houses were empty. It had not a schoolhouse or meeting-house. There were not a dozen Methodists in the town. There was an old frame building in which a school was taught, and sometimes preaching had. The quarterly-meeting was held up-stairs in a dilapidated frame house. Armstrong preached on Saturday at eleven A.M., and George Randall preached at night, Mr. Warner, who kept the only hotel, a small frame house, said if Armstrong would preach Monday night he could have the hotel dining-room, and Armstrong preached there that night.
>
> Things here looked discouraging; few members, and no leader; the circuit preachers, Revs. W. H. Smith and George Randall, with clothes well worn out.[22]

John Shrader had been preaching in the area since 1819. One of the first meetings that he conducted was at "Hugh McGary's double log warehouse."[23] The few practicing Methodists in Evansville had been meeting at McGary's Ferry since 1809.[24] There was also a group of English who had settled in the area. Among them were three educated "regularly ordained ministers, Richard and Joseph Wheeler, and Robert Parrett."[25] The Wheelers had studied under Adam Clark in England. Joseph Wheeler's wife, "when a small child, had recited a long psalm while sitting on John Wesley's knee in her father's house in Witney."[26]

In 1821 Dr. John W. Shaw gave the Methodists permission to meet in the front room of his new home, which was in the process of being built. The Methodists met at Dr. Shaw's residence until 1824, when the group moved to Warner's tavern. Iglehart found that Warner's tavern was called the "den" because men generally met here to "play cards and drink, but the tavern-keeper, when it was time for the preacher to come around, had it vacated, swept and cleaned."[27] Meetings had to form in such places, "whether in the tavern, the courthouse or the log-cabin, for there were up to 1830 no churches in Vanderburgh county."[28]

Joseph, Armstrong, and Orceneth Fisher went to Boonville after preaching in Evansville.[29] Tarkington preached the sermon, and Armstrong followed "with an exhortation." The preachers then went to Rockport, located in Spencer County, and Armstrong preached at 11:00 A.M. in an "old-brick courthouse." Kentuckian Rev. George Locke preached at night from "Arise and shine, your light having come."[30] Armstrong again conducted the Sunday morning meeting and then went to Kentucky with Locke and Rev. James L. Thompson. Joseph and Fisher were left in Indiana to finish the quarterly meeting.

Tarkington preached at the courthouse, and Fisher governed the altar call. Seven were converted. On Monday, Joseph and Fisher "started for an appointment in Pigeon Creek." The men stopped at Mr. Barnett's home for breakfast. After they were finished Fisher prayed for the family while Joseph got their horses. Joseph recalled the event: "Fisher and the others got to singing and shouting, and I held the horses at the gate for half an hour, waiting. They had a happy time. After they had calmed down, Fisher and I started; but on the way he got happy and shouted, and in his ecstasy fell off his horse Charley, who stood still, as if used to the occurrence, until his master got ready and mounted."[31]

Joseph described Fisher as "the most diligent man in pastoral work" he had ever met. Fisher would visit families in the manner of a missionary. Tarkington related an incident in which Fisher was preaching at McCoy's, located between Rockport and Boonville. After he had completed his message, Fisher crossed Pigeon Creek during a severe rainstorm that rose so high he could not recross until the next day. Joseph and elder Joseph Arnold conducted the meetings in Fisher's absence. When Fisher returned he reported that he had visited ten families and had prayed and preached to each of them. Several of the families joined the church after Fisher's visit.[32]

A camp meeting was conducted by Joseph and his associates between Boonville and Evansville. Armstrong, the presiding elder, attended and "preached with much power." After the meeting had finished, Armstrong took Joseph and Fisher with him on an extensive evangelical trip. The men first went to the Paoli camp meeting, which was on the Blue River circuit, then to the Bloomington circuit camp meeting, and on to the Illinois conference, "which met in August that year, 1825, at Charleston, Indiana." The Illinois conference, which had just been carved out of the Missouri conference in 1824, included Indiana, Illinois, and parts of Michigan. The conference was divided into four districts. The Madison district had John Strange as presiding elder; Charleston had Armstrong; Wabash had Charles Holliday; and Illinois had Samuel Thompson.[33] Six new circuits were created—Rushville, Salem, Paoli, Boonville, Vermillion, and Mt. Vernon. The old Blue River and Mt. Sterling circuits were absorbed into the new circuits.[34] At the close of the conference there was a total of nineteen circuits in Indiana.

Prior to 1801 the Methodist conference in the West was known as the Kentucky conference. Later in the year, the name was changed to the Western conference, which existed until 1813, when it was divided into the Ohio and Tennessee conferences.[35] In the year 1816, all of the settled parts of Indiana was encompassed in the bounds of these two conferences.[36] In 1801 the Kentucky district of the Western conference contained nine circuits located in Kentucky and Ohio. The circuits were "manned by fourteen preachers and one Presiding Elder, the redoubtable William McKendree." None of these circuits were found in Indiana in 1801, but William Warren Sweet contends that early Methodist services were conducted by local preachers "who came into the Indiana country among the first settlers."[37] In 1818 the parts of Indiana where Joseph Tarkington later preached were placed in the Missouri conference. In 1824 the Missouri conference was divided, and the states of Indiana and Illinois were placed in the Illinois conference.

One of the most important features of the annual conference meeting was the examination of a preacher's character. Even at the quarterly meetings, in which regular members were brought to trial, a common question was asked: "Are there any complaints or appeals?" The Methodist *Discipline* had a mechanism for "disciplining its ministry and church members," which began with John Wesley's "General Rules of the United Societies" as follows:

> These are the General Rules of our societies: all of which we are taught of God to observe, even in his written Word, which is the only rule, and the sufficient rule, both of our faith and practice. And all these we know his Spirit writes on truly awakened hearts. If there be any among us who observes them not, who habitually breaks any of them, let it be known unto them who watch over that soul as they who must give an account. We will admonish him in the error of his ways. We will bear with him for a season. But, if he then repent not, he hath no more place among us. We have delivered our souls.[38]

Although lesser charges were brought against preachers, such as "improper tempers, words, or actions," and the most common charge "during the first twenty years of the Illinois Conference was immorality," Robert H. Williams states that "[t]he charges of immorality are quite interesting. They reflect the general society as well as the church's standards on the frontier." Immorality did not only apply to sexual offenses in the first years of the Illinois conference, although prenuptial fornication was generally grounds for suspension of preachers and members alike. The term "immorality" pertained to "falsehood or lying, slander, taking bribes, drinking, fighting on the Sabbath, violation of contracts, and non-payment of debt." Sexual offenses did occur and ministers were sanctioned for them. As was common practice, preachers frequently stayed in members' homes. On September 28, 1837, a preacher named Simon Peter (his real name) was invited to the home of Mrs. Forsythe "for the night service after the evening services at the conference session." When Peter was shown to his room he embraced Mrs. Forsythe and kissed her. Mrs. Forsythe ran to a neighbor for assistance and charges of "Immoral Conduct" were issued against Peter. On September 30, he was brought before the conference and pleaded guilty. Peter was expelled from the church. In 1847, Reuben Plummer was expelled from the church for placing his hand between a Miss Ogden's legs and "twice in the same night" visiting the bedside of Mrs. Kizzard.[39]

A common charge brought against church members and preachers was the misuse of spirits. Sweet claimed, "Undoubtedly the basic moral problems which confronted the average frontier community grew directly or indirectly out of the abundant supply of intoxicating liquor which was to be found on every new and raw frontier." Peter Cartwright "caused many a liquor seller to go to jail for selling on the camp-grounds" of the camp-meetings.[40] The Baptists and Presbyterians also sanctioned their members for moral offenses, especially for the use of spirits. In 1816 the Synod of Pittsburgh took action against whiskey users in their congregations, and they assessed the "use of ardent spirits": "The excessive use of ardent spirits produces sickness poverty and wretchedness; it destroys health and reputation; introduces discord into families and larger communities; it enervates the strong and changes many of the wise into idiots; it threatens to sweep our land as with a besom of destruction, and calls loudly on all the friends of religion, order, science and humanity to exert their influence in checking an evil so alarming in its progress and so vicious in its effects."[41] But whiskey was always a threat. It was commonly found everywhere, which is not surprising when even part of some Presbyterian ministers' salaries were paid with spirits. Church members regularly complained that preachers "smelled very strong of whisk[e]y." Regardless of the abuses and excessive personal liberties of some church members and preachers, the frontier churches were in most instances the only guardians of morals in the small communities.[42]

At the Illinois conference in 1825, Joseph along with Philip Cole, William See, Eli P. Farmer,[43] James Hadley, and Asa D. West had their characters examined and passed.[44] Joseph commented that the "examination at Conference of candidates for admission was very strict in the early days. They were called before five to seven of the clearest heads of the Conference. Well do I remember my time, when Dr. Allen Wiley, Revs Calvin Ruter, Thomas Hitt, Samuel H. Thompson, George Locke, and James Scott put us 'through the flintmill.'" After the examination Joseph was appointed to the "Patoka Circuit, in the Wabash District, with James Garner in charge." Tarkington states that Garner had a wife and five children, and he could not support them on the twenty-eight dollars a year that he received on the circuit preaching. Part of the amount was paid in "leather, linsey-woolsey, and flax." Joseph received only "nine dollars and a pair of trousers."[45] He adds that he had to "draw on" his father for other clothing.

Despite his poverty, Tarkington and the other circuit riders continued to gain church members through their efforts. Joseph's circuit included New Harmony, where Robert Owen had established his communal settlement. Tarkington disliked the commune and described the atmosphere:

Robert Dale Owen had bought out Mr. Rapp, and tried to establish his system of living in common harmony, which proved a failure. He erected a chapel and hall, which all denominations of Christians and all free-thinkers and infidels were alike welcome. I preached in the chapel while a ball was going on in the hall, connected with the chapel by a door. When the door opened to the other, the fiddling and preaching mingled in both rooms. Mr. Jennings, one of Mr. Robert Owens's followers, used to rise in the religious assembly and catechize and contradict the preachers. This he did to Mr. Beck, of Illinois; also to Rev. James Armstrong, who got even with him. He asked Armstrong, "Mr. Armstrong, how do you know you have a soul?" Armstrong answered, "I feel it." "Did you ever smell, taste, see, or hear your soul?" "No." "Then there are four senses against you." Then asked Armstrong, "Mr. Jennings, did you ever have a toothache?" "No" "Then you have four senses against you." The doctrines of Mr. Owen were "of man and came to naught." Now where his chapel of reason stood, is a Methodist station preacher, preaching "Jesus and the resurrection."[46]

The Patoka circuit that Joseph worked included five counties. The first day on his circuit he came to Archibald Campbell's, located one mile from Petersburg. It was dark upon his arrival, and he asked Mrs. Campbell if he could stay overnight. Mrs. Campbell told Tarkington that he could not stop for the night. She said the family was sick and no one could take care of Joseph's horse. Tarkington informed Mrs. Campbell that he could tend to his horse.

Mrs. Campbell then gave her consent for Joseph to spend the night, but she declared that he would have to wait on himself "and do without supper."[47]

Archibald Campbell had a high fever and was very sick. When Joseph entered the home, he asked if the young preacher was traveling. Tarkington admitted that he was. Joseph then asked Campbell if he knew any of the Methodist preachers, telling Campbell that the "presiding elder was Rev. Charles Holiday from Kentucky." After a conversation about other church figures, Campbell instructed his wife to give Joseph "some cornbread and cabbage." Tarkington then conducted several home meetings on the circuit at the close of 1825 and the first months of 1826.

One of the home meetings where Joseph preached was in the vicinity of Bruceville in the home of Richard Posey. Home meetings were also conducted at Posey's son-in-law William Hargrove's home until 1832, when a church was built.[48] When a small meeting house was available, they were generally log churches. At the meeting houses where Joseph preached, "[s]eats were log slabs with pegs fitted in for legs; the seats on the side of the church where women sit had backrests—another heavy hewed board scraped smooth."[49] On occasion the primitive churches were dangerous to the parishioners. In one event at the Asbury Chapel, which was lit by candles held by tin reflectors, burning tallow fell on the long, fluffy hair of a woman, setting it on fire "and almost causing a tragedy in the church."[50] Because of the great distances between locales, Joseph usually only conducted services every three or four weeks at each church. People would arrive hours early on horses or spring wagons in order to get news or to make business transactions with their neighbors before church.

The 1826 Illinois conference was held in Bloomington, Indiana, and started September 28. The Bloomington circuit at the time of the conference consisted of 670 white members and "5 colored."[51] Bishops Roberts and Soule presided over the meeting. Joseph Tarkington was appointed to the Sangamon circuit in Illinois, where Rev. Richard Hargrave was preacher in charge and Peter Cartwright was the presiding elder. After the conference concluded, Joseph reports that about ten preachers stopped at his father's house in Stanford for the night on their way to their appointments.[52] Joseph states that some of the men lay on pallets on the floor. Joseph found out while he was in Stanford that his father and his brother Sylvanus were planning to become trustees in the Ebenezer Methodist Church. In November 1826, they were elected, as the following document reveals:

Be it remembered that on the 29th day of November, 1826 the following instrument of writing was filed by one of the trustees to be made a matter of public
record to wit: At an election held at Jesse Tarkington's in Monroe County, State
of Indiana, according to advertisement on the 18th day of November, 1826 for
trustees of the Ebenezer Methodist Meeting house the following persons, members of the Methodist E. Church were duly elected. Thomas Freeland, John Whaley,
Samuel Hite, Jesse Tarkington, Sylvanus Tarkington.

Samuel Hite
Judge of the present election[53]

The morning after the preachers spent the night at Joseph's father's house,
they left en route to their appointments. Joseph rode with them. He remarked
that he was left alone before reaching the White River. The first night, Joseph
stayed with a black man, "twenty miles from Terre Haute." The next morning
he rode to John Dickson's place on Honey Creek, where he ate breakfast.
Tarkington then rode to Mr. Wayo's residence in Edgar County, Illinois, and
preached that night. The following day he was joined by Cartwright and
Hargrave. The preachers rode fifteen miles and stayed overnight with a man
who gave them "venison and roasting-ears to eat."[54] The next day the circuit
riders traveled forty-five miles to a cabin on the Okaw River owned by a Mr.
Sedoris. Joseph reflected on their night in the Sedoris cabin:

Cartwright had called for quarters for himself, Hargrave, and me but a few minutes before three others rode up to stay all night. The landlord told them he would
have to put them on the floor, and they were willing to take the floor; for they said
there was not a house to stay at within forty-five miles. When bedtime came, the
landlord said the first three who came should lie on and the last three under the
bed. And so it was; the three under the bed slept with their feet out. The man and
his family occupied the rest of the floor, the table having to be moved out of the
house for room. I slept between Cartwright and Hargrave on the bed, and was well
flattened out by morning.[55]

The next morning the preachers arose and ate a meal of cornbread and
venison for breakfast and the same for supper. Tarkington and the frontier ministers were charged fifty cents for their lodging. Many times the circuit riders
were required to pay for their lodging, and the Methodist Church did not reim-

An 1842 portrait of Bishop Robert Richford Roberts. DePauw University Archives and Special Collections.

burse them for their expenses. In a newspaper advertisement for Washington Hall in Indianapolis, Samuel Henderson listed his rates as follows:

Without lodging, per week	$2.00
including lodging, per week	$2.50
Legislative members and other during session	$3.50
If lodged separately	$4.00
In separate rooms	$5.00
Transient persons under one week self and horse per day	$1.25
Over one week, per day	$1.00
Rate of horse keeping, per day	.50
rate of horse keeping, per week	$2.00[56]

Regardless of room rates, Tarkington states that traveling expenses were cheap in the mid-1820s. In one instance, it only cost him $2.75 to travel from Bloomington, Indiana, to Springfield, Illinois. Even though travel was inexpensive, it was difficult, and as soon as wagon roads were opened the stagecoach appeared.[57] Traveling by stage was often worse and slower than by horseback.[58] Joseph Wheeler Walker's account of Methodist minister Thomas Goodwin's trip to Asbury College from Brookville in 1837 provides ample proof of the difficulties of traveling by stage:

> He reached Indianapolis too late for the stage west and had to lay over for a day in the capital. He took the St. Louis Limited Stage at ten o'clock that night and arrived in Plainfield in time for breakfast the next morning, having traveled a distance of fourteen miles. They had not gone far on this fourteen miles when the stage stuck in the mud.
>
> The passengers were requested to get out and get fence rails and pry the stage coach out of the mud. They obeyed. After getting out of that mud hole, the driver told the passengers that they had better carry the rails on down the road with them, because they would need them again.[59]

There was little danger in traveling by stage during this period. Nevertheless, there were accidents, usually caused by "drunken drivers or factious horses." Communication was slower than travel. The mail was carried on horseback, and the interval between mail service was "not less than a week and often more than two weeks, when the mails were regular."[60]

The day that Tarkington, Cartwright, and Hargrave left the Okaw River, Joseph and Cartwright killed a wolf. Both Joseph and Cartwright pursued the animal, but it was Cartwright's blow to the head with his stirrup that brought the animal down. Hargrave rode up to the men and demanded, "What are you doing?" Joseph answered, "Taking the wolf out of the way, so he won't trouble your sheep!"[61] Hargrave responded, "If you felt as I do about my horse's back being skinned by the saddle, you would not be after wolves." Tarkington comments that Hargrave was in "one of his blue moods, which fell to his lot often." Hargrave could not help his depression because he was dyspeptic, suffering from severe digestive problems.[62]

The preachers then rode forty-five miles that day and stayed at Mrs. Stevens's home, which was thirty miles east of Springfield, Illinois. The next day, Joseph stopped at Mr. Larkin's home on the Sangamon circuit, while Cartwright and Hargrave went on to Cartwright's home on Richland Creek.

Hargrave and Joseph made arrangements to meet near the middle of the circuit, at Mr. Clark's home near Sangamontown. There, the two reported to each other about their work.[63]

After traveling the circuit a "round or two," Tarkington and Hargrave visited a man who was to be hanged at the Springfield jail in November 1826. The prisoner had murdered his wife "in a drunken spree." After he was executed, Joseph claims that Hargrave stood and delivered the "greatest exhortation" that he had ever heard to the thousands of people assembled. In April 1827, Hargrave's dyspepsia caused him to suffer so much that he was forced to go to his father's home in Pike County, Indiana, for rest. Joseph was left in charge of the circuit, but Cartwright sent Rev. James Johnson to assist him.[64]

The 1827 Annual Conference was held at Mount Carmel, Illinois, on September 20. At this conference, Joseph, along with Eli F. Farmer, Asa D. West, and James Hadley were admitted to "full Connexion" and "Deacons orders" in the Methodist Church after they "were called in and questioned and admonished by Bishop Roberts as the Discipline Directs."[65] Joseph was reassigned to the Sangamon circuit with Isaac S. House. The following year at the 1828 conference held at Madison, Indiana, Joseph was assigned to the White Lick circuit. While at the 1829 conference at Edwardsville, Joseph was examined for "Elder's Orders" and approved. Also, Joseph's brother Hardin was admitted as a circuit rider on a trial basis.

Joseph and William Evans were appointed to the Rushville circuit in 1829–30 as preachers, and Allen Wiley was named presiding elder.[66] The circuit was so large it was known as the "four weeks circuit."[67] The Rushville circuit was located in the Madison district. Money was scarce during this period, and ginseng, coonskins, and small amounts of grain became legal tender for debts, especially the preacher's pay. The circuit included the small towns of "Rushville, Greensburg, St. Omer, New Castle, West Liberty, (now Knightstown), and Shelbyville." At some of these sites classes had not been formed, and it was Joseph's duty to build classes. Joseph left quite an impression upon young George Curtiss of Shelbyville, who later became a preacher. Curtiss described Joseph as "a genial man, a true friend, a sincere christian, a good preacher, and a careful disciplinarian."[68]

Tarkington found much religious enthusiasm and "community of feeling" at places like Sugar Creek when he was assigned to the Sangamon circuit. John Mack Faragher found that "regardless of their denominational proclivities," the residents of Sugar Creek attended the singing schools and sang to the "strictly religious" hymns found in the *Missouri Harmony*.[69] Faragher added: "Psalm-songs, practically unchanged from versions in the English Psalters of the six-teenth century, constituted the core of the *Missouri Harmony* collection. In singing schools and churches the leader 'lined-out' these metered verses, and the people sang them to familiar modal melodies like 'Old Hundreth': Before Jehovah's awful throne, / Ye nations bow with sacred joy ; /Know that the Lord is God alone, / He can creat[e], and He destroy."[70]

The Methodists continued to gain large numbers within the Illinois con-ference. In Indiana, Ruth Price discovered that "[w]hen the preachers made their reports in 1817, it was found that they had completely overcome the great loss in members caused by the war with Great Britain in 1812. The year 1817 showed an increase of 849 over the preceding year, and 580 over the number before the war began. In 1810 the population of Indiana was 24,520, and Methodism numbered its members at 755. In 1820, the population had increased to 144,178 and Methodists to 4,410."[71] Camp meetings continued to play a large role in gaining members. At a camp meeting at Crooked Creek, which was four miles from Madison, "there was one hundred and forty conver-sions."[72] The meeting at Crooked Creek went so well the preachers were re-quired to stay three extra days. It was near Madison that Joseph met his future wife.[73]

Chapter Five

A Young Preacher Weds

In the year 1830–31 Joseph was appointed to the Vevay circuit along with George Randle. Allen Wiley claimed that both preachers were "well received and labored with acceptability and success until spring, when Randle brought charges against one of the members in the circuit who was acquitted; and this acquittal so displeased Randle, that he left the work and went to farming."[1] Wiley did not tell the entire story why Randle quit preaching. Randle was an Englishman by birth and came to America as a preacher. Around 1830 Randle married a woman, "Miss Eubank," a marriage that was not approved of by her friends or her father. They eventually took their complaints to the quarterly conference. As a result Randle was "located"—that is, moved to another circuit—in 1831. However, neither party was satisfied with the action of the church, and thus two societies withdrew from the church. The event became known as the "Radical Secession." Randle moved to Dearborn County following the dispute and left the Methodists shortly after his location.[2]

Courtship and marriage for the circuit riders were often complicated and often ended in controversy. Marriage was not allowed to the circuit riders during their first four-year itinerancy. Unmarried preachers were required to discuss marriage with their brethren (usually the presiding elder) "before mentioning matrimony to a young woman."[3] If a preacher was even suspected of being in love before he had served his four years on the circuit, he risked being located to another circuit. T. A. Goodwin, who was the first graduate of Indiana Asbury, claimed that preachers often found themselves caught between two opposing forces—"one declaring that he must not marry until an arbitrary time had expired; and the other officiously, not only suggesting marriage, but proffering help in the selection of a 'suitable companion.'" The circuits generally encompassed several counties, and the appointments were often fifty miles apart. Each preaching engagement was usually autonomous, or "a sort of social center, distinct from all others." The locales almost always offered a "pious young sister" who met the qualifications for becoming a first-class preacher's wife. In 1899, Goodwin adds that as "strange as it may appear to this generation, most of these were heroic enough to be willing to endure all the hardships of the itinerant if they might providentially be called to it."[4]

To make matters worse, the preachers were often required to stay in members' home while on the circuit, so frequently they dwelt with these "self-sacrificing young sisters." When a young preacher stayed in a member's home, "common politeness required him to be courteous to all, and the instincts of a gentleman would lead him to be respectful to the grown daughter, who never failed to be in her best attire and on her best behavior during his stay." Goodwin reported:

> Before the year was out, the local gossips, encouraged perhaps by the hopeful mother, had the preacher engaged to this local belle, as they had to two or three of his predecessors. No prudence, short of boorishness and bad manners, could prevent this; and it was probably duplicated, on the same authority, over in the other county, or at one or more of the appointments twenty to fifty miles away. It is almost inconceivable at this time how many men and women of that period became meddlers in the matrimonial matters of unmarried preachers, under the impression that the preachers were bound to consult them.[5]

If the young preacher left the circuit without marrying, and with "no prosecution for a breach of marriage contract following him" to the conference, the frustrated girls "lay in wait for the next young preacher." Goodwin pointed out that if a young preacher did marry one of the girls on his circuit, it was likely that one or more of the disappointed ones would file a charge against him at the conference. Goodwin also found one young girl who had filed a grievance at "two or three successive Conferences against as many different preachers, who had shown her only common politeness when guests at her father's house."[6]

If a young preacher did find a potential bride but was not in a position to marry, he often turned the young woman over to unwed fellow itinerants. Rev. Elnathan C. Gavitt recalled his experience at Monroe, Michigan, in 1832:

> There was some of the most refined and intelligent young ladies belonging to this charge, and one of Whom would have been competent to have filled the place of a Methodist minister's wife. But knowing the law of the church and the penalty if a young minister married before he had served his full four years in conference, I dared not as much as squint at any one of them, much less to make any propositions. However, like the Quaker whose conscience would not permit him to fight in the defense of his country, but who could tell others where to shoot and not likely to miss their man, I referred my successor to one of these young ladies, William Sprague took a prize in Miss Zeruba Hall; and soon after Miss Aremintha Stoddard followed her good example.[7]

Almost all of the first circuit riders were unmarried. Bishop Asbury discouraged his preachers from marrying because of the hardships marriage would place on the circuit rider and his family. Many of the early preachers ceased to travel while they were young because they married and settled in a certain locale. Moreover, those who continued to ride after marrying faced straitened circumstances: the Methodists provided little money for the circuit riders, and they were required to provide their own horses and equipment. In 1825, Bishop McKendree advised Rev. Edwin Ray not to marry "for the reason that the unmarried preacher could go anywhere, and go further, easier, and cheaper."[8] Few circuits could provide for a preacher and his family. Tarkington was paid sixty-three dollars in 1829, while Rev. William Evans, who was married, also received sixty-three dollars.[9] The Methodists had a rule that attempted to keep young preachers single: preachers who married within four years after joining the conference "received no additional allowance."[10]

Not only women were competitive in their efforts to land a preacher husband; many times the preachers were just as aggressive in pursuing mates after serving their four years of celibacy. Goodwin recalled one occasion when three young preachers who had served their four years were in love with the same woman. All of them wanted to marry her, and they approached the presiding elder. None of them knew the other's intentions. Goodwin reported the event:

> One obtained an early interview, presumably to the others, to talk over the next year's appointment; but he began by telling the presiding elder that his term of four years celibacy was about to expire, and he had been making it a matter of prayer, and the Lord had evidently made it clear that he ought to marry.

"That seems very probable, and I see no objection to it," said the fatherly official, "but may I ask who is the happy girl?"

"Cora ———," was the reply.

"A splendid girl—will make any man a good wife," was all the young man could wait to hear.

In less than an hour he was on his horse, making haste to break the news to Cora, and begin the work of courtship.

The second soon had an audience, and made substantially the same speech, and received the same indorsement of Cora; and he, too, started to tell her the news, not knowing that No. 1 was on the same errand, or, if he was hoping to outride him.

Later in the same day, No. 3 had a hearing. He made substantially the same speech, winding up, as the others had, with Cora ———.

"Now you see her, my young brother," said the presiding elder; "there must be a mistake somewhere. Cora ——— is a splendid girl; but you are the third man who had to-day said the Lord had indicated her for a wife. Somebody must have misunderstood the Lord."[11]

In spite of the Methodist leaders' position on the undesirability of marriage among young preachers, many preachers, of course, did get married. Ministers' wives played a vital role in the spread of Christianity to the American West. A minister's wife generally became her husband's "right arm sharing many pastoral responsibilities and functioning as an extension of his ministry; and the Partner, who ministered with both her hands, developed a ministry alongside her husband, and often served as the pastor's pastor."[12] The important role that ministers' wives played was only natural. Historically, the number of women in most congregations was higher than the number of men from the founding of the country. Cotton Mather observed in 1691, "There are far more godly women in the world than there are godly men." Mather also remarked, "In a church of between three and four hundred Communicants, there are but a few more than One Hundred Men." Frances Trollope related, a century and a half later, that she "never saw, or read, of any country where religion had so strong a hold upon the women, or a lighter hold upon the men."[13] Most preachers hoped that women in their congregations "would influence men and the next generation, they focused much of their proselytizing zeal on women."[14]

During the American Revolution and after the Great Revival, the female component of most congregations significantly increased. Richard D. Shiels found that men "might find personal support in other circles," whereas women were "excluded from politics and commerce and many of the new organizations which competed for men." Women's activities were "restricted to membership in churches and evangelical societies." They defined themselves "in religious terms" and found personal support in religious company. In the East religion was not given full time interest. There "were more non-religious activities to fill women's days."[15] On the Indiana frontier, religion played a central role in women's lives, and they were expected to be role models. Women were believed to be intrinsically morally superior to men, and it was surmised that their superiority would be used to lift the morals of the country.[16] Like clergymen, women were expected to care deeply about the family in a period in which men were encouraged to succeed in the amoral worlds of government and business. Women and clergymen were restricted to similar "overlapping spheres of activity."[17]

Joseph Tarkington served his four years of celibacy without becoming entangled in any romantic affairs. On several occasions, certain mothers tried to match him up with their daughters, and others attempted to find him a companion, while "more than once it was supposed that a match had been made." But Joseph avoided the snares successfully without making any enemies. The 1830 conference was held in Vincennes. Tarkington was appointed to the Vevay circuit. While he was working the circuit, Joseph became attracted to Maria Slawson, eldest daughter of Simeon and Martha Wood Slawson.[18]

Maria had been converted to Methodism three or four years prior to her marriage to Joseph. She described the event: "I was converted at a prayer-meeting in a little log house up the branch of 'Indian Kentuck,' at the home of Mr. Marlow, three or four years before I was married. No preacher was there, but the neighbors had simply gathered for prayer."[19]

In the fall of 1818 the Slawsons had moved to Switzerland County, Indiana, from Orange County, New York. No reason is given for the decision to move, but it is possible that Simeon was influenced by his second cousin Ezra Slawson, who had migrated to Switzerland County earlier. When Simeon and Martha arrived in Indiana, they had six children.[20] They had traveled from New York on the Ohio River and stayed in the small village of Rising Sun the first winter. The next spring they moved to their 160-acre farm, about nine miles north of Vevay. Thirteen-year-old Maria helped her father with his work "piling and burning brush and logs" while also helping her mother "about the house."[21] Maria's sister Malissa was given the job of chasing off the squirrels that attempted to steal the corn that was being planted.

Martha described the Slawson property in a letter to her nephew. It was "first rate land and is a very level countery the black swamp as some call them but which is neither swamp nor upland is I think the best land of all the rest it is timbered with large black walnut from 2 to 3 feet diameter."[22] Shortly after settling, the Slawsons bought their neighbor's 160-acre plot also.[23] Simeon Slawson and his family stayed in a small cabin for three years. Then he built a "hewed-log house, of one large room, about twenty feet square, and a shed room on the first floor, and a room up-stairs over the large one."[24]

In 1830 Simeon began burning bricks for a new and larger house, but tragedy struck in the winter of 1830–31. Five of the children died of cholera between December 27, 1830, and January 30, 1832.[25] The deaths were devastating to the family. Ten-year-old Matilda wrote a poem after the death of the first two children:

When Shall We Three Meet Again

When Shall We Three Meet Again
Oft Shall glowing hope expire
Oft Shall weary love retire
Oft shall death and sorrow reign
Ere we three shall meet again

The Slawson House, circa 1900. Courtesy of R. D. and Cathy Slawson.

Though in distant lands we sigh
Perched beneath the hostile sky
Though the deep between us rolls
Friendship shall unite our souls
And in fancy's wide domain
Oft shall we three meet again

When our burnished locks are gray
Thinned by many a toil spent day
When around this youthful pine
Moss shall creep and ivy twine
Long may this loved lower remain
Here may all three meet again

When the dreams of left are past
When its wasted lamps are dead
When in cold envisions shade
Beauty wealth and fancy are laid
Where immortal spirits reign
There may we three meet again[26]

In the early nineteenth century, poetry in the style of Matilda's "When Shall We Three Meet Again" was one of the few ways that the Methodists could express themselves. Theaters and reading novels were strictly off-limits.[27]

After so many children died, Martha Slawson lost much of her enthusiasm for her new home. Nonetheless, the house was finished in a couple of years. Simeon described the house to an unnamed nephew in 1834. The house was a large two-story structure: "I have been building a brick house 48 feet by 22 two story with a kitchen or ell 22 by 24 and a wash house adjoining the back of the kitchen 15 by thirty feet all of which except the wash house is nearly completed except plastering the cost of which is between 2 and three thousand dollars."[28]

Regardless of the depression that the Slawsons suffered over their losses, Joseph and Maria were attracted to each other even as the children's deaths were occurring. In the spring of 1831, Maria was riding home by horseback from John Cotton and Amanda Clark's wedding when Joseph rode up beside her and asked if she "had any objections to his company."[29] Maria responded

Maluda Slawson's poem. Courtesy of the Indiana Historical Society.

that she did not. This was not the first time the couple had met. Joseph had been stopping frequently at her father's home following his rounds to visit and to provide spiritual guidance to the Slawsons over the recent loss of their children. In regard to Joseph's visits, Maria stated that their house "was one of his homes."[30]

Maria's father had a fairly good library and ample facilities for studying, which gave Joseph a perfect excuse for spending so much time at the Slawsons' home. But Maria had set her "head and heart on capturing the young preacher." She always dressed in her best clothing when Joseph was visiting, and she entertained him with "literary and theological discussions, leaving her mother to care for the domestic matters, the mother apparently consenting."[31]

One day while Joseph was studying in the Slawson library and Maria was busy at the spinning wheel clattering and buzzing away, the noise of Maria's work "strangely affected him, as it came mixed with a treble voice singing, 'Give joy or grief, give ease or pain,'" which was one of the most popular hymns in Methodism at the time. Joseph then turned to the thirty-first chapter of *Proverbs*, and started reading: "She seeketh wool and flax, and worketh willingly with her hands. 'That's Maria!' he added. 'She layeth her hands on the spindle, and her hands hold the distaff.' 'Maria again!' 'She maketh fine linen and selleth it, and delivereth girdles unto the merchant.' 'More Maria!' And he found his heart strangely warmed; but he told nobody about it. Old as he was, he would have loved to see his mother about that time." He asked Maria to marry him, and she gave her consent. Joseph then approached the presiding elder about marrying Maria. The elder at the time was Allen Wiley, who was fond of both Joseph and Maria. Joseph revealed to Wiley that he was thinking of getting married before the next conference. Wiley replied coldly, "I reckon you are old enough, if you ever intend to." Joseph was approaching thirty-one years of age and Maria was twenty-six. When Wiley found out who the proposed bride was he acted surprised and said: "Then I must use the ceremony in full, as is given in the Discipline." "Very well," said Joseph; "if you can stand it we can."[32] After Joseph had consulted the presiding elder he was "permitted to proceed with his courting."

The *Discipline* did not allow preachers to marry until the bride's parents were consulted. While departing the Slawson home on one particular day he handed Maria's father a letter that read:

August 30, 1831.

Dear Brother and Sister,—You, by this time, expect me to say something to you concerning what is going on between your daughter and myself. You will, I hope, pardon me for not saying something to you before I ever named anything to her, though she is of age.

Notwithstanding all this, I never intended to have any girl whose parents are opposed. Therefore, if you have any objections, I wish to enter them shortly. I know it will be hard on you to give up your daughter to go with me; for I am bound to travel as long as I can, and, of course, any person going with me must not think to stay with father and mother.

Yours very respectfully,

J. Tarkington.[33]

Maria's father had some concerns about the marriage because there were "Many dangers, with suffering and poverty, in being a preachers wife." However, Maria's father reluctantly gave his consent as expressed in the following letter.

September 4, 1831.

Reverend Sir,—You express a wish to know if I have any objections to you forming an affinity with my daughter Maria, to which I would reply: If you and my daughter are fully reconciled to the above proposition, which I have no reason to doubt, I do hereby assent to the same; nevertheless, if such a union should take place, it would be very desirable, if you should settle yourself down here, that you would not be too remote from us,

Yours most respectfully,

S. and M. Slauson.[34]

Reverend Allen Wiley. Courtesy of R. D. and Cathy Slawson.

Margaret Wiley, wife of Rev. Allen Wiley. Courtesy of R. D. and Cathy Slawson.

On September 21, 1831, Joseph was married to Maria at her father's home, nine miles north of Vevay. Rev. Allen Wiley, the presiding elder, "solemnized the wedding." Goodwin described the service: "The elder read the form in full as it appears in the Discipline, stopping to emphasize 'You both,' as it appears in the charge, which asks them to 'confess' if they know of any 'impediment why they may not be lawfully married.' Instead of the usual silence, which is taken as evidence there is none, Mr. Tarkington responded, in a distinct voice and with much emphasis as the elder had put on 'you both,' 'I know of none,' and the bride answered, 'I know of none,' and the ceremony proceeded to the end."[35]

Immediately after the couple was married, they attended a camp meeting on Crooked Creek. After the event closed two days after the wedding, the Tarkingtons started for Joseph's parents' home, "a bridal-trip on horseback."[36] Tarkington states that it was "customary among those in high life, in that day (and we were of that respected class), to enjoy wedding tours, in order that the young couple might begin life under as favorable auspices as possible."[37] Maria rode a five-year-old horse, given to her by Rev. James Scott of the Madison circuit, that she had raised from a colt. Joseph states that Maria had a "bridle, saddle, and saddlebags, paid for by her own weaving of linen on a common loom."[38] Tarkington described their difficult journey:

> The first night we reached a hotel on the old Madison and Indianapolis road, twelve miles from Columbus, Indiana. The house was of hickory logs, with the bark stripped off. The next morning I left it to her to breakfast where we were or go on to Columbus, and she decided to go on to Columbus. From Columbus we started through what is now Brown County. Soon we passed White River, it began to rain, and it continued until night. As my horse was a very fine traveler, we changed horses. We had some thirty miles to go to get to the first cabin. Just at dark we got to Jackson's Lick, on Salt Creek. I asked for quarters of the man at the Lick, and he referred us to some cabins ahead. We went to the first, and the woman there told us that her husband had gone to the settlements for breadstuff, and there was no place for our horses; to go to the next. We went to the next, and they were all sick, with no place for the horses. So we went to the third, and they were in the same condition with the last. We went back to the first of the three, and the woman said we could come in ourselves, and go to the Lick with our horses. So the bride alighted, and I went back to the Lick, where the man said horses were being stolen about there when left out. So we built a pen around the horses, got some green corn and fed them. The man offered to share his buffalo-skin and blanket with me; but I went back to the cabin. I asked the woman of the cabin if she ever got to Church, and she said she had not heard praying or preaching since she left Kentucky. After prayers we went to bed, without anything to eat since leaving Columbus. The bed was made by driving forks into the ground, between the puncheons forming the floor, and laying poles in the forks, and across the poles boards. I asked my bride if she was hungry. She said: "What if I am, there is nothing to eat here; but I have one little biscuit in my pocket I brought from home." Upon her insisting, we divided it. Next morning by daybreak I was up, looking after the horses at the Lick, and found them safe, and soon be started. At three o'clock P.M. we got to my father's, and we soon had dinner, and it was sweet. A bride these days who would go through such as mine did for her bridal tour, would be thought worthy to be trusted in any mission where the gospel should be preached.[39]

The following day, Joseph left his bride at his parents' home and went to the conference at Indianapolis with his brother Hardin and Rev. Enoch G. Wood. At the conference, Bishop R. R. Roberts presided and preached the

Sunday sermon. Rev. John Strange preached a funeral sermon for Rev. Edwin Ray, who had died during the year.[40] Joseph was appointed to the Wayne circuit at the conference. His colleague was Rev. James Robe. Rev. Allen Wiley was the presiding elder. He returned to his father's home and with his new wife started out on horseback for "Old Wayne," which is the area around present-day Richmond.

Chapter Six

Joseph and Maria Begin Their Long Life Together

It took the newlyweds four days to reach their destination. Upon arrival the Tarkingtons boarded for four weeks in Centerville with Israel Abrams, who was "one of the leading stewards of the circuit."[1] They later rented a small house that consisted of two rooms. After a short stay in this house, they obtained part of a house owned by the brother-in-law of Gov. Oliver P. Morton.

From the outset of their marriage, Joseph and Maria were separated due to his preaching responsibilities. Joseph never complained of the physical hardships and deprivations. He seemed to thrive on the loneliness of the circuit. Joseph wrote letters, but seldom. The correspondence with Maria that exists reflects his loneliness, but Tarkington embraced the sporadic nature of his relationship with her. His duties as a pastor increasingly consumed him. He had become an ambitious man, being driven by respectability instead of material gain, and viewed the ministry as his way to succeed in life. And his challenges were great. There was much religious competition in Wayne County. All denominations were battling to gain converts. Upon Joseph and Maria's arrival, according to historian Chelsea Lawlis, Wayne County contained seven religious sects: "Quakers, Methodists, United Brethren, Baptists, Dunkers, Universalists, and Presbyterians."[2] His ambition was his source of great strength, enabling him to endure the hardships of the circuit life.

Maria never protested Joseph's absences. She idealized him. After the

Portrait of Maria Tarkington, painted circa 1832 by John Inscoe Williams.

Portrait of Joseph Tarkington, painted circa 1832 by John Inscoe Williams.

marriage Joseph and Maria underwent a transformation similar to the one psychologist Charles B. Strozier ascribes to Abraham and Mary Lincoln: they merged themselves, causing "each partner to rise above his or her existential loneliness."[3] Most preachers' wives became martyrs to their husbands' ministries. Their lives were lonely, and most "achieved their identity through great suffering and passive servanthood."[4] Maria's family did visit her. Indeed, her sister Matilda practically lived with her.

In many cases, if a preacher's wife was not burdened with children, she often followed her husband to his preaching sites, frequently sleeping on the ground and being exposed to extreme weather conditions. When children were born, a wife generally had them without the accompaniment of her husband. Leonard I. Sweet comments that "when children were born, baptized, or buried, itinerants were not usually around to celebrate, to weep, or to lift the burden." Sweet adds that preachers such as Bishop Joshua Soule "wore as a badge of dedication his absence at the births of his eleven children. He was so seldom at home (between 1804 and 1806 he spent only three weeks with his wife) that his children did not recognize him when he did manage to show up."[5]

Maria was more than the woman at home. She was strong and hardened to the frontier. For most of her life she had prepared for the position she occupied as a minister's wife. While living in New York as a child, she gained a good primary education. After moving to frontier Indiana, she had learned the hardships of pioneer life. Maria had also helped her mother care for her younger brothers and sisters and occasionally helped her father with his farming chores. Her training made her almost perfect for the life of a minister's wife. Joseph, for his part, developed a strong attachment to his young wife. Maria supported and encouraged her husband's thirst for upward mobility in the ministry and provided him with a home that granted him a strong sense of security.

Shortly after Tarkington arrived on the circuit, Allen Wiley transferred Joseph's colleague, James Robe, to Connersville and Rev. A. Beck in exchange for Elijah Whitten. Robe was described as being mild compared to Whitten. Another Methodist preacher, Thomas Hitt, commented on the situation, "what a mistake to put men like Whitten and Beck on one circuit! Either would blaze on ice in a minute." Whitten and Joseph worked well together. Joseph stated that "[o]ne held the reins, and the other cracked his whip from the word 'Go!'"[6]

Exactly nine months after Joseph and Maria's marriage, their first child was born. Joseph described the birth: "On June 24, 1832, on Sunday morning, while I was preaching, I saw the doctor called out of the meeting, and when I went home at the close, I found something new, and we called him John Stevenson Tarkington."[7] Glenda Riley points out that most women on the frontier were expected to bear children. "This expectation was reinforced by popular literature, which assured women that motherhood was a highly desirable achievement."[8] Riley adds that "children appeared with great regularity. A study of childbirth patterns in Missouri during the pioneer period indicates that a child was born every two or three years in most families."[9] Conditions were similar in Indiana. In addition to Maria's domestic duties, her position as the minister's wife required that she entertain other ministers and travelers. She was often required to let other ministers stay in her home, cook for them, wash and mend their clothes. Maria generally received little gratitude for her deeds.

Tarkington described the year at Centerville as successful. He was paid $144 for the year and was elated about the birth of his first son. Although Joseph was not paid much, he utilized the farming skills he had learned from his family. He generally moved from a preaching assignment to tending his cows and chickens. He even impressed his father-in-law with some of his farming possessions. Simeon tried to acquire an egg tress like the one Joseph had earlier purchased. He told another son-in-law, Augustus Welch, to buy him one, as "Tarkington got one in good times for $2 50 cents."[10]

While Joseph kept up his farming skills and loved farm life, he had no desire to copy the life of his father. Tarkington had genteel aspirations and used the respectability of the ministry to achieve his goal. Even though he was paid little during his first few years of preaching, he still needed the circuit to support his material aspirations while freeing him from his former life on the Tarkington farm at Stanford. In fact, Tarkington returned to visit his parents' family in Stanford few times. When he did call on his parents, he did not take his children or Maria with him. No records exist indicating that Maria ever visited Stanford after the wedding trip. The few times Joseph actually called on his parents occurred when the circuit drew him near them. Joseph and Maria spent their visiting time with the Slawsons; the Slawsons were cultured and respectable according to the standards of nineteenth-century Indiana.

Even though Joseph had rejected his rural roots, he was at his best among ordinary citizens. He always reached back to his past as a source of strength to identify with a congregation. Tarkington's sense of the needs and mood of the ordinary citizen came from his lifelong immersion in their ways. Knowledge of the frontier way of life made men like Tarkington essential to the Methodists. He had a personality that attracted people.

Allen Wiley also found the ministry preferable to the hard life on the farm. Referring to Wiley, Goodwin wrote:

He was an average farmer on a quarter section of only medium land in Switzerland County, living in a cabin two miles from any neighbor. By dint of hard work, chopping or plowing by day, and burning brush, or husking corn, or making splint brooms, or pounding hominy, by night, he was succeeding in feeding his wife and five children, and in adding a few additional acres to his cleared land every year; studying English grammar by taking his book to the field when plowing, or to the woods when chopping; and preaching acceptably as a local preacher in his own cabin, or in some neighboring cabin, on Sundays. Did it require any great heroism to exchange all these for the less laborious but more conspicuous calling of a traveling preacher, uninviting as that calling was at that period, yet furnishing opportunities for mental improvement such as his soul longed for? . . . Allen Wiley sacrificed the hardships of a frontier farmer, with its huskings and log-rollings and house-raisings, for the position of a travelling preacher, with its opportunities to study and with the best entertainment that the country afforded.[11]

In the fall of 1832 the annual conference was held in New Albany and Joseph was appointed to the Whitewater circuit.

Even though Joseph was happy about his marriage and the birth of his son, he was concerned about the cholera epidemic that was taking lives throughout the country. He commented that "in 1832 the cholera prevailed more or less in the country, and in the cities to a great extent."[12] In the spring of 1833 the disease broke out in the southwest with intensity. Charles E. Rosenberg indicates that "Americans prided themselves on their railroads, canals, and steamboats,"[13] but these methods of travel were instrumental in spreading the epidemic throughout the country. In addition, cholera did not show preference for warm weather as yellow fever did.[14] Cholera was primarily found in the poorer sections of the cities, where filthy and adulterated food was prepared, few took baths, sewage was dumped by early corporations into the streets, and prostitution and intemperance flourished.[15]

To many, cholera was a consequence of sin: "man had infringed upon the laws of God, and cholera was an inevitable and inescapable judgement." Many cases of death seemed to prove the disease was a scourge of the immoral. "To die of cholera was to die in suspicious circumstances."[16] Even American physicians advanced the idea that religious, god-fearing people who kept God's law did not need to worry about cholera. The doctors believed the disease was a plague of the lower classes, who indiscriminately were involved in "sins" such as drunkenness, sexual perversions, and a variety of other wrongs.[17] However, these beliefs began to change as people from the respectable classes began to contract the disease. In 1835 thirty-seven-year-old James H. Wallace, a member of the Indiana legislature and one of the editors of the *Republican and Banner* died eight hours after onset of the illness.[18] Many other respectable people, including Methodist preachers and their families, contracted cholera.

In August of 1833, "while holding a sacramental meeting at Carmichael's three miles west of Brookville" Joseph became infected with the disease at Williams Hendrickson's home. Dr. Haymond of Brookville was the attending physician. Rev. Greenbury Becks took Joseph's horse home, and Mrs. David Price took Maria and the baby to Brookville. From there, Rev. Samuel Goodwin took them to Hendrickson's home. Joseph claims that "their coming was my medicine." Maria attended her sick husband until his health was regained.[19]

In 1832, the Illinois conference was divided into the Indiana and Illinois conferences.[20] Joseph remained in the Indiana conference. He continued to make large gains in adding to Methodist membership. At a meeting house at Connersville in 1832, Maria's twelve-year-old sister Matilda experienced conversion under Joseph's ministry. She was living with the Tarkingtons at the time while attending school.[21] The 1833 conference was held at Madison, and Joseph was sent to the Greensburg circuit. Joseph described his new route: "The Greensburg Circuit was cut out of the Rushville Circuit in 1828. In 1833 it had appointments at Greensburg, Robbins's, Burke's, W. Braden's, Cox's,

George Miller's, J. Truesdale's, Joseph Henderson's, J. Lower's, Biggot's, Gray's, Sharpe's, T. Perry's, and also Burney's, south of where Milford now is."[22] The Methodists had been holding services in Greensburg for ten years when Joseph arrived. The first sermon was preached in 1822 by James Murray. The first church was organized in 1823 with nine members. Aaron Wood (appointed 1823) and James Havens (appointed 1824) were the regular preachers.[23]

When the Tarkingtons arrived in Greensburg, they found that many had died from a recent outbreak of typhoid. There had been no religious services for "some time," and no Methodist church building had been constructed. Joseph preached in private houses and in a cabinet shop owned by a local named David Gageby.[24] On occasion he preached in the "old court-house." Joseph also visited the sick and prayed for them. In the spring of 1834, Joseph was given thirty dollars by local citizens, which he used to purchase a lot on Franklin Street.[25] With help of the "feeble Church," he built a house. On February 24, 1934, Joseph became a father for the second time: a daughter, Mary, was born.

In Greensburg the Methodists, Presbyterians, and Baptists conducted services at the same meeting house. Tarkington commented that the preachers worked together. "One would preach, another exhort, and the third pray." Some people would come a distance of "eight to ten miles to attend."[26]

The 1834 Annual Conference was held in Centerville. Bishop Roberts preached the funeral sermons for three ministers who had died during the year: Reverends Locke, Griffith, and Joseph's friend Armstrong. Joseph was appointed to the Charlestown circuit. He paid sixteen dollars for a Dearborn wagon that the family traveled in and drove their cow to their new home. Joseph sold five hundred dollars' worth of religious books to his new congregation. He stated that "[o]ne can judge of the religious standing of a family by the books they read." He added that he would see what books were read when he made the first round of a circuit.[27] The Methodists expected people in their congregations to read materials that assisted them in their religious convictions. On November 7, 1834, a Methodist woman apologized in the *Western Christian Advocate* for reading novels. She stated that novels did improve manners but gave a false impression of the world. The woman contended that the books represented "characters that never existed. . . . Walter Scott benefits no one in a religious sense."[28]

The 1835 conference was held in Lafayette, where Bishop Roberts presided. Tarkington was sent to the Greenville circuit, which had been part of the old Corydon circuit. On the circuit was a man named John Hancock, who lived in Harrison County. Hancock owned a "double log-cabin." Hancock and his family lived in half of the house, and the Tarkingtons moved in to the other, which consisted of two small rooms. Joseph described Hancock as a man who was "six feet four inches tall." He added that the Hancocks were a "good family of plain Methodist folk." The Hancocks had seven children, five sons and two daughters. The Tarkington children became very attached to John Hancock. On February 17, 1836, Joseph and Maria became parents of their third child, a second daughter, named Martha. Maria made more money over the year than the circuit paid Joseph: she "made and bleached bonnets for the women and stocks for the men."[29]

The 1836 conference was held in Indianapolis with Bishop Soule presiding. Joseph was assigned to the Vevay circuit. Rev. Lewis Hurlbut was sent with him. When the Tarkingtons left Harrison County for their new assignment, there was sadness; John Hancock rode in the wagon with them for "some distance." Tarkington's children loved the old man and cried when he left the wagon. The Tarkingtons' son, John, said, "Grandpa Hancock had to cry, too. Poor grandpa! I am sorry for him; he has no little children to play with now."[30]

On the first night of their journey, they stayed at Mr. Kettley's home, and the following night at Rev. Edward Ames's home. As Ames helped the Tarkington children out of the wagon, he commented, "What I would give if my children were as healthy as these!" In response, Joseph told him to keep a cow for his children's nourishment.[31] Mrs. Ames was described by Joseph as "delicate of health but noble spirited." Joseph also recalled that Mrs. Ames had never learned to cook and wanted Maria to teach her. Tarkington gave his assessment of the situation in a manner that would cause twentieth-century readers to label him a sexist:

> How many ladies regret, when the charge of a household comes upon them, that they never learned the art and mystery of cooking! Children should be brought up to be independent in their line of life, to practice unto knowledge all the things which may be proper, as well as necessary, to their after enjoyment of the gifts of man and God, and in this to consider work honorable in all persons in all grades of society. Knowing how themselves, they may teach others what they are not compelled to do with their own hands. All women should know how to keep house.[32]

The following day, after leaving the Ameses' home, the Tarkingtons stopped at Rev. William H. Goode's place, which was located four miles from Madison. Joseph's in-laws lived on this circuit, and the next night they reached Maria's father's home, "nine miles north of Vevay."[33]

The conference for 1837 was held in Indianapolis, and much business was conducted: the "question came up as to the establishment and location of a university."[34] Several colleges had been started in the West by the Methodists, but most had collapsed due to the "lack of adequate financial support."[35] Three places were nominated for the site of the planned university: Rockville, Indianapolis, and Greencastle. General Tilghman A. Howard "represented Rockville" and made a good argument in favor "of the location at his place." Calvin Fletcher "spoke for Indianapolis" but, Tarkington commented, he "did not labor hard for it, saying it was not good for boys to be away from home, and in as large a place as Indianapolis would be some day." Dr. Tarvin Cowgill won the university for Greencastle after General Howard admitted that "there were some chills and fever at Rockville."[36]

The first generation of American Methodists had rejected formal education, but by the 1830s they "perceived its importance to the retention of their young people and the advance of the church."[37] Joseph added that another reason for building a college was that there was little money in circulation and the Methodists wanted the security of knowing that they could send their children to a facility where "they would be cared for by the faculty."[38]

In 1837, the Presbyterians controlled the "board of trustees and faculty of Indiana College at Bloomington." The Presbyterians had also established colleges at Wabash and Hanover. Since the Methodists outnumbered the Presbyterians in Indiana four to one, they tried to gain some control and representation in the state university system. They "attempted the stratagem of placing the election of the hitherto self-perpetuating university board in the legislature." Samuel Bigger, a Presbyterian lawyer from Rushville, was sarcastic about the matter and doubted the Methodists' ability to manage a university. He declared: "When Ohio University wished to get a Methodist professor, they had to send to Europe for him."[39] Bigger gained the support of his fellow legislators, and the Methodists lost their requests.

In response to being denied representation at Indiana College, the Methodists launched the idea of building a school of their own. One preacher wrote in the *Western Christian Advocate* that the Presbyterians had only four thousand members in Indiana and controlled three schools. The Methodists, on the other hand, had twenty-four thousand members and "no voice in any" institute of higher learning. After a struggle in the legislature, "a committee of the Indiana Annual Conference secured a charter and opened a preparatory school in Greencastle." The school was named Indiana Asbury University, and in 1839 the trustees selected Matthew Simpson, a vice-president and professor of natural philosophy, as its president.[40] William C. Larrabee was elected professor. The preparatory school was opened in the fall of 1836 by Rev. Cyrus Nutt, and the first classes were conducted in the old Methodist church and town seminary until the university buildings were completed. Rev. H. B. Bascom laid the cornerstone of the first building on June 20, 1837.[41]

In 1837, agents for the university had received pledges for $60,000, and another $20,000 was expected before the fall term opened. Before the year was over, the economic depression that had struck the entire nation also hit Indiana, resulting in a shrinkage of pledges.[42] At the end of Matthew Simpson's first year, he reported a deficit of $449.02 to his trustees. By 1843 the amount had increased to $4,610.26, which caused the board to pay its professors in scrip.[43] Due to the hard times associated with the depression, the trustees of the college appointed agents to "solicit contributions and subscriptions for scholarships." A plan was implemented to sell one-hundred-dollar scholarships. Tarkington related, "[T]he purchaser paid twenty dollars cash, and the remainder in four annual installments with interest." Joseph bought one of the scholarships, and the payment took one-third of his salary.[44] The university received thousands of these subscriptions.

In the fall of 1837 Joseph was struck down with another illness and became "superannuated," or retired, for the year from his preaching duties while remaining at his father-in-law's farm near Vevay. During this period, Tarkington helped clear and cultivate a small field of corn. He also taught school. Many of these early frontier teachers taught children to read and write from the Scriptures.[45] Most teachers were not of the laid-back, Ralph Hartsook type, as portrayed in Edward Eggleston's *Hoosier Schoolmaster*.[46] James Albert Woodburn commented that the early teachers were "densely ignorant" and often used profane language while carrying a bottle of whiskey to school with them. Many of the teachers were brutal, and Woodburn adds that he was familiar with one who "would walk around in front of the class, and if things didn't go off to please him he would grab the little fellows by the hair and shake out everything they had in their heads."[47] Joseph must have been a welcome sight to the students.

While the Tarkingtons were living at Maria's father's home, they had their fourth child. Joseph Asbury was born November 25, 1837. Augustus Welch's aunt Armilla, a native New Yorker, made cheese and brought it to the family in celebration of the event.[48] To Joseph Tarkington's disgust, Armilla had papered her cheese room "with the show bills and poster of the Brother Rufus Welch's Circus, Theater, and Hippodrome." The Methodists thought the theater and circus were evil, but Armilla was proud of Rufus Welch, her husband

Aruna's younger brother, whom she had help raise.[49] After the preachers were out of sight, many of the Methodist paid twelve and one-half cents to see the shows.[50]

During this stay at the Slawsons' home in 1837, five-year-old John S. Tarkington was first exposed to slavery. Indiana was not a slave state, but many runaway slaves passed through Switzerland County after crossing the Ohio River and escaping their bondage in Kentucky. The hotly discussed issue of slavery was inflaming Gallatin County in Kentucky, directly across the river. Slavery was a divisive issue as early as 1820, when a group in favor of colonizing slaves and sending them to Africa to rid Kentucky of slavery met staunch opposition from slaveholders. The agitation about colonization and emancipation caused conflicts among church members in Gallatin County, who then fled to Switzerland County. Baptist preacher John Pavy, for instance, "espoused the cause of emancipation, to avoid the turmoil occasioned by the difference of opinion, in 1823 removed from Fredericksburg, (now Warsaw) to Switzerland county, where he continued to preach for many years."[51]

A group of slave catchers visited the Slawson home one evening while John Tarkington was there. He recalled the event years later:

> [D]uring a visit at my grandfather's on the high plateau which ends in the great hills which merge and confine the Ohio River, a half-dozen tall horsemen rode up to the gate in the dusk of the evening and asked for entertainment, His house was large, the barn capacious, and grandfather's hospitality in proportion. I took and hung up in the hall, the heavy overcoat of one of the Kentucky gentlemen, and, as I did so, happened to slide my hand down the skirt of it and felt the outlines of a large horse-pistol. Presently, meeting my grandmother in the hall I showed her the bas-relief, and with visions of highwaymen in my mind, asked her what that meant? She answered with the scorn of a Connecticut North-woman: "They are hunting runaway slaves." John "They won't kill them will they?" Martha "Yes, if the poor things run." . . . After supper the slave-hunters went to the cross-roads to watch for their game. All night long I shuddered in dread lest they return bearing the bodies of their dead slaves. But the next morning I found the overcoats in the hall, the gentlemen at breakfast and their horses saddled and bridled at the gate; and I asked grandmother: "Did they kill any?" How she smiled at my simplicity and the fact: "They did not find any."[52]

The circuit caused Joseph to be an absent father, and his ties to his children were complex. At the most superficial level Joseph clearly seemed to love and appreciate his children. But he had to leave the responsibility of raising them, along with other domestic duties, to Maria. However, Joseph taught his children many lessons, and, as one might expect of a preacher, he had a talent for instructing through the use of metaphor. During the year that the Tarkingtons stayed with the Slawsons, Joseph gave young John more than his share of parables. In the woods directly across from the Slawson house, John built a dam that blocked a stream that flowed from a spring and built a miniature sawmill. Young Tarkington claimed his mill had the power to "cut saw-logs of elder pith. . . . I was a wheelwright!" John commented that he "would lie down on the bank and watch my handiwork with the satisfaction of a Fulton launching his first steamboat." Following a downpour of rain one evening, John's dam and mill were washed away. He was crushed, and "bewailed" the loss to his father. Joseph offered his assessment: "There was the foolish man who built his house upon the sand, and the rains descended and the floods came, and the winds blew and smote upon that house; and it fell, and great was the fall thereof."[53]

By the fall of 1838, Joseph had regained his health and attended the conference at Rockville. He was assigned to the Lawrenceburg station. Young John regretted leaving his grandfather Slawson's farm. He later commented: "The happy year at grandfather's came to an end. We left the great brick house with its twenty by twenty-five foot rooms, the fields, 'The orchard, the meadow, and deep tangled wildwood, and all the dear scenes that my infancy knew,' and made our home in a town near a river."[54]

Joseph remarked that he was the first "station preacher" appointed for Lawrenceburg station, located on the Ohio River.[55] There was no parsonage, and the Tarkingtons moved into the "old banking house on High Street." Maria would tie John to her rocker with a clothesline to prevent him from joining swimmers who went to the river. On one occasion, after giving up on escaping, John crawled under the large rocker, and a neighbor woman who was visiting sat in the chair. John realized that he was trapped and began squirming to elude his predicament. He then bumped his head against the bottom of the seat. John's jolt startled the unsuspecting woman, and she screamed. Maria had a good laugh at the neighbor's expense.[56]

Shortly after the rocking-chair episode, John was caught in another embarrassing situation when his playmate Johnson Hunter attempted to teach him how to suck eggs. John later recalled the event: "The suffocating horror of it when the yoke broke in my mouth! I proved to be only a Hoosier and not a Sucker, as mother laughing to tears, beheld my egg-nostic face and clothes."[57]

Maria was generally responsible for the children's upbringing even on

matters of religion. Being the station preacher at Lawrenceburg for a year enabled Joseph to be at home with his family and to provide some religious training for his children. On one winter evening, John was sitting on the hearth by
the fire, eating hickory nuts, when Joseph, who was reading his *Western Christian Advocate*, noticed that his son was tired. Joseph said to John, "My boy,
hadn't you better say your prayers and go to bed?" As John arose from the
hearth, Joseph inquired, "What do you say when you pray?" John rubbed his
eyes and said, "Oh, 'Now I lay me down to sleep.'" Joseph responded, "What!
don't you say the Lord's Prayer?" John told his father, "I hardly know it." Joseph
then instructed his son to "take the testament and learn it before you sleep."
John took the Bible and read the Lord's Prayer several times, but recalled years
later that he did not think he said it before creeping into bed.[58]

If Joseph had precious little time to devote to his children's upbringing, he
did struggle with the larger social issues that dominated frontier life. Joseph
rejected the strains of nativism that were common in nineteenth-century Indiana as well as in the rest of the country. In the area around Lawrenceburg,
there were many German-speaking families. Joseph was concerned that the
Germans had no church in the area that could accommodate their native tongue.
On a trip to Cincinnati to the Methodist Church offices, Joseph visited the
bookroom. There, Joseph met Rev. Adam Miller.[59] Miller was on the North
Bend circuit of the Ohio conference. After Joseph learned that Miller could
"preach in German," he invited Miller to preach in Lawrenceburg. Miller took
up Joseph's offer and, along with Rev. John Kissling, established a German
Church "in a little house on High Street."[60]

While Joseph was located at Lawrenceburg, he was haunted by an abundance of whiskey in the town. Pioneers regarded whiskey "as one of the prime
necessities" of life. Elizabeth K. Nottingham comments: "It was thought to
have great medicinal value. It cured rheumatism, it dispelled ague, and miti-
gated the possible ill effects of impure water. Socially it was also indispensable.
No boat was launched, no cabin raised, no logs rolled, nor wedding celebrated
without the copious libations of whisk[e]y."[61]

In *The Alcoholic Republic*, W. J. Rorabaugh contends that the first three
decades of the nineteenth century produced the "greatest per capita consump-
tion of spirits in United States history, and by 1830 the average American was
lustily quaffing an astounding five gallons of whiskey [per year], or its equiva-
lent."[62] American political leaders, including Sam Houston, could frequently
be found drunk. The famous orator Daniel Webster was ordinarily so inebri-
ated "on the floor of the Senate that he could not articulate his mother tongue."[63]

James Monroe's vice-president, Daniel D. Tompkins, was several times drunk in front of the Senate. Andrew Jackson's first inaugural reception broke out into a drunken brawl that resulted in much damage to the White House.[64] Vice-President Andrew Johnson was intoxicated at Abraham Lincoln's second inauguration, as most pictures of the event clearly display.

During the early part of the nineteenth century, distilled spirits became the third-leading industrial product of the United States, and excessive drinking was so common that local temperance societies were formed by the hundreds to combat it. The National Temperance Society was founded in 1826.[65] But alcohol would prove difficult to fight: due to the shortage of currency in the West, whiskey was often used as a medium of exchange. Nottingham adds that "many a house or piece of land was paid for in whisky at the regular price of forty cents a gallon."[66]

Whiskey certainly made its presence felt in Switzerland County, Indiana, and was available at the camp meetings. It was also used as a treatment for a variety of illnesses. Perret Dufour recalled one occasion:

> At one of those camp meetings held near the residence of Judge Cotton on Indian Creek, there was a great awakening and many converts. One lady was so much overcome, that she fainted and a great crowd gathered around her—the weather being warm Jean Daniel Morerod seeing such a crowd around the fainted lady made his way to the crowd, and urged them to stand back and let her have her fresh air—many were disposed not to heed the request, but some fell back. Mr. Morerod seeing the pale face of the lady exclaimed "My God she is dead or dying" and drawing from his pocket a bottle with some Whiskey or brandy in it stepped forward to wet her face with the liquor when he was drawn back by one of the preachers and told not to attempt such a thing as that. Mr. Morerod said "the woman will die if you do not do something for her soon."[67]

Bishop Asbury found it necessary to expel many preachers who failed to refrain from drinking whiskey. Ten of the twenty-one preachers expelled for drinking from 1817 to 1825 "were from the Tennessee, Ohio, Missouri, Mississippi, and Kentucky, Conferences."[68] John Wesley had not been completely opposed to the use of alcoholic beverages. Indeed, he consumed some wine almost weekly at the sacrament of Holy Communion and drank "some hot mulled wine only weeks before he died" for medicinal purposes.[69] Moreover, his use of wine was not limited to the medicinal and sacramental. Ivan Burnett Jr. states that "it is certainly clear from Wesley's writings that he saw neither the Bible nor the Christian faith as demanding abstinence from wine." What

Wesley was opposed to was drunkenness. Methodism in nineteenth-century America "departed from Wesley's position decades before the Eighteenth Amendment was passed; and, as the temperance movement grew in momentum it repeatedly chose to remember only that part of Wesley's writings with which it was comfortable."[70]

Joseph was conducting a meeting when, as Sweet relates, a "well-to-do Methodist farmer and distiller arose to speak. He began by saying , 'I have been governed by two spirits; one is the good spirit, that prompts me to be good and do good. The other is ———!' Here Tarkington called out 'Whiskey' at the top of his voice. 'No,' said the distiller, who was at the time under the influence of his own homemade goods, as he often was, 'nobody ever saw me drunk,' 'Some people never get drunk,' was Tarkington's reply, and the half-drunken Methodist took his seat." This rude treatment by Joseph was effective, for within a few months the distiller had abandoned his trade and became a total abstainer.[71]

In 1824, the first organized temperance society in the state surfaced. The group pledged "not to furnish whisk[e]y at raisings and log rollings."[72] By 1828 other societies were established, and in 1829 there was an attempt to keep alcoholic beverages out of Indianapolis.[73] Allen Wiley was probably the first to preach "tee-total temperance" in Indiana. Wiley hated whiskey and virtually declared war on any kind of alcohol. In the late 1820s, he transformed his quarterly meeting conferences into temperance societies.[74] It was a custom to provide whiskey at harvests during the pioneer period, and Wiley disliked the practice. At his farm near Vevay, he declared that no whiskey would be served in his harvest field. "When the harvesters arrived with sickles and cradles, he served cold buttermilk to quench their thirst and 'Wiley's Buttermilk Harvest' became the joke of the countryside. However, the Christian men and women appreciated his courageous attack upon an evil custom and in a few years whiskey harvests were out of date."[75]

Methodist preachers also fought the use of snuff and tobacco. Posey reported a preacher named James Axley who "stood out again as the leading preacher-reformer of his period in the entire West."[76] Axley frequently preached his "Sermon on Abomination" to congregations. In his message he attacked "masonry, slavery, whiskey, tobacco, and fashions." On one particular day, he directed his theme to tobacco. Since smoking was prevalent among women, he recited a poem that he had written.

> Tobacco is an Indian weed,
> And from the devil did proceed;

Joseph Tarkington around 1850. Courtesy of the Indiana Historical Society.

It spoils a woman, burns her clothes,
And makes a chimney of her nose.

An old woman in the crowd became so enraged by Axley's rhyme that she left the meeting house. As she proceeded out of the gathering, the woman turned and said, "I wish to God I had my pipe, I would smoke this minute for spite."[77] Posey reports another rollicking tale concerning tobacco use:

In the midst of a class meeting Axley once inquired of a pious German as to the condition of his tobacco crop. Upon receiving the answer "Very well," Axley teasingly said, "You are the meanest people in this neighborhood I ever saw. It's all tobacco, tobacco, and you do not raise corn enough to feed my horse when I come around." Whereupon the German retorted, "Brudder Axley, if you vill not teach your horse to eat derbacker dat is not our vault. Deach his dis, and den ve give him blenty." "Never!" said the indignant Axley. "If Bob was to chew tobacco, I would never speak to him again."[78]

During the 1840s and 1850s, the temperance movement continued to gain momentum. At Evansville, during the early 1840s, John Ingle Jr. kicked over a barrelful of whiskey which "was being served, free, in tincups in front of the courthouse on Main Street." It was the only polling place in town at the time. Ingle was "sued for the value of the whiskey."[79] In the year 1841–42 temperance revivals were conducted throughout Indiana. Rev. George Curtiss of Shelbyville commented that the revivals had a big impact in his town, adding that revivals "commenced in the East and like a tidal wave swept over the country."[80] In 1853–54 at the second quarterly conference at Shelbyville, a resolution was passed "condemning the trafficking with distillers of ardent spirits" in an attempt to force members to stop selling corn and barley to distilleries.[81]

Chapter Seven

From Preacher
to Presiding Elder

At the conference of 1839, which met at Lawrenceburg, Joseph was appointed to the Richmond station. Joseph was then given the duty of appointing the other preachers to their new locations. John claimed the circuit riders "came trooping up to our house to get their billets." John and young neighbor boys watched the event until the local bully told him, "You go in the house or I'll lick you." John, who was suffering from whooping cough, replied, "Come on and try it, and I'll give you the whooping-cough!" The bully did not press the issue, so John felt that he had fulfilled the Scriptures: "Rejoice in tribulation!" and "Resist the devil and he will flee from you!" Young Tarkington assessed the event: "I was very proud of my whooping-cough which, as 'a smooth pebble from the brook' had slain my Goliath. It whooped up my courage. My challenge had been in accord with the natural law of compensation, balance; it was in agreement with the fairness of the universal code of give-and-take, but the young bruiser declined the tourney!"[1]

The conference that met in Lawrenceburg was a significant meeting. It is regarded as the most important conference conducted in Indiana. "The Conference included the entire State and one district in Michigan."[2] The meeting was held in the courthouse, and some preaching took place in the "little church on Short Street." Three bishops were present, Robert R. Roberts, who presided over the meeting, Joshua Soule, and Thomas Morris, who was the "president of the conference." Thirty-one preachers were received on a trial basis, while twenty-one were received into full connection. Allen Wiley, E. R. Ames, C. W. Ruter, A. Eddy, and Aaron Wood were elected as delegates to the General Conference. The church reported 8,694 new members. Many preachers had arrived at the conference after traveling a distance of more than two hundred miles. The issue of the preachers' apparel was raised. Most were dressed in seedy "home-made goods" that were quite worn after traveling so far on horseback. After a lengthy discussion, the preachers were allowed to dress as they pleased.[3]

A significant person at the meeting was Matthew Simpson, the president of Indiana Asbury University. Few of the preachers had met Simpson, and his initial personal appearance was disappointing to them. Not only was he "too youthful," Simpson was also wearing jeans. Simpson soon changed their first impression. He preached to the gathering on "Ezekial's vision of the waters flowing from the sanctuary" and preached on the millennium. Simpson's pulpit oratory was full of fire and caused many preachers to be overcome with emotion. One woman, described as being "intelligent" and not easily excitable, "jumped to her feel waving her parasol, and looking upward exclaimed, 'Sun, stand thou still, and let the moon pass by,' repeating the sentence until someone started to sing, while her immediate friends took her out of the congregation."[4] After Simpson delivered his message to the conference, he was regarded as the "prince of pulpit orators."

Joseph's stay at Lawrenceburg was one of the best periods of his career. He reported that "he could rejoice in that as the best class of men and women joined the church and most of them lived well and died well."[5] Joseph comments that he worked hard during his year there, and two hundred had joined the church. Rev. John Maffitt held "a series of meetings." He baptized ninety-eight in the meeting house while Joseph baptized twenty-eight in the Ohio River.[6] The river, incidentally, was not always the best place to conduct baptism. On occasion a pastor lost one of his flock, as illustrated in the following article from Alfred Berry Nisbit's diary:

A Man Drowned While Being Baptized

(Correspondence of the Cincinnati Gazette)

SAND HILL, KY., December 5.—One of the most melancholy and heartrending accidents which it has been our duty as a news-gather to chronicle, occurred near this village on Sunday last. The particulars, in brief are as follows A few week since Dr. A. P. Powell was married to Miss Mary J. Wilson, also a resident of this place. Shortly after his marriage Dr. Powell united with the Christian Church, and Sunday last was appointed as the day of his baptism, he having requested his pastor, Rev. J. B. Hough, to perform the rite. At the appointed hour a large number of persons had assembled on the banks of Crooked creek, the place chosen for immersion. After singing and prayer, everything being in readiness, the Rev. Hough entered the water, leading the Doctor, and the descent being very gradual, they were obliged to proceed some distance from the shore in order to reach sufficient depth, but suddenly both were seen to go down, having stepped over a bank concealed by the water; both soon arose to the surface, and the Rev. Hough regained the bank, but the Doctor being unable to swim was swept under a flood-gate only a short distance below. Every exersion [sic] was made to save him, but in vain.

The body was soon found and brought to the shore, amid the most heart-rending screams from his young wife and friends. Ever[y]thing possible was done to resuscitate the doctor, but alas! the vital spark had flown. This sad occurrence had cast a gloom over the country for miles around, all joining in extending their sympathy to Mrs. Pownall. As I before remarked, the doctor had been married but a short time, his marriage being published in the *Gazette* at the time. J. T. H.[7]

At the conference Joseph was appointed to the Richmond station. The Tarkingtons' goods were sent by "canal to Brookville, thence by wagon to Rich-

Interior of Hamline Chapel, built during the mid–nineteenth century at Lawrenceburg, Indiana.

mond." Joseph stayed at the Richmond station for two years, until the fall of 1841. Tarkington's three oldest children were sent to school, which was conducted in the basement of the church by a six-foot-tall schoolmaster named James Poe. Poe was an Ichobod Crane type of teacher who instilled education by "free use of apple tree sprouts."[8]

When Joseph arrived at Richmond, the meeting house was in need of repairs, and many of the church members volunteered their labor in making improvements to the building. The church was enlarged and additional seats were made. The Quakers who were living in the area were not very friendly toward the Methodists, but would sent their children to the Methodist Church on Sunday nights. Joseph claimed that he could "[s]ee their little smooth white caps close by the door, and sometimes they got to the altar of prayer."[9] Joseph became popular among the Quakers, and "he was welcomed by many of the best Quaker families."[10] Some of the Quakers joined the Methodists. However, resistance still existed, and very few adults attended Joseph's services. "They could not think of listening to a paid minister, or hear singing in worship; while, to them, the mourners' bench was unbearable."[11] Regardless, after Joseph's tenure in the Whitewater Valley, relations there between Friends and Methodists were harmonious.

During 1840, the first year of Joseph's appointment at the Richmond station, Maria became sick "nigh unto death," but Joseph claimed that "God stood by her, and saved her to raise a family."[12] The second year Joseph himself contracted an illness (probably cholera again) during a camp meeting near Centerville. The meeting was conducted during the month of August. Joseph had made the journey in an open buggy. His son John remembered that "the sun was hot, the roads dusty, and the wayside ponds were green with the scum of decayed herbage." Joseph was stricken with a fever and was taken home to Richmond, where it was believed that he could not live. On the third day of the illness, the doctor decided that "the crisis of the disease would come in the following night,—if he lived through the night he would recover." Maria and the children gathered by Joseph's bedside to hear what would probably be his final words. Joseph "made provision" for Maria's future and spoke tenderly to his children. To John he said: "Love God and your mother; fear no man." Joseph's doctor instructed the family not to give the preacher cold water to drink. However, Joseph told Maria that he wanted "[c]old water from the bottom of the well!" He added: "If I must die I want to die comfortably." The doctor yielded to Joseph's demands, and Maria prayed. Joseph drank the water and with great thankfulness said: "And the Spirit and the Bride say come. And he that heareth let him say, Come. And he that is athirst let him come; he that will let him take the water of life freely." He then fell asleep and broke into a "profuse perspiration" and recovered in "due time."[13]

Members of the community stayed with the preacher until his condition improved. One man named Mark E. Reeves stayed with Joseph during the critical nights of the illness. When Joseph improved and was able to "step out," Reeves took him riding in his carriage every day for weeks.[14] A couple of days following Joseph's illness, John became sick with the fever. After watching his father drink the cool water during his bout with the sickness, young John attempted the same remedy. John's method failed, and he was put to bed as his mother and the doctor cared for him. John complained about the smell of the camphor that was used by the physician in treating him. After a long ordeal with the illness, John also recovered and was allowed to "weakly walk about." John was also visited by the schoolmaster during the sickness, which young Tarkington saw as unnecessary. When John had recuperated he found his world shattered; his "pet rabbit had eloped and my tame pigeons had taken themselves wings and flown away, but the world was all interestingly new, for I was living in it."[15]

During the 1840s, when cholera made its second major strike, Methodist opinions concerning the disease began to change. Even though many Methodists still viewed cholera as God's vengeance on the destitute and corrupt sinners, the disease was approached as a social problem that could be prevented with proper sanitary and hygiene methods. When the third major cholera epidemic appeared in the 1860s, Charles E. Rosenberg states: "Cholera, a scourge of the sinful to many Americans in 1832, had, by 1866, become the consequence of remediable faults in sanitation. Whereas ministers in 1832 urged morality upon their congregations as a guarantor of health, their forward-looking counterparts in 1866 endorsed sanitary reform as a necessary prerequisite to moral improvement. There could be no public virtue without public health."[16] Many preachers had their own remedies for the treatment of cholera. Rev. Alexander Douglass entered his in his diary on Friday November 14, 1857:

Cholera Specific

1 oz. Tincture of linaman

1 oz. Peppermint

1 oz. Compound spirits of lavender

1 oz. spice tincture of rubarbe

2 oz. camphor

2 oz. laudium

2 oz. number six

2 oz. sulphuric Ether[17]

In the fall of 1841 the conference was held at Terre Haute. Joseph was appointed to the Liberty circuit. Due to his illness, Joseph was still unable to ride on horseback. A man named Daniel Burgess took the Tarkingtons to their new assignment by carriage. George Havens was Joseph's colleague. Havens had a brother, Landy, who assisted him in meetings. Joseph comments that the Havenses could start much excitment in a meeting. George was the son of James Havens, who had two brothers, Joel and John, who helped him with his pastoral duties. Joseph said that James preached, Joel exhorted, and John led class. "If nothing moved, no one else need try for that time."[18]

Five days after the Tarkingtons arrived at their new home and "got into the parsonage," they were burned out. A girl had been cleaning ashes out of their smokehouse with a wooden vessel, which caught fire from the hot coals. The smokehouse was attached to the house. Once the fire started, neither structure could be saved from the flames.[19] Four days after the fire, November 5, 1841, Maria gave birth to the Tarkingtons' fifth child, a son. He was named William Simeon Reeves Tarkington.

In July of 1842, Joseph, Maria, and the family visited the Slawsons. Matilda wrote her husband, Augustus: "We have a visit from Br. Tarkington and family they were very friendly and also invited you and I to come and see them."[20] The conference of 1842 was conducted at Centerville. Rev. James Finley of Ohio preached and recalled when he saw James Havens's conversion to the church in the mountains of Kentucky. Many of the other preachers delivered messages. Joseph expressed the desire to stay on the Liberty circuit, but was appointed to Centerville. Centerville was the county seat of Wayne County, "the largest county for population in the state."[21] Centerville was a difficult circuit to be in charge of, and heavy preaching was demanded in Centerville on Sundays.

Thomas A. Goodwin was made Joseph's colleague. John Robbins was also sent to the circuit to help Joseph. Tarkington described Robbins as being "easily depressed." Robbins had a large cornfield in the bottoms of the White River. In early summer, when his corn had reached a height of three feet, a heavy rainstorm caused the river to overflow. Robbins's corn was swallowed by the rising water. As a result, he told his wife that he was ruined. He went to bed and stayed until the next day. Robbins's father-in-law told Joseph about the situation, and the preacher visited his colleague. Robbins complained to Tarkington that his corn was destroyed, but Joseph told the man that the overflow would only fertilize his crop. Joseph then took Robbins by the hand and "brought him out of his bed."[22] Robbins later told Joseph that his corn yield for that year was higher than any of his previous harvests.

On October 23, 1843, Maria wrote Joseph a letter from Centerville while he was at Crawfordsville. She reveals clearly the loneliness that she and the family felt in his absence. The letter also reveals Maria's intense religious convictions. Joseph received the letter four days after it was mailed:

> Centerville Ind.   October the 23 1843
> My very dear husband we recieved your letter this morning and was very glad to hear from you, we are all well and doing as well as I expected the first sabbath after you left Br Robbens preached at eleven oclock Br Reed at night and yesterday on the barren fig tree. I think he done beter than when you heard him Br Jemmerson just called to see us and sends his love to you and sais that he thinks Religion is very dull hear, we had a tolerable good general class meeting yesterday I feel resolved to be more dedicated to God I have resolved many times but never roat it down before O pray for me that I may be faithful the children all sends there love to you little William sais pappa go way to Croffensville he must come home I have nothin intarresting to write. I am ever your affectionate wife.
>
> Maria Tarkington[23]

Maria gave birth to a daughter, Ellen, at Centerville on December 18, 1843. She was the sixth child born to the Tarkingtons.

The conference of 1845 was held at Lafayette. Prior to the meeting, Joseph took his family to his father-in-law's home for a visit and then left Maria and the children in Switzerland County while he went to Lafayette. Bishop Hamline presided, and Dr. Charles Elliott, editor of the *Western Christian Advocate*, attended. Elliott traveled to the meeting with Hamline, Joseph, and Rev. Samuel T. Gilbert. Joseph claimed that he never had a "more pleasant travelling companion than Dr. Elliot." Joseph described the routine they enjoyed: "Bishop Hamline would have prayers, and he would keep on until we were called to dinner or supper, as the case might be, calling on each preacher in turn to pray, omiting himself, until Dr. Elliot turned on him, and called on him to 'lead in prayer.' It was amusing and interesting to be with these two good and wise men."[24] On the second day of the meeting Joseph received news of the death of his brother-in-law, Delanson Slawson.

During the year 1845 Joseph was transferred to the Indiana conference from the North conference, and he was sent to the Brookville circuit. Greenly H. McLaughlin was his colleague and Allen Wiley was the presiding elder. Joseph claimed that the year "passed off well." The 1846 annual conference was held at Connersville, and Joseph was sent back to Brookville "with Thomas C. Crawford coleague, and Lucian W. Berry presiding elder." Again Tarkington claimed, "We had a prosperous year on the circuit, with, as during the former year, an increase in membership."[25]

In the fall of 1847 the conference was held at Evansville. Joseph went to the meeting by boat, traveling on the Ohio River from New Albany. The river was low, and only small boats were running. Around twenty-five preachers were with Tarkington. Due to the size of the party, they were required to sleep on the floor. It took two days and a night to reach the end of their journey. Joseph was required to preach on the boat going down the river, while Rev. F. C. Holliday assumed the duties on the return.[26] While staying at Evansville, Joseph stayed with Dr. Elliott, who lived in Evansville.

Bishop Waugh, the presiding bishop at the conference, dined with Tarkington one day and told him that he was looking for "someone for the Vincennes District." Joseph told him that he "had six children and there was no way to move but by wagon." Allen Wiley volunteered, but his wife "was helpless, and had not walked a step for years." Waugh told Joseph that he "could go with a healthy wife and six children better than Wiley with his wife as she was."[27]

The Vincennes district "reached from the corporation line of Greencastle to the neck between White River and the Wabash, in sight of Mt Carmel, Illinois."[28] Joseph moved from Brookville to Greencastle, which was located beyond the north end of the district. Joseph paid a man forty dollars to move the family's household goods from Brookville to Greencastle. The reason Joseph moved to Greencastle was so that the children could go to school there. As a result, John graduated from Asbury. Mary and Martha attended Mrs. Larrabee's school in Greencastle.

The circuit was very difficult; it took five weeks to visit all the stops. Joseph described one of his trips:

Taking my clothes books in my saddle-bags, I attended five quarterly-meetings, including Vincennes as the last. At Vincennes I stopped with Brother David Bonner, and on Monday morning before day he had my horse fed, and I rode eight miles before sunrise, and fifty miles that day. At night I called for quarters at the

Rev. Thomas Manwarren's, in whose house I preached in 1833, at New Trenton, Franklin County, Indiana. I did not know he had moved. He did not seem willing to let me stay. It was dark. He wanted to know who I was, traveling so late in the night. I told him I was Joseph Tarkington, and had traveled fifty miles that day. "O," he said, "I know you; come in!" So we met unexpectedly, and talked over the "old times."[29]

After Joseph had left Manwarren's place, he started his journey home. He stopped on the National Road at a hotel for dinner, and found the landlady to be longtime friend, Rebecca Sedgewick, who had belonged to the group that he headed as "a class-leader" in Stanford, Indiana, some twenty-five years before. Joseph had been the best man at her wedding when she had married Thomas Freeland. Freeland had died, and she had married a Mr. Mason, who owned the hotel where Tarkington had stopped. Joseph then returned home for a day and a half, and then went to the Spencer quarterly meeting. Joseph's old friend, Rev. Henry S. Talbot, was the preacher in charge of the meeting.[30]

In the late 1840s many progressive changes had occurred in Methodism, but most congregations still insisted on a demonstrative religion that emphasized the need to see proof of God's work. In the early autumn of 1848, two camp meetings were held near Terre Haute. One was conducted on the "farm of Jacob D. Early, some five miles above the city; the other, in Brother Durham's grove, below the city, in the bounds of the Indiana conference, on Prairieton circuit."[31] The pastor of the Prairieton circuit was Elijah D. Long, and Joseph was the presiding elder. At the meeting held at Durham's grove, Rev. John L. Smith witnessed events that he would never forget. One involved a child.

On the Sunday night of the camp meeting, a little girl around seven or eight years old who was the daughter of a Doctor Hamilton was converted with "a large number of others." Approximately one hour after her conversion, she came on the stand, "her face all lighted up with joy, and in her childish way, meekly asked the question, 'Wouldn't you let me talk to the people?'" The child was lifted to the stand and stood on a chair. She delivered a message, "so clear and impressive, that it sent a thrill throughout the large assembly." The consensus among the gathering was that the girl was "directly inspired." Reverend Smith stated that "as a result of her talk more than fifty souls were there and then so convicted of sin that they came rushing to the altar, to find peace and pardon in believing."[32] Among those who were converted was her grandfather, a Hicksite Quaker whom Reverend Smith described as "not to say a downright infidel."[33] When the child had finished her address, she said to Smith

"Now I'll go to the tent and see if I can find grandpapa." Smith elaborated on the event: "She did go, and, while seated on the old gentleman's knee, with one arm around his neck, looking him intently in the face through her tears of joy, she talked to him about his soul as only one soundly converted to God can talk; and before the close of the meeting the poor old man was happy in the Lord, and in turn, he, too, talked to the people, telling them what a dear Savior he had found."[34]

Whether or not the girl's performance was an act of divine intervention, much of the Methodist religious creed was learned by this kind of oral transmission. While visiting the Slawson farm as a boy, John Tarkington recalled a story about a young six-year-old boy who had been taken to the Center Meeting House to hear the Rev. John Miller preach. During the sermon the preacher "waxed to a climax with a shout 'Salvation!'" The boy "swallowed up the sermon," according to John. Later "on a chilly evening in the Autumn following," the young boy was visiting the Slawsons. Simeon was sitting in front of the fireplace "meditating in the firelight." Martha was knitting while Joseph was reading his *Western Christian Advocate*. Maria Tarkington was holding her son Joseph in her arms, and Ezra Slawson was asleep on a stool. With an audience enough for the boy to perform, he stood in a chair and began delivering a sermon "with the whoop of a wild Indian."

John pictured the scene: "Grandfather awoke from his trance with a jerk; grandmother dropped a stitch in her knitting; the *Advocate* fell to the floor while the hands which had held it remained suspended in the air; mother clutched the baby to her breast, and old Ezra, toppled sprawling onto the floor: all a gratifying tribute to the conceit of the young orator."[35] The boy's voice rang out while his arms and hands shook. As if in a "Delphic trance," the youngster had the family "awe-stricken." With his face "aflame with accumulated energy and vehemence, he slammed his tiny fist down on the family Bible that lay on the stand, and cried out with all the strength of his lungs, 'Salvation! Salva-a-tion!! Salva-a-a-tion!!!'" Joseph was amazed at the young preacher and whispered: "Out of the mouths of babes and sucklings!" At that point Maria relaxed her hold on the baby and said: "Tut, tut! Ezra, what have you been putting the child up to? This is your doing." Ezra then went and got the boy and began hugging him, saying: "Why he's a Word Builder just from the tower of Babel." Martha then said: "Well Ezra, suppose you take the Reverend Johnny Miller and his 'Salvation' up to bed." As Ezra took the boy up the stairs he said: "You got *one* word all right."[36]

In 1848, Rev. Matthew Simpson resigned the presidency of Asbury University. On Commencement Day of that year, Simpson baptized the Tarkingtons' newest son, Matthew Simpson Tarkington, the Tarkingtons' seventh child, who was born at Greencastle, on July 16, 1848.[37] Joseph remained on the Vincennes district until the fall of 1851, when Bishop Waugh assigned him to the Greensburg district.[38] For the next two years Joseph was presiding elder of the Shelbyville station and J. W. Sullivan was the preacher. "The membership of the station was 200, with forty probationers, and 3 colored members, making a total of 243. In Sunday School were 30 officers and teachers, and 100 scholars."[39]

Chapter Eight

From Circuit Rider to Established Minister:

Tarkington's Residence in Greensburg

In 1851 the Tarkingtons moved to what would be their permanent home, the 162-acre farm on the Michigan Road, one mile northwest of Greensburg, which Maria's parents had given them. In a later sale bill the farm was described as composed of "all tillable black walnut and sugar tree land, no better producing land in the country." Joseph's sons Joseph A. and William drove the cows from Greencastle to Greensburg. Joseph described the journey:

> The first night we stopped at Stilesville, at Brother Kelly's. The next day we dined at Mooresville, and that night we were kindly entertained by Mr. Christian and family. It was dark when we got to his house, and the boys had some trouble driving the cows. William said, "Others may have tribulation, but nothing like Joe and I had driving cows after dark." The next day we reached Rev. James Ray's, and some of us stopped with him, and others went on into Shelbyville to Dr. Robbins's. The people were very kind to us seeing we had to move so far. The next day at sundown we got to a little cabin on the farm which my brother Eli had built and had lived in for seven years. He had bought land near Kokomo and moved on it. The cabin was empty. We lived in it until we built adjoining it the next year the house we now live in.[1]

Joseph hired a carpenter named John B. Trimble to build a house.[2] Trimble built the house for twelve hundred dollars. Joseph states that weatherboarding for the structure was obtained for "fifty cents per hundred" boards.[3] The Tarkingtons new home reflected their affluence. The house de-emphasized intimacy and reflected the family's genteel aspirations. It was an elaborate structure with five bedrooms and two stairways. One stairway was a "servant's stairway" that led from the upstairs hallway to the kitchen. Since the early 1840s Maria had occasionally enlisted the aid of young women to help her with the many domestic duties that faced her daily. The new home also had a sewing room, parlors, gaslights, hardwood floors, beautiful trim throughout the house, and a grand staircase leading to the upstairs bedrooms.

Tarkington built a large fifty-by-one-hundred-foot barn behind the house, with several outbuildings and corncribs. Just as his father had near Stanford, Joseph also grew an orchard of apple and peach trees. What Rhys Isaac terms the "evangelical revolt" in American society was clearly waning by mid-nineteenth-century Indiana.[4] By 1851, Joseph Tarkington had become a prosperous man, reflecting that the Methodist clergy had evolved into a professional class from their log cabin days.

After settling at the farm in Greensburg, Joseph continued with his preaching duties. He was presiding elder of the Greensburg district, which kept him

The Tarkington house at Greensburg as it appeared in June 1994.

on the road constantly. Maria, Joseph A., and William managed the farm. Daughters Mary and Martha taught school at the farm following construction of the house. John was left at Asbury to graduate the following year. The Indiana Asbury University (which became DePauw University) *Register of Students, 1837–1875* indicates that John was a good student who undertook a difficult curriculum. His deportment was also excellent. Another of Joseph's sons, Joseph Asbury, however, did not finish the Indiana Academy and records reveal that he was somewhat ornery.[5] Mary and Martha attended Mrs. Larabee's school for young women between the years 1848 and 1851 and graduated. On July 15, 1850, the books listed for their courses included McGuffey's *Spelling Book*; McGuffey's *Reader*, 1, 2, 3; Parley's *Geography*; Wilson's *Juvenile History*; Ray's *Arithmetic*, 1, 2, 3; and Parley's *Universal History*.[6]

The education that Martha and Mary received and their subsequent careers as teachers reflected a national trend toward educational reform. Reformers such as Horace Mann, the first superintendent of education in Massachusetts, were fearful of the moral decadence they perceived in the country, even though seminaries were spreading in the United States. Churches and their schools could no longer be the sole source of uplifting the morals of society. Around 1850, public schools began to play a large role in education. Classical education, however, played a small role in early classroom instruction in mid-nineteenth-century Indiana. A future generation of farmers and mechanics was taught moral habits with standard classroom texts, such as Webster's *Speller* and McGuffey's *Reader* along with the Bible.

Prior to 1853 there were no single free schools in Indiana. All schools were supported in part by tuition.[7] Early education in Decatur County was generally conducted for three months, and the usual school day, such as Martha and Mary taught, began in the morning and lasted until evening. Pupils often studied "out loud," and another teacher in Decatur County established in rhyme the rules she expected her pupils to live by: "No rippin', no tearin', / No cussin', no swearin', / No clingin', no swingin', to trees."[8]

In 1853, under law, civil township trustees began to establish "a sufficient number of public schools to care for the education of all white children." African Americans and mulattos were not admitted to the schools. A small consolation to this injustice was that "neither could they be taxed for school purposes."[9] In one case a "very light in color" African American girl did attend school, which caused a stir. Trustee "Doctor" Moody handled the matter with "true Solomonic wisdom." Lewis Harding reported the event: "One of the patrons of the school came to [Moody] and protested because a little negro girl was attending the school. He said he would take his own daughter out unless the colored pupil was removed. The colored girl was very light in color, while the protesting citizen's daughter was a very dark brunette. 'Very well,' said Doctor Moody. 'We will send a man around tomorrow to pick out the negro, If he picks out the negro, she goes out, and if he picks out your child, she goes out.' The irate citizen was content to drop the matter."[10]

With the rapid commercialization that Jacksonian America had ushered in, Indiana society had become stratified. The Methodists were not immune to these changes. They found increasingly wealthy people within their ranks. The growing wealth of the Methodist Church and many members of its congregations often conflicted with the Methodists' earlier emphasis on egalitarianism. The upper-class Methodists often resented the traditional and poor church members.

Individualism was also beginning to end in what Charles Sellers calls "the market revolution."[11] The changes brought together businessmen with farmers and rural people who had traditionally practiced a subsistence lifestyle along with the practice of barter. In many cases farmers had been required to haul their produce and other goods to markets. In the winter of 1844, when Joseph was acting as presiding elder of the Centerville district, he reported seeing a "wagon standing in water and mud, with a woman seated with a child in her arms on top of the load of hoop-poles. She said they had stalled, and her husband had gone for help to pull the wagon out. They were taking hoop-poles to Cincinnati to exchange for goods."[12]

Even though traditional farmers and businessmen were brought together by a market economy, the middle and upper classes severed the social ties that had once bound them together. Ministers also became separated from the laity with the changes that were occurring. Nottingham comments: "increasing wealth, increasing 'settledness,' brought with them the desire for church building and an atmosphere of ecclesiastical respectability. . . . There was a desire for a stable form of administration, and it is perhaps for this reason that Methodism . . . was not more torn than it actually was."[13]

By the middle of the nineteenth century, the revivals that had been so useful in gaining converts to the Methodist Church had begun to lose much of their earlier flavor and productiveness. Allen Wiley wrote in 1846 that there had been two great camp meetings during the year. Wiley added, "When, however, we say they were good, I could not be understood to say they would compare with the former meetings during the year. There was much more preaching talent at those meetings than the former; but there was not the same zeal in the preachers or people."[14] The Methodists were still gaining large numbers of members during the 1840s, as a letter from Matilda Welch to her husband, Augustus, indicates: "Our meeting commenced and still is going on I think there is about seventy joined the church and a great many professed religion among those who have joined is Aunt Mary and Norman Hatch and his wife and a great many of the neighbors. I cannot mention how long it will continue I cannot tell. Br. Durbin says so long as there is one sinner that will come to the altar for mercy he will try and labor with them."[15]

In his study of camp meetings in the South, Dickson D. Bruce claims that "[i]n spite of their great success, camp-meetings virtually disappeared in the 1840's." Bruce adds:

> In part their discontinuance may have been because of the fact that increasing population density in many areas made the establishment of "located" churches feasible so that it was no longer necessary to draw people from over a large area in order to make a religious meeting worthwhile. A good-sized congregation could be attracted from the immediate neighborhood . . . the disappearance of the camp-meeting was just as likely a product of larger historical and social forces, for it paralleled other significant changes in both the Methodist and Baptist churches. Both groups were changing status from that of sects offering alternatives to the status quo to that of denominational institutions within the existing Southern social order.[16]

However, the changes were also occurring in the North. Congregations insisted on having a regular or "located" preacher that could be on hand to help with problems or needs. In most cases, as the population grew, circuits got smaller in order that a preacher could better serve a more concentrated population. A complementary trend, which Randy Sparks documents among evangelicals in Mississippi, was that "[a]s the evangelicals moved from sect to denominations, many ministers sought a higher status—more recognition as professionals—an ambition that necessitated separating themselves from the laity and elevating their position within the churches and society."[17]

The desire for professional status was clear among graduates of seminaries. When the building of a seminary was discussed during the 1832 conference at New Albany, many lay people worried that such a place would be a factory for preachers. However, Allen Wiley, who had learned Latin and Greek at Indiana Seminary at Bloomington, argued that there was "nothing further from our minds" than the mass production of preachers.[18] Even though it was not Wiley's intent to produce seminary-trained preachers, the numbers of lay preachers were declining by the 1830s. Seminary-trained clergymen were gaining a hold on the pulpit.

The changes that occurred in the 1830s had a profound effect on the style of worship within congregations. Randy Sparks comments that "[t]hese modern clergymen were changing basic aspects of evangelical worship and creating what can be called a clerical ministry as opposed to a congregational one."[19] This change was reflected in the very words that church members used. During the first years of Methodism in Indiana, preachers were generally called "brother" by fellow lay members. However, after the mid-nineteenth century the clergy were often called "father." Class meetings and love feasts, which had been practiced in the state since Methodism was introduced, virtually disappeared. "Hot preaching," as had been found at the camp meetings—punctuated with shouting, hand clapping, and foot stomping—yielded to prepared and intellectualized sermons. Even Joseph, who had relied on the "Divine" to help him deliver unrehearsed and spontaneous sermons in the 1820s, was prepreparing his messages by the mid-nineteenth century. By the 1880s, he even used a typewriter. Nevertheless, he had not completely lost his evangelical style. While preaching in Indianapolis on August 6, 1865, at Robert's Chapel, Calvin Fletcher, one of the city fathers, was in the congregation. Fletcher entered into his diary: "This is a pleasant day went to church heard a Mr. Tarkington 60 + over old fashioned minister."[20]

A reduction in lay participation greatly reduced women's roles in church services, but the changes did give women opportunities to take part in activities such as Sunday schools. As Christopher H. Owen found in Georgia: "Early Methodist women normally did not pray in public, but class meetings, love feasts and other Methodists institutions gave them opportunities for public expression of religious feelings."[21] Regardless of Calvin Fletcher's assessment of Joseph, he was a reform-minded preacher who was not even against letting women in the pulpit.

At a quarterly conference in 1843 on the Centerville circuit, a woman was scheduled to preach when Allen Wiley objected. T. A. Goodwin responded to Wiley, "I have published it." Wiley replied, "I will not be present; for if I do, it will be published that I have women preaching at my appointments." Tarkington intervened in the argument and said, "Brother Wiley, it will not militate against you going to the General Conference. I will be present, and see that the ark shall be safe." Wiley reacted to Joseph's pledge by proclaiming, "You may but I will not." The woman delivered her message from the text "Mary hath chosen that good part." Some of the church members took Wiley's position and left, while others accepted the woman preacher.[22] Joseph gave his assessment of the situation: "You can see women engaged in the work of the Church in trying to save souls. They are eloquent in the pulpit, busy as doctors and lawyers, and go on great missions to the end of the world. May the time come 'when all God's people will be prophets!'"[23]

One of the main reasons that Joseph supported women working in the church was because many were reform-minded, and some, such as "Mrs. L. O. Robinson and Mrs. Governor David Wallace," toiled for the cause of temperance.[24] Many times throughout his pastoral career, Joseph was appointed to give the report on temperance at the conference meeting. At the 1853 Southeast Indiana conference, the report was read, and the Methodists were urged to "[a]dmire and applaud the humane and patriotic Christian conduct of all coopers who refuse to make whisky barrels of all farmers who refuse to sell hogs or grain to distillers; of all businessmen who disclaim any and all connection with the traffic; and of all politicians who exhibit the moral courage and patriotic honesty to advocate the Temperance cause . . . [they] should also warn the foreign immigrant about the 'drunkards grave.'"[25] Growing numbers of immigrants—Germans with their beer-drinking traditions and whiskey-drinking Irish—caused temperance advocates to become more fearful of the harmful effects of alcohol. As church groups preached against alcoholic beverages, many reform-minded women's groups joined their cause. The attacks on alcohol were not confined to the Methodists. The cause even penetrated popular literature. Timothy Shay Arthur's work, *Ten Nights in a Bar-room and What I Saw There* (1854) was second in sales only to Harriet Beecher Stowe's *Uncle Tom's Cabin* in the 1850s.

During the first part of the nineteenth century, Sydney E. Ahlstrom contends that "nothing in America was safe from the reformer's burning gaze. Everything from diet and dress to the social structure itself—even the family and motherhood—were up for critical review, while panaceas and nostrums ranged from graham crackers and bloomers to free love and socialism. Crackpots and dreamers, sober philosophers and millennial prophets had their moment if not their day."[26] Communitarianism flourished in the early part of the century with Robert Owen's New Harmony, the transcendentalist Brook Farm, and the Oneida Community, which established a complex marriage system. During the Jacksonian era, communal experiments began to wane, and reform movements surfaced. So did alternative religious crusades, including spiritualism, which was sympathetic to women's rights.[27] Mormonism, Millerism, along with other new religious traditions, were also born during the period.[28] Even Abraham Lincoln experimented with spiritualism. During his presidency, he attended at least five séances. At one of the events, held on February 5, 1863, at Georgetown, a piano allegedly "rose and fell a number of times," to Lincoln's amazement. Lincoln stated that he was "perfectly satisfied that the motion [of the piano] was caused by some 'invisible power.'"[29]

By the middle of the nineteenth century, Methodist preachers were no longer clad in buckskins. The pastors generally dressed better than the laity. From the onset of Methodism in Indiana, clothing had symbolic meaning. Leigh Eric Schmidt remarks: "Clothes, to play upon an anthropological trope, were good to think with. They helped people express ideas about hierarchy, equality, gender, clerical authority, community, ritual, purity, repentance, redemption, sin, pride, shame and last things. They offered a powerful channel of communication through which people—whether literate or illiterate lay or clerical—conveyed various messages to one another." Schmidt provides an example of the Methodists' changing views on clothing. In 1855, William Winans, who had left Indiana for Mississippi, previously had "expelled women from the church for dressing in finery, gave up the battle but continued to criticize; he wrote, 'I found Georgiana Carter, who had, I believe, but six rings on her fingers besides considerable other jewelry. Such are many modern Methodists!'"[30]

At the 1839 Indiana conference, which was held in Lawrenceburg, dress became an issue. Rev. John S. Bayless had recently married a well-to-do young woman at Vincennes. He brought her to the conference with him on a steamboat but left her at the small town of Rising Sun. T. A. Goodwin recollected what followed:

With no fear of tradition before his eyes, he had had his wedding suit made by a tailor in the height of the fashion. The fact that it was made of store-goods was not of itself to be censured; for Edward R. Ames, William H. Goode, and a dozen or more others, wore store-goods; but the style of the clothes gave offense. The pants were 'tights,' with narrow falls; the coat was 'pigeon-tailed;' and the hat of the stovepipe variety, giving the wearer a unique appearance in a body of Methodist preachers in regulation uniform. This was too much of a departure from traditional Methodism to go unrebuked; hence, Samuel C. Cooper offered a resolution that every member of the Conference be required hereafter to wear to Conference straight-breasted or shad-bellied coats, and breeches with broad falls. It passed without a dissenting vote; but more and more, from that on, preachers dressed as they pleased, so that the cut of the coat or pants is no longer a distinguishing badge of a Methodist preacher.[31]

As early as the 1820s Illinois Gov. Thomas Ford commented that "neighborhood after neighborhood" was abandoning "buckskin, homespun, and moccasins in favor of cloth coats, calico dresses, and shoes." Governor Ford also observed that the "young ladies" no longer walked barefoot to church as Joseph Tarkington had reported in early Monroe County, Indiana; they "now came forth arrayed complete in all the pride of dress, mounted on fine horses and attended by their male admirers." The Illinois leader thought that the changes at least "taught young men as well as women to admire and wish to be admired. Each one wanted to make as good a figure as he could."[32]

The Methodist churches became elaborate structures by mid-century, reflecting an ebbing of simplicity. Christopher H. Owen states: "By mid-century, Methodists in Indiana towns owned 'the finest and most costly Protestant churches,' replete with immense steeples and melodious bells." Many of the traditional members did not like the new buildings. The first bell that Francis Asbury saw on a Methodist church in 1806 at Augusta, Georgia, made him hope that "the bell would break and that he would never see another on a Methodist church."[33] However, the evolution of church architecture during Joseph Tarkington's lifetime embodies almost a century of social and religious change. The early churches were simple and often small log cabins; these were transformed into opulent brick buildings that were often Gothic in taste. Richard Bushman claims that the Methodists "lagged only a step or two behind the Congregationalists and Presbyterians in this cultural competition."[34]

With the rapid industrialization of the nineteenth century, many businesses gave philanthropic support to their churches. In Greensburg the first Methodist Church of 1834 was replaced in 1849 "when a two-story brick, forty-five by sixty feet, was built."[35] In 1875 an ornate structure was constructed. The new churches reduced lay participation in most congregations. By the middle of the nineteenth century, organized choirs took the place of congregational singing. As instruments such as the organ were introduced in churches, some resistance resulted. Greensburg and the Tarkington family were not sheltered from these battles. In 1865 the First Methodist Episcopal Church in Greensburg organized a choir and "introduced an organ into the church," and a schism occurred. Many of the congregation believed the organ was an instrument of the devil and "withdrew their membership on March 1, 1866, and organized a second Methodist congregation." Among church members, 100 of 273 joined a splinter group and formed a new church over the issue. Among them were Maria's sister Maluda and her husband, Rev. John S. Winchester, who was appointed pastor of the new church for the years 1866–67. The new church was known as the Centenary Methodist Church because 1866 was the one-hundredth anniversary of Methodism in America.[36] Joseph and Maria Tarkington avoided the battle over the new organ. But Joseph was still preaching in rural churches during the period. Despite Winchester's dislike for musical instruments in churches, the Mason and Hamlin Organ Company attempted to sell him an organ on February 2, 1870.[37]

Traditional preachers such as William Winans, who had moved to Mississippi because of his pro-slavery stand, were critical of the changes occurring in Methodism. He was especially harsh on the subject of the newly educated preachers and elaborate church structures that had evolved. Winans commented:

> They have other refined and elevated tastes that must be accommodated. The churches where they condescend to hear the gospel must, if possible, be magnificent piles of Gothic architecture. The seats must be pews, to keep apart the elite and vulgar, and must be carpeted and cushioned. The music must be the scientific performance of a well-trained choir, accompanied by the deep, solemn, awe-inspiring tones of the organ. Nothing less than all this can match the pretensions of such excelsior Methodist taught graduates.[38]

Along with the changes in the churches, many of the traditional Methodists did not like the remodeling of society that industrialization was bringing, believing that industrial development would break down society's moral safeguards, which would lead to crime and the decline of morals among the general populace. The Indiana Methodists' feelings were not unique. When the cotton mill industrialists were attacked in Georgia, Judge Joseph Henry Lumpkin countered with his own paternalistic argument: "I am by no means ready to concede that our poor, degraded, half-fed, half-clothed, and ignorant population, without Sabbath-schools, or any other kind of instruction—mental or moral—or without any just appreciation of the value of character, will be injured by giving them employment. . . . After all, the most powerful motives to good conduct, is to give suitable encouragement to labor, and to bestow proper rewards upon meritorious industry."[39]

The rapid changes that were occurring even penetrated politics. In the pioneer period of Indiana, most settlers felt that government should stay out of local affairs. However, as early settlements matured, Hamiltonian notions "that the political state might be extremely useful to those who 'knew how to control its policies to their own particular ends'" had taken root. Traditional Methodists tended to remain aligned with the Jacksonians, as opposed to the modernist Whigs, who "looked favorably on the emerging capitalist system and the market economy."[40] Maria Tarkington's father, Simeon Slawson, had long favored a strong central government. In the 1812 presidential election, he favored Federalist candidate De Witt Clinton over Democratic-Republican James Madison.[41] In the 1824 presidential election, Slawson and a group of Switzerland County voters met at the courthouse in Vevay and again gave their support to De Witt Clinton as their choice for president, with Andrew Jackson as their preference for vice-president.[42] Slawson and his friends efforts failed, and Jackson was elected president. The reason Slawson favored Clinton was due to his support of internal improvements. As governor of New York, Clinton had launched several projects that had helped those living on the frontier. His main achievement was the construction of the Erie Canal, "which created a water highway from the Great Lakes to the Atlantic and opened the vast interior of the North American continent to commercial exploitation."[43]

After Jackson's victory, the Slawsons continued to support Whig candidates. In a family register loaned to me by Simeon Slawson's descendant R. W. Manuel, virtually all of the family voted with the entrepreneurs and remained with the Whig Party. Later they became Republicans after the formation of the Republican Party in 1854–55 from various political components that were opposed to the Kansas-Nebraska Act of 1854.[44] Mr. Manuel's records also reveal that other families that the Slawsons married into, such as the Grahams, Mansers, and Welches, were also mainly Methodists with Whig and later Republican political affiliation. By the 1840s political barbecues were held in Switzerland County in support of the Whigs.[45] Edward Eggleston gave an account of a Switzerland County political rally in his novel *Roxy* during the 1840 presidential campaign between William Henry Harrison and Martin Van Buren. People had come from miles around in camp meeting style, shouting slogans: "Hurrah for Harrison and Tyler! Beat the Dutch or bust your b'iler!"[46] Eggleston adds that some did not know anything about politics: "Now and then one of them stops, and looking over the valley and the village, swings his cap and cries out: 'Hurrah for Harrison and Tyler!' or 'Hurrah for Tippecanoe and Tyler too!' Not, perhaps, because he knows or cares anything about the candidates for the presidency, but because a young cock must flap his wings and crow."[47]

There were other modernizing tendencies, too. Improvements in travel made it easier to reach areas in Indiana during the mid-nineteenth century that could only have been reached by horseback or stage earlier. In 1836 Gov. Noah Noble signed a bill named the "Mammoth Internal Improvement Bill," which created the Whitewater Canal, the Central Canal, and extended the Wabash and Erie Canal. A railroad was constructed from Madison located on the Ohio River to Lafayette. Turnpikes were also built in conjunction with other transportation projects. The appropriations for all these undertakings totaled a massive ten million dollars.[48] The transportation revolution resulted in a highly mobile population.

Advancements in communications also helped recast the Indiana countryside. The introduction of the rotary press in the 1830s made printing relatively inexpensive. The development of the "penny press" "made it possible to flood the mails with religious tracts, political broadsides, abolitionist propaganda, or testimonials to patent medicine. Anyone with a message and modest capital could now bypass established local leaders and address himself to the ordinary reader. The Communications Revolution was giving birth to popular mass culture."[49] Circuit riders such as Joseph Tarkington were no longer the chief sources of news to communities. The faster press produced cheaper editions of earlier printed books and periodicals. Less expensive reading materials reached a wider audience. William Warren Sweet claimed that 174 religious periodicals appeared in the United States in 1830, as compared to 10 in 1800. "One of them, the *Christian Advocate and Journal*, claimed in 1829 a circulation of 25,000, the largest circulation then reached by any newspaper in the world, not excepting the *London Times*. . . . It was a religious, specifically Methodist journal, but its editors understood, or learned, what a newspaper had to be in order to appeal to a large audience. It carried stories and anecdotes, advertisements, bank note tables, and a list of New York prices."[50] R. Laurence Moore summarizes the effects of this new, widely available reading material:

> antebellum ministers and their close allies, determined to foster the habit of reading, were a major force in creating a commercially exploitable reading public in America and in determining its tastes. Religious organizations distributed a vast quantity of cheap, even free, print material in the first part of the nineteenth century . . . the American Bible Tract societies *created* mass media in this country, pointing the way, in the period before 1830, to innovations later used by the penny press and large publishing houses. Their activities help explain the rela-

tively early arrival of mass reading audiences in the United States, in comparison with France and other European countries.[51]

Moralistic novels were produced with "warnings against conventional vices—adultery, gambling, murder, dishonesty." Some warned about the evils of visiting brothels or of adolescent male masturbation. Different ways of peddling religious messages were found, dispersing cultural values other than the pulpit. The Bible had a symbolic presence in homes. With the less expensive editions of the Bible, "with handsome engravings, could tempt people to buy again."[52]

By mid-century religion was no longer the chief source of entertainment. Secular amusements posed a threat to the churches. As mentioned, however, novels and theatrical productions that flourished were, in many cases, like those written by Mason Lock Weems: they "remained bound up with Christian concepts of sin, redemption, and eternal life."[53] The novels used sensationalism to attract readers just as circuit riders like Tarkington had used a demonstrative religion to gain converts in the past.

Chapter Nine

A Preacher Faces Slavery and the Civil War

By the 1850s, the Tarkingtons had become prominent citizens. Maria and Joseph's children married into notable families. John married affluent Elizabeth Booth of Terre Haute, the sister of the future governor of California, on November 19, 1852.[1] On May 18, 1858, Martha married Daniel Stewart at her father's home. Before Martha had decided to marry Stewart, she had considered marrying Elmer Croy of Carrolton, Kentucky. Croy was a cousin of the Welches. Stewart simply took Martha away from Croy. Unaware of the situation between Martha and Stewart, Croy wrote Augustus Welch on August 30, 1857, stating that Martha had not written him and that he "had the 'blues' and burnt brandy does one no good."[2] Croy was simply wasting time by worrying about Martha. He was a common man and being the wife of a farmer did not appeal to Martha. She had no desire to play the role of so many other farm wives, who found back-breaking work, annual childbirth, and early graves. A cultured and refined man like Daniel Stewart was what appealed to her.[3] In 1863 the Stewarts moved to Indianapolis in order to expand their business, and their family became one of the wealthiest in Indianapolis.[4]

The rest of Joseph and Maria's children also married well. Mary wed Dr. John Alexander at her father's home on December 9, 1856. Joseph Asbury married Elva Meridith Yeatman in 1885 at Washington, D.C. Elva was a famous concert pianist and harp player. She played many times at the White House. William Simeon Reaves married his first cousin at the home of his

Elizabeth Booth Tarkington, mother of the author Booth Tarkington.
Courtesy of Patricia Cochran.

grandfather near Stanford, Indiana, on June 2, 1870, and Matthew Simpson Tarkington married Clare Williams Baker, the daughter of a large landowner, at Greensburg in 1878.[5]

Along with their rise in status, the Tarkingtons embraced a strong sense of social responsibility. One of the preachers in the Centerville district when Joseph was presiding elder in 1843 was a local elder named Jonathan Shaw. Tarkington described him as a man "well posted in theology by reading Wesley, Fletcher, and Watson." Shaw was opposed to slavery. However, people on the circuit called him an "Abolitionist, and said he was crazy." Tarkington simply said the man was "ahead of his time."[6] Another preacher, Dr. T. H. Lynch, came to Indiana from Kentucky because of his opposition to slavery. He was also a free-soiler, deeply opposed to allowing new slave states and territories into the Union. During the denominational split between northern and southern Methodists in 1844, Lynch was a member of the Kentucky conference.

Lynch worked hard to change the slaveholding stand of the Kentucky church; when it was evident that his efforts were not going to work, he left Kentucky and settled in Shelbyville, Indiana.[7]

Joseph had seen slavery during his youth in Tennessee, and he had also seen people who freed their slaves as they moved near his father's home in Monroe County, Indiana. As was his father, Joseph was opposed to slavery. But he was not an abolitionist, due to the Methodist Church's resistance to abolitionism. Some Methodist preachers, however, actually purchased slaves and gave them their freedom. In one case, as William Warren Sweet relates, John Ray, a strong anti-slavery advocate and Kentucky circuit rider and the father of Indiana preacher Edwin Ray, gave "$50.00 to the American Colonization Society, and $50.00 for the redemption of James Thompson, a slave, who understood the Wyandotte tongue and had been acting as an interpreter in the Methodist Wyandotte mission. The *Western Christian Advocate* urged his purchase, in order to prevent his sale, and this was finally accomplished for $1,200."[8]

William Cravens, who had been sent to Indianapolis in 1821 to organize a circuit, found some Hoosiers who were slaveholders. Sweet comments: "He found some residents in Indiana who hired out their slaves in the slave states, and were drawing their wages, while many more had sold their slaves and had purchased homes for themselves in Indiana with the price of their slaves. These he denounced as 'hypocrites, and worse than the actual slave holder.'"[9] Holliday states that Cravens had a "special abhorrence to sins of drunkenness and negro slavery."[10] While he was living in Virginia prior to moving to Indiana, he had a slaveholding neighbor referred to as "Mr. T." Cravens worked hard trying to get the man to become a Christian and also attempted to get him to free his slaves. Mr. T. became ill and believed that he was near death. He sent for Cravens. When the preacher arrived, the sick man asked Cravens to pray for him and to indicate what he must do to be saved. Cravens inquired, "Ah, Mr. T., I thought it would come to this. What have you done with your negroes?" Mr. T. responded, "I have provided for them in my will." He added, "I have divided them among my children, as I wish them to remain in my family." Cravens answered, "I can not pray for you. . . . God will never have mercy on you until you are willing to do justly. You will never get religion until you set your negroes free." Cravens then left the ailing man but was shortly summoned again. Mr. T. knew that death was rapidly approaching. When Cravens arrived the second time, Cravens asked, "Well, Mr. T., how is it now?" The sick man informed Cravens that he had altered his will and had provided for his slaves' emancipation. Cravens then prayed for the man. Holliday comments that Cra-

Joseph A. Tarkington, circa 1885. Courtesy of Jeanette Tarkington Stokely.   *Elva M. Yeatman Tarkington, circa 1885. Courtesy of Jeanette Tarkington Stokely.*

vens "made an impression in favor of Methodism, and against slavery and intemperance, that has never faded out."[11]

Antislavery advocates such as William Cravens began to draw serious attention to the slavery issue during the 1840s and 1850s. At the 1842 Indiana conference, the York resolutions were passed without the sanction of the General Conference. The York resolutions prohibited selling or hiring out slaves to slave states. As Sweet reports: "The York resolutions were taken up, and on the first viz.: 'The buying or selling of men, women, or children, with an intention to enslave them, or the holding of them as slaves in any State, Country or District, when the laws of such State, Territory or District will admit emancipation, and permit the liberated slave to enjoy freedom,' was concurred in by the Conference by a vote of 92 yeas, 34 nays."[12]

After the General Conference of 1840, antislavery feeling among preachers in the North increased. By the 1840s Methodists had passed Episcopalians as the "slaveowners church, with the Baptists running a close second."[13] Abolition had become an issue that could not be ignored. Robert H. Williams reports a Methodist Church trial in Illinois where a "Dr. Worrell" brought charges against a man for having abolitionist leanings. The "Presiding Elder replied that the plaintiff was not eligible to bring charges, and that in any case his charges were not serious enough to involve more than reproff." Dr. Worrell refused to accept the presiding elder's decision and wrote to Bishop Andrew. An investigation was conducted and Nichols was located, "after considerable debate."[14]

Michigan circuit rider Elijah Holmes Pilcher drafted a series of articles on slavery "which were influential in the formation of public opinion." Pilcher, like his father, Stephen, before him "stood on the side of humanity and freedom." Pilcher's father freed his slaves and worked actively among his Virginia neighbors to get them to adopt his views. "In one meeting a pro-slavery advocate, in a fury over his inability to cope with Pilcher polemically, rushed upon him with the intention of substituting violent action for words in the argument. But his companions intervened and restrained him. Pilcher, smiling and undisturbed, tranquilly resumed his remarks."[15]

During the colonial period, slavery was a "recognized legal institution in every one of the thirteen colonies." For several years after constructing the Methodist Episcopal Church, the faith expanded more rapidly in the South than in the northern states.[16] In the three decades prior to the Civil War, as Mitchell Snay contends in his work *Gospel of Disunion*, the South was not a monolithic culture but a diverse society with different concerns, and religion was the key ingredient in forming a distinct sectional identity.[17] Snay also holds that religion strengthened significant components in southern political culture, caused sectional politics to take on an increased religious significance, and advanced a moral view that made secession possible by convincing southerners to believe that slavery and their civilization could best be maintained as a separate nation.

During the 1830s abolition became a large element of the Jacksonian reform era. Abolitionists demanded immediate emancipation and were opposed to both gradual liberation and the colonization societies. Nonetheless, most Americans were opposed to immediate emancipation of slaves. In the northern states, resentment toward slavery, which was expressed in a highly religious tone, increased during the 1830s with the rise of abolitionist propaganda. The abolitionist postal campaign of 1835 marked the shift in American antislavery reform from moderate action to instantaneous action. Abolitionists met major resistance from the slaveholding states. Southerners burned antislavery pamphlets and became active in fighting abolitionist literature by other means.[18]

After the invention of the cotton gin by Eli Whitney in 1793, cotton cultivation boomed in the South, creating unparalleled demand for slaves. Following the War of 1812 and the opening of the "Black Belt" of Alabama and Mississippi, cotton crop production reached one million bales by 1835. In an attempt to arrest any further spread of slavery into Missouri, Senator James Tallmadge Jr. of New York introduced the famous "Tallmadge Amendment" on February 13, 1819. After considerable debate between North and South, bills were adopted for the admission of Missouri and Maine as slave and free states respectively with the additional provision that slavery be prohibited in the Louisiana Purchase territory north of 36°30′. The compromise held for two decades, but the Kansas-Nebraska Act of 1854 organized two territorial governments for portions of the Louisiana Purchase north of the 36°30′ line and, in effect, repealed the Missouri Compromise by allowing settlers in the territories themselves to decide whether the territories would be free or slave. Further, the Supreme Court's Dred Scott Decision of 1857 declared Congressional prohibition of slavery in the territories unconstitutional.

Active reform toward the abolition of slavery in the United States began in 1808 when Congress abolished the African slave trade. During this period, several northern states voided slavery within their borders, but immediate abolition had not become a major issue. In the early 1830s the British abolitionist movement gave new hope to those pushing for instantaneous emancipation in the United States. British emancipator William Wilberforce's convictions were reechoed in New England in 1832 when the New England Anti-Slavery Society was formed. Only a very few people joined the society initially. In 1833 a national society was formed after Nat Turner's revolt made William Lloyd Garrison's abolitionist views famous throughout the United States. Nationally, newspapers began reprinting Garrison's editorials, and his name became synonymous with emancipation. During this period some of the Methodist Episcopal Church's preachers were becoming "abolitionist agitators," and the authorities attempted to avoid dissension within their ranks by enforcing disciplinary measures against those "who engaged in abolitionist activities."[19]

American abolitionists were not generally from the eastern intellectual circles, such as Harvard president Edward Everett, who pushed only for educating blacks. Most abolitionists drew their inspiration from religious reformers like Garrison. Garrison himself had worked with Quaker abolitionist Benjamin Lundy during the 1820s before establishing his own antislavery newspaper, the *Liberator,* in Boston in 1831. Garrison denounced the churches for tolerating slavery and burned copies of the Constitution because it accepted the institution.

Another abolitionist, Theodore Dwight Weld, also entered the antislavery campaign because of his extreme religious beliefs. After experiencing conversion under Charles G. Finney, Weld devoted his life to reform. In 1834, while attending the Lane Theological Seminary at Cincinnati, Weld arranged debates with his fellow students on the subject of slavery. After arguing the subject for a couple of weeks, the students decided that immediate emancipation should be granted to those held in bondage. Weld and forty of his classmates left the seminary after offending authorities at Lane and attended Oberlin College. Oberlin became a center for abolitionist activities. By employing the machinery of the camp meetings and revivals, thousands of converts in the East and Northwest were gained by the abolitionists.

While concerted action against slavery based on religious belief awaited abolitionist leaders like Weld and Garrison, there had been a long history of individuals who had rejected slavery on the basis of religious belief. Freeborn Garrettson, a native of Maryland, was probably the first Methodist in America to take action against slavery. In 1775, following his conversion, he announced one day during family prayers: "It is not right to keep our fellow-creatures in bondage. . . . It was God, not man that taught me the impropriety of holding slaves." American-born local preacher Philip Gatch also freed his slaves in 1780.[20]

In the early nineteenth century, Donald Matthews argues that "Southern Methodists had grown accustomed to slavery and, as early as 1824, had commended it in no uncertain terms, they had, for the most part, kept silent."[21] In the 1750s George Whitefield built an orphanage in Georgia with the assistance of slaves. A century later, Matthew Simpson offered a sympathetic apology for Whitefield's actions, stating that "he appears to have been persuaded that not only was slave-holding right, but that the slave-trade itself might be looked upon favorably."[22] On March 22, 1751, Whitefield wrote a letter to Wesley offering his position on the legality of slavery:

As for the lawfulness of keeping slaves I have no doubt, since I hear of some that were bought with Abraham's money, and some that were born in his house. I also cannot help thinking that some of those servants mentioned by the apostles in their epistles were, or had been slaves. It is plain that the Gibeonites were doomed to perpetual slavery; and though liberty is a sweet thing to such as are born free, yet to those who never knew the sweets of it, slavery, perhaps, may not be irksome; however this be, it is plain to a demonstration that hot countries cannot be cultivated without negroes. What a flourishing country might Georgia be had the use of them been permitted years ago! How many white people have been destroyed for want of them! And how many thousand pounds spent for no purpose at all!

Though it is true they are brought in a wrong way from their own country, and it is a trade not to be approved of, yet as it will be carried on, whether we will or not, I should think myself highly favored if I could purchase a good number of them, in order to make these slaves comfortable, and lay a foundation for bringing up their posterity in the nurture and admonition of the Lord. I had no hand in bringing them into Georgia, though my judgement was for it, and I was strongly importuned thereto; yet I would not have a negro upon my plantation, till the use of them was publicly allowed by the colony. Now this is done, let us diligently improve the present opportunity for their instruction.[23]

At the time of Whitefield's death, he owned seventy-five slaves and willed them to the "Rt. Hon. Selina, Countess Dowager of Huntingdon."[24]

Wesley, it should be noted, did not accept Whitefield's position on slavery. In his journal dated February 12, 1772, he expressed his sentiments: "I read a very different book published by an honest Quaker on that execrable sum of all villanies commonly called the slave-trade. I read of nothing like it in the heathen world, whether ancient or modern; and it infinitely exceeds in every instance of barbarity what Christian slaves suffer in Mohammedan countries."[25]

As early as 1772, Englishman Granville Sharpe had begun to incite action over the issue of slavery in England. In 1774 Wesley joined Sharpe in denouncing the institution and published his famous work, "Thoughts on Slavery." Shortly after the publication of the pamphlet in England, it also surfaced in Philadelphia. Wesley received much ridicule over his stand in England and some opposition in American, but it was not until the 1780 conference in Baltimore that slavery started receiving considerable attention. All sorts of questions were raised, and members considered whether a preacher who held slaves should promise to set them free, and "[d]oes not this Conference acknowledge that slavery is contrary to the laws of God, man, and of nature, and hurtful to society; contrary to the dictates of conscience and pure religion, and doing that we would not that others should do to us and ours?"[26] The prevailing answers to these questions condemned slavery. While these issues caused much excitement, they were not raised again until the 1783 conference, when it was decided that Methodists who bought and sold slaves would be expelled. Further demands were made and actions taken in the following conferences. In 1789, the Discipline incorporated the following phrase: "that those desiring admission to the Methodist Church should avoid evil of every kind, such as 'the buying or selling of men, women, or children, with an intention to enslave them.' So it remained until the time of the Civil War."[27]

In 1785 Bishop Francis Asbury visited Virginia and began attempting to get slaveowners to free their slaves. On Thursday, May 26, Asbury and Dr. Coke met George Washington. Asbury said that Washington "received us very politely, and gave us his opinion on slavery." Asbury claimed that Washington "shared their sentiments on emancipation," but did not think it was proper to sign a petition demanding freedom for slaves that was presented to him.[28] In Halifax County a grand jury determined that Asbury was a seditious person for preaching against slavery. Another county also brought action against him. One man actually pursued him with a gun because he was so irate with Asbury's preaching.[29]

By 1796 the conference had developed elaborate rules concerning slavery in local church organizations. Following the 1796 conference, no slaveholders were admitted to the church until their local preacher discussed the subject with them. The conference also determined that male and female children born to a woman in servitude should be given their freedom at ages "twenty-five and twenty-one respectively." After the conference, the quarterly conferences served as a "court of equity" on the slavery issue.[30]

By 1844 most preachers in the North contended that their churches had always been antislavery. At the General Conference in 1844, Peter Cartwright asserted: "Now, sir, I will say that in all my long years of relation to, and acquaintance with Methodism and Methodist preachers, I never heard one that did not oppose slavery from stem to stern." Lewis M. Purifoy contends that if Cartwright had not heard antislavery feeling expressed in Kentucky and Illinois, he heard such expressions at the 1844 conference. William A. Smith of Virginia defended the institution of slavery by saying: "we feel justified in our course, and, indeed cannot avoid it. And we feel that we should be doing an infinitely greater wrong by altering the condition of the slaves, under present and existing circumstances."[31]

For several years the Baltimore conference supported the efforts of the American Colonization Society and other state groups that promoted the idea of sending blacks to Africa to form a colony in Liberia. Even Kentuckians such as Henry Clay, who believed that blacks and whites could "not live together harmoniously," supported the Kentucky in Liberia society, which "regarded this as the sanest plan by which the state could rid itself of slavery and free Negroes."[32] Chief Justice John Marshall expressed similar sentiments.

In 1828, as Homer Calkin relates, Stephen Roszel and Peter Cartwright "proposed a resolution which would permit the Church to discipline masters who mistreated their slaves. It provided for objurgation, suspension, or even expulsion for treating slaves with 'inhumanity, either in not supplying them with comfortable and sufficient food or raiment, or in separating husbands and wives or parents and children by buying or selling them in an inhuman traffic.'"[33] However, the General Conference denied their proposal.

Cartwright was an "acknowledged leader of antislavery forces in the Kentucky-Tennessee Conference, where he was even once put on trial for expelling slaveholding members from his district." In 1826 Cartwright was dismayed as he watched his presiding elder, Samuel Thompson, be defeated as a candidate for lieutenant governor of Illinois in 1826 for his antislavery position. Other antislavery candidates were also defeated. In 1828 Cartwright succeeded Thompson as presiding elder and did "some electioneering for himself as he traveled" to his preaching assignments. As a result he was elected to the state legislature from Sangamon County. In 1832 he was reelected to the post, defeating Abraham Lincoln.[34]

On October 18, 1843, the final session, or "Twelfth Annual Session" of the "old Indiana Conference" was held in the Old School Presbyterian Church in Crawfordsville. Bishop James O. Andrew presided, and a "deep anti-slavery sentiment was manifest among the preachers."[35] Joseph Tarkington was not passive in his feeling against slavery by the 1840s. The conference records reflect that he served on a committees to colonize slaves. At the 1855 conference at Connersville, he served on the "Committee on Slavery." Tarkington was also against the Kansas-Nebraska Act and the Dred Scott Decision, and he favored making the nation stand on the Missouri Compromise. At the Greensburg quarterly conference in August of 1854 it was decided that the Methodists would not support any candidate for Congress "who would not pledge himself to restore the Missouri Compromise line and that the extension of slavery over free territory would be a disgrace to our government."[36]

At the General Conference of 1844, a schism occurred between northern and southern Methodists. The question of slavery arose early in the meeting over the appeal of a member of the Baltimore conference, Francis A. Harding, who had been dismissed from his ministerial position for refusing to free slaves. He had come to own the slaves through marriage. The General Conference upheld the Baltimore conference by a vote of 117 to 56. The debate on slavery was launched with the report of the committee on Episcopacy on May 21, but the real trouble started when it was pointed out that Bishop James Osgood Andrew owned slaves. Andrew had become a slaveowner when his first wife died, leaving him a young mulatto slave woman "on condition that he should liberate her and send her to Liberia, with her consent." When the young girl became old enough to be sent to Liberia, she refused and remained the property of Bishop Andrew. The bishop had also received a slave boy from his first wife, and upon his second marriage he wed a woman who had inherited slaves from her dead husband's estate.[37] The committee requested that Andrew free the slaves, but Georgia law prohibited manumission.

Northern conservatives attempted to appease the South "by explaining that Andrew's morality was not at issue. They argued that his being a slaveholder would needlessly antagonize Northern antislavery men, change the policy of having no slaveholding bishops, and condone slavery by precept and example. The church had the power to control this situation and it therefore should."[38] The committee requested that Andrew resign from his office, but after some discussion a substitute resolution was offered, stating that it was the sense of the General Conference that he "desist from the exercise of this office so long as this impediment remains."[39] The action was sustained by a vote of 111 to 69. The southerners responded that "the General Conference was not empowered to call bishops to account."[40]

A convention was called in Louisville, Kentucky, on May 1, 1845, in regard to a "Plan of Separation." Bishops Soule and Andrew presided, and "after full deliberation, it declared the Southern Conference a distinct church, under the style of 'The Methodist Church South.'"[41] As a result, the Methodist Episcopal Church South was formed. The following year the first General Conference met in May of 1846 at Petersburg, Virginia. Other churches also split over the issue of slavery. In 1845 the Southern Baptist Conference was formed when northern Baptists informed southerners that they could no longer tolerate slavery.[42] The Presbyterians had split over slavery in 1837.

By 1860 the Tarkington family saw no middle ground on the slavery issue. Joseph and his sons believed in total abolition. Surviving family letters reveal an increasing interest in politics during the period. Family members used the Bible to predict that the end was near for the South.[43] Augustus Welch's uncle Stephen Greenleaf wrote to Welch in January of 1861: "Give love to all Friends Relatives and Consanguinity whatever. And tell them all for me, who Sympathize in Nigger Propagation, as the South designed. Let them go South immediately, and join the Desparatos of the South, whose end is near unless they retract. They will overthrow themselves like the Barley Cake that overthrew the Midnights under the sword of the Lord and of Gideon. See Judges Chapter 6 and 7 also How the Walls of Jerico fell."[44]

Greenleaf also wrote to Runy Welch, stating that he saw an inscription in large capital letters: "OLD ABE LINK AN HONEST MAN WE THINK." Greenleaf added that he had been to a political rally where "4 or 500 had gathered in a mass." He also believed Lincoln would be "elected but Douglass would carry Missouri." Greenleaf said he thought Lincoln would clean up the "stink of the bad eggs that have been smashed at the capital."[45] Lincoln was elected and stopped in Greensburg on his fifty-second birthday (February 12, 1861) on his way to Washington. Lincoln appeared at the rear of the train and briefly spoke to a crowd of two thousand that had gathered to see him.[46] The crowd sang "The Flag of Our Union," and the local band, with Joseph Asbury Tarkington among them, played "Hail Columbia" to the president.

On Saturday morning, April 12, 1861, shots from the Confederate batteries at Charleston, South Carolina, were directed at Fort Sumter. When it was learned that the Union garrison had fallen, cries went out in the North to crush the rebellion. On the following morning, there was hardly a preacher in a pulpit in the North who did not speak of the event. Almost all of Indiana's ministers from all congregations demanded that active steps should immediately be taken to smash the revolt. On the morning of April 15, President Lincoln issued a national proclamation, requesting 75,000 volunteers to serve the cause. On the same day, Gov. Oliver Morton telegraphed Lincoln to offer the services of 10,000 Hoosiers. Every county in the state was called on by the governor to provide troops. Although Indiana's quota was only 4,683, 10 days after Lincoln's request, 12,000 men were in Indianapolis ready for service.[47]

To add more worries to Joseph and Maria Tarkington's lot, Joseph Asbury was a member of the Greensburg regimental band, which was a drum-and-fife corps. The band volunteered and was immediately accepted into the Seventh Regiment. William S. R. and John Tarkington also enlisted in the Seventh Indiana Regiment; William was a private.[48] John wrote Joseph a letter stating that "he would furnish blankets and private pistols—revolvers—for the boys." He added that he would "rather they had waited for the next call." John did not like their regiment. He wanted them in the "Zonave Regiment," which had the best arms.[49]

The Tarkington soldiers left for Virginia on September 14, 1861. Family members corresponded with the young men. On September 16, 1861, John wrote William and Joseph A., telling them that he had sent cartridge boxes of eighty cartridges each. John had bought them at the arsenal for one and one-quarter cents each. John also instructed his brothers, in typical big-brother fashion, not to let anyone handle their pistols to avoid accidents. He also told them who to associate with. If problems arose, they were to check with John's friend, Quartermaster Dick Johnson. John advised his brothers not to let their cartridges get damp and that they should practice firing with balls and flask powder. Finally, he reminded William and Joseph that they had forgotten their Bible, but he would send it to them.[50]

Martha wrote her brothers on December 15, 1861, relating that the Children's Aid Society had sent about forty orphans to Decatur County in an attempt to find the children country homes. Martha stated that "Papa took a German boy that talks English very well." The boy's name was Bowler, and he helped perform many of the farm tasks, such as cutting wood. On one occasion, when he was putting the horse, Sam, into the stable, he disappeared and was found crying in the kitchen exclaiming, "He kick me! He kick me! I no touch him." Matthew Simpson Tarkington put the horse in the stall after the incident.[51] In Martha's letter to her brothers, she recounted family news, such as "Cattie will be a year old tomorrow" and "Dan and I with the children and mother went up to John's thanksgiving day."[52] Daniel Stewart wrote Joseph Asbury a letter on December 19, 1861. He told Joseph that he had eaten a roasted turkey with cranberry sauce and asked, "Don't you want some?" Daniel added in the letter that he could "beat anyone in the Seventh in horseshoes."[53]

John wrote his brother Joseph Asbury on January 20, 1862, revealing that family member John Slawson had left Greensburg to join them and that he was bringing Joseph a harness. John had also bought his brother a coat and trousers and paid twenty-two dollars for them. John told Joseph that his daughter "Hauty speaks of him."[54] He added that she did not want her father to go to the war and was suspicious when he tried on Joseph's new coat. John finished the letter with his typical instructions, telling Joseph to practice his drills, such as fencing with sticks. He added that Joseph should not let his pistol nor his spirit rust.[55]

By February 13, 1862, the Tarkingtons were at Cumberland, Maryland. Joseph A. Tarkington was paid thirty-four dollars for his service of less than a year. He was sick. Various diseases passed through the armies, which took a heavy death toll. Three members of Joseph's regimental band died from sickness: John H. Howard on December 6, 1861, William H. Criss on February 13, and G. W. Hiver, whose date of death is unknown. The Seventh Regiment was involved in the fighting from the start. They were in some brief skirmishes around Cheat Mountain and then fought an intense battle at Kernstown, Virginia, on March 22, 1862, against Gen. Stonewall Jackson's forces. The Seventh "lost nine men killed and thirteen wounded, of whom six died." On June 8, they fought at Port Republic and then at "Cedar Mountain, Manassas, South Mountain, Antietam, Chancellorsville, Gettysburg, Cold Harbor, Wilderness, Petersburg, and ending with the battle at Weldon Railroad on August 23, 1864."[56] However, Joseph A. and Will stayed in the army only a short time; the young men were mustered out of service after it was determined that a regimental band was not necessary.

Joseph and Maria's son-in-law, Dr. John Alexander, the husband of Mary Tarkington, enlisted in the "Twenty-seventh Regiment, Indiana Volunteer Infantry, under Col. Silas Colgrove, and was promoted to surgeon, July 15, 1864, having been commissioned assistant surgeon September 27, 1862."[57] Joseph visited his sons, along with a party from Indiana, sometime during the fall of 1861. The trip was hard and dangerous. Tarkington wrote to his mother-in-law, Martha Slawson, that a hard rain had caused the road to wash, causing him to "walk some and ride some." In places the mud was twelve inches deep. It was so dark that a wagon came within six inches of falling "some hundreds of feet twice." As a result the party "lit some fifty newspapers" as a source of light.[58]

Joseph wanted to keep in touch with his sons during the war and instructed his daughter Martha to keep the young men supplied with envelopes.[59] Mary went to Cincinnati to visit her husband, John Alexander, but he left shortly to go to Pittsburgh to assist the wounded who had fought at a recent battle.[60] As her father had requested, Martha did keep her brothers in envelopes and wrote them constantly. In a letter to William, Martha told him that Lincoln had issued a proclamation for preachers to deliver a "thank sermon for the victory." Martha said that they had raised seventy dollars for hospital supplies to help wounded soldiers who had fought in Tennessee. She also asked for a picture of Will and said she was glad that his regiment had won a battle.[61] In another letter, Martha wrote in a letter to Joseph Asbury Tarkington that Joseph had a soldier who had fought in two battles working for him. She also told her brothers that her daughters, Mary and Martha (Cattie), had gotten in a fight over a chair. She told the girls that "Joe has to sleep on the ground and Mary would cry."[62]

In 1860 U. S. Grant had claimed "that in the United States there were three political parties, the Republican, the Democratic, and the Methodist Church." Prior to the Civil War, Joseph Tarkington's friend and ex-president of Indian Asbury College Matthew Simpson had become a powerful man. In

1843 Simpson had successfully kept Gov. Samuel Bigger of Indiana from being re-elected.[63] Elizabeth Cady Stanton and Susan B. Anthony constantly asked Simpson's advice on promoting woman's suffrage. Frances Willard used Simpson as her advisor at Evanston when she founded the Woman's Christian Temperance Union. During the Civil War, Simpson won many converts to the cause of the Union with his war speech, "The Future of Our Country."

Simpson also had an influence on Lincoln. Lincoln never liked the idea of slavery, but, prior to the war, he had believed that he and the government did not have the right to interfere with it. In fact, in the debates with Stephen A. Douglas, he had admitted the constitutionality of slavery. However, Matthew Simpson did not accept the idea of slavery. On April 8, 1861, Simpson told Lincoln that "he would have to get rid of slavery before God would ever let him win the war."[64]

In a later discussion, Lincoln told Simpson that he had always opposed the extension of slavery into new territory, but it was unconstitutional to emancipate the slaves where slavery existed. Simpson responded:

> We are doing many things now that in peace times would be unconstitutional. . . . For instance, we are shooting down American citizens. The Constitution guarantees them life, liberty and the pursuit of happiness. When the Constitution is imperiled and a rebellion is on, the first right the constitution has is self-preservation. There is only one question, Shall the Constitution survive or perish? Whatever saves the Constitution now is constitutional; and what ever destroys it is unconstitutional; and if granting freedom to the slaves would help to preserve the Constitution, I care not whether the act goes over the Constitution, or under the Constitution, or around the Constitution, or through the Constitution; if it will save the Constitution, it is Constitutional.[65]

Simpson made his point. Lincoln told him "I will do this thing at the earliest practical moment. . . . Let us get down on our knees and ask the Heavenly Father to guide us as to the time, place and circumstances of its promulgation."[66]

The war caused financial strain on most families. Because her husband, Augustus Welch, had joined the fighting on the side of the Union, Maria's sister Matilda rented her farm out for a year to a David Shaddy, as an agreement between her and Shaddy reflects.[67] Joseph complained that the "war has taken much of our time and all of our money." The absence of Joseph's sons was hard on the family, especially in regard to farm labor. Joseph and Maria were not the only parents all of whose sons enlisted in service of the Union. At the opening session of the Southeast Indiana conference in 1864, which was held in Shelbyville, Rev. E. G. Wood delivered one of the most powerful "prayers the Conference ever heard." Two of Wood's sons were already serving in the army. Wood had learned earlier in the morning that his remaining son had been drafted. Rev. George Curtiss commented:

> The father, loyal to the heart, was much moved, and pronounced a blessing upon the sons, and all the "Boys in Blue" who had gone fourth to defend the honor of the nation, and sustain the glory of the stars and stripes. As he prayed, he asked a special blessing upon the nation and her union soldiers. He prayed that "when puny man attempts to measure his unholy arm with the arm of Jehovah, and uphold human slavery and destroy the best of governments, may be paralyzed, defeated, destroyed, and may lives be spared, the nation saved, and God glorified." To this earnest, heart-felt prayer of faith, there were hearty responses from as loyal a body of ministers and laymen as ever lived.[68]

Any preacher who criticized the war effort in any way found himself in hot water. A preacher named S. B. Chamberlain made several statements that got him in trouble with the Indiana conference. Chamberlain said: "Our Generals are not fighting for the country, but for the money they are making out of this war." He also argued, "There is as much mourning over the South as there is in the North. Women love their husbands, sons and brothers as fondly as we do, and mourn as sadly over their fall. Every rebel that is slain, carries desolation to home and friend." Finally, he commented that "[t]he South fully believes that she is right as much as we do—she has fought desperately for those rights, and she will fight it out to the last." Lt. George Johnson tore into Chamberlain's views in an article written in the *Indiana Weekly Visitor*. Johnson said Chamberlain's sermons, taken as a whole, were "perfectly rotten, stinking and magotty, with disloyalty and treason." Johnson also commented that a Methodist preacher should not be making such announcements and that Chamberlain had said "[n]ot a word that the South were the aggressors, and brought down all this desolation and mourning and woe themselves, both North and South. Not a word that Southern women spit in the faces of our brave Union boys, who offer them the protection of the Stripes and Stars; nor even that they wear finger rings and neclaces [sic] carved out of the bones of our brave, patriotic and fallen friends—not a word."[69] As a result of Chamberlain's sermons—and on the pretext that he was preaching funerals and lecturing on the Sabbath—he was expelled from the ministry.[70]

In May of 1864, John Tarkington helped form Company A of the 132nd Indiana Regiment in order to combat John Hunt Morgan's raiders. In July of 1864 John was at a stockade that was holding Confederate prisoners to be shipped to prisons in the North. John noticed a man who was attempting to escape and ordered him to stop, but the escaping prisoner kept running. The sentinel on duty then shot the man. John believed the man was dead and left him to a surgeon for burial. The man was not dead; he recovered and was sent to a prison in Columbus, Ohio. John later found out that the man was Albert Crippin, a boy whom his Uncle Delanson Slawson had adopted and with whom John had spent several of his boyhood summers during his childhood.[71]

In Joseph Tarkington's youth, he had witnessed slavery in Tennessee. The Tarkingtons' dislike of the institution had contributed to their move to Indiana in 1816. After Joseph Tarkington married Maria Slawson, whose family also abhorred slavery, Joseph's feelings about keeping people in bondage were reinforced. Even though northern Methodists had tried to keep their preachers from becoming involved in Abolition, after the great schism in 1844 northern pastors saw no middle ground between the rejection of slavery and its acceptance, so they demanded its end. Even Abraham Lincoln was influenced by the Methodists' demand. Following a civil war, and now in his sixties, Joseph finally saw slavery in the United States end.

Chapter Ten

Final Years

The war years were hard on the Tarkingtons. To compound their miseries, Joseph and Maria lost their youngest daughter, Ellen, during the conflict. On May 22, 1861, Ellen died at the farm. She was only seventeen years and five months old at the time of her death. Ellen's cause of death was simply listed as a lingering illness that had kept her confined to bed for several weeks. Ellen was a refined daughter, reflecting the changing view of the family toward the arts. She was described as a "devoted admirer of music and literature." A newspaper clipping recounted that "she was regarded by her parents, and numerous circle of friends, as having more than ordinary prospects, and affording unusual promise of happiness and success in the world." Even though Ellen was a refined young woman, she did not turn her back on Methodism, and she fully accepted the Tarkingtons' religious values. Only a month before her death, "in a neat note written in her own hand, in her sick room, she requested the privilege of becoming a probationer in the Church."[1] There is a copy of Ellen's obituary from an unnamed newspaper in the Slawson-Tarkington Papers:

Obituary

Died—On the 22d of May at the residence of her father, near Greensburg Ind., after a lingering illness several weeks, Ellen M. youngest daughter of Rev. Joseph and Maria Tarkington, aged 17 years 5 months and 4 days.

Reared under the parental roof of true piety, she instantly embraced the cause of Christianity and bid fair to become a useful member in the Church of Christ. Love was the motive of her heart, and neither passion nor envy ever ruffled the calm source of her thoughts. The gentleness of her manners and sincerity of her intentions, with a retiring and unassuming disposition won the admiration and love of all who approached her, yet those who knew her but slightly were ever conscious of her rare personal and intellectual charms. A true friend, a devoted admirer of music and literature. Society has lost one of its choices gems. With her "Outward loveliness was index fair, of purity with in."[2]

Joseph and Maria had felt the sting of death many times in their lifetimes. Joseph's father, Jesse, died on October 20, 1854, and his mother, Mary, passed on April 2, 1859, at the old homestead near Stanford, Indiana. Five of his eleven brothers and sisters had died before 1861. Maria's father, Simeon Slawson, died on January 22, 1858, and only two of her ten brothers and sisters, Maluda Winchester and Matilda Welch, were living in 1861. Maria's mother, Martha Slawson, lived until July 7, 1866, and died at her home in Switzerland County. Prior to her death, Martha had been suffering for the previous few years with illnesses associated with old age. Her granddaughter Mary Welch wrote to her brother Albert Welch on September 12, 1864, that "Grandma [Martha] is some febler [sic] than she was when you left home, she is very helpless and cannot help herself in the least bit."[3] In Martha's obituary, which was included in the *Western Christian Advocate* on October 3, 1866, W. S. Mahan described her: "Mother Slawson was a woman of God—she loved religion, and though a great sufferer for years previous to her death, 'she endured as seeing Him who is invisible,' and now sleeps in Jesus."[4]

Nothing hit Joseph and Maria as hard as Ellen's death. She was the youngest daughter of the family and was favored by everyone. After Ellen died, Joseph made references to her death for the rest of his life. As late as 1889, Joseph entered into his diary that Ellen had died "28 years ago."

In the fall of 1864, Joseph and Maria almost lost their daughter Martha when she was thrown from a horse that fell on her. The mishap broke "two or three" of Martha's ribs and "mashed her hips."[5] Martha was maimed as a result of the fall. She also received internal injuries that kept her from having additional children. In a letter dated January 8, 1865, Augustus Welch informed Matilda that John Tarkington told him that Martha was in Greensburg for a visit and "is still a cripple."[6]

In spite of the loss of Ellen and injuries to Martha, Joseph continued his

The Stewart family, 1860s (left to right): Mary, Martha, Martha ("Cattie"), and Daniel. Courtesy of the Indiana Historical Society.

preaching duties. Prior to Ellen's death, he was the preacher of the Wesport Methodist Church from 1860 to 1863. He preached at St. Omer from 1863 to 1865 before taking over the Indianapolis City Mission in 1865. Tarkington did mission work in Indianapolis under the direction of the Ames Institute, "an association of young Methodists, representing all the Methodist churches in the city." He did the missionary work for two years, "preaching and organizing suburban churches." Many became strong churches. Joseph raised money and organized the Ames Church into a "tabernacle made of boards from Camp Carrington barracks; and the Hall-place Church in the schoolhouse on Tinker, now Seventh street." The *Indianapolis Journal* reported that Joseph had built a frame church on Third Street, which returned it to the corner of Seventh and Hall-place.[7] While Joseph was in Indianapolis, he also visited every home in the city, encouraging residents to attend church.[8]

After leaving Indianapolis, Joseph held various positions in the Methodist Church and was honored on occasion for his work. At the 1857 conference held in Aurora, Joseph was honored, along with C. W. Ruter, James Havens, John Miller, and Enoch G. Wood, as "Our Conference fathers." The presentation was described as "solemn with tears . . . a session . . . which will be long remembered . . . they commenced traveling before any conference was called Indiana."[9]

During the 1870s Joseph was superannuated, but retained his position as a respected church father. He continued to be active in the church conferences. The 1876 Southeast Indiana conference was conducted at Greensburg, and Joseph was elected treasurer of the conference. He was also elected president of the Board of Control of Preachers Aid Society. Maria attended the conference too, and she showed her generosity by giving five dollars to make her friend Belle Adkinson a life member of the South East Indiana Conference Missionary Society.

The 1880 conference, which began on September 8, was held at Greensburg. When the morning session of the conference's first day adjourned, Joseph delivered the benediction. The following day Joseph presented his conference treasurer's report, which referred to the auditing committee. The committee examined the "receipts and disbursements" and found no problems. Joseph was elected treasurer for another year. He had few adversaries, even though he did go against the majority on some occasions. At the 1883 conference in Columbus, a resolution was passed to remove the limitation of the pastoral term of three years to an indefinite period. Tarkington stated his opposition in the following manner: "Resolved, we the members of the South-East Indiana Conference, hereby declare that we are opposed to so radical a change in the economy of our beloved church."[10]

Throughout the 1870s and 1880s, Joseph spent time on the road as a special judge or conducting other church business. While he had become a most respected leader in the church, many of his expenses were paid directly out of his pocket. On February 2, 1872, F. C. Holliday wrote to T. A. Morris of the Indianapolis, Cincinnati, and Lafayette Railroad asking for the railroad to grant Joseph "half fare" travel, which was typically granted to working preachers. The railroad denied the request, since Joseph was not in charge of a congregation.[11]

As a special judge, Joseph often sat on church trial committees and severely admonished his fellow preachers if they were found guilty of bad conduct. Generally, these trials were conducted to investigate and reprimand preachers for sexual improprieties, drinking, or other infractions of Methodist immorality rules. In one church trial that Joseph presided over, charges were brought against the Rev. Francis S. Turk, preacher of the Palestine Methodist church and an elder in the Southeastern Indiana conference.

On October 19, 1877, Turk was charged with immoral conduct. A special judicial conference was formed to deal with the case. Turk allegedly put his hand under the dress of a young woman named Mary Eaton and acted with "imprudent conduct." Miss Eaton was a member of his church. Turk answered the charges as "not guilty." Mary claimed that, near the end of April 1877, Rev. Turk had visited her house when she was alone, bringing a Sunday School book with him. Rev. Turk asked Mary to sing and play some of the hymns on her organ. The organ was in the parlor, which was located upstairs in the house. As Mary began to play, she charged that the preacher put his arms around her waist, obstructing her playing. As a result Mary left her seat at the organ and sat on the sofa. Reverend Turk then took a seat beside Mary. As the two were looking at some cards and pictures, the preacher pulled her on to his lap. Mary then got up and sat in a chair near the sofa. Mary told what occurred next: "Soon I arose from the chair and he took it, and again pulled me onto his lap. He then put his hand under my dress as far as my knees. We then went immediately down stairs, and he left the house. He said nothing bad to me. He did put his hand as far as my knees under my dress. He held me very tight each time he had me in his lap, and with difficulty I got away from him. We went downstairs immediately after he put his hand under my clothes, and he left the house."

When Mary was cross-examined, she repeated her original story. After she was asked about the preacher putting his hands under her dress, Mary did say that she "did not tell him to stop, but got away from him." She also stated that she did not tell Reverend Turk to leave the house "nor ask him to return." Mary told a friend, Miss Gates, and her grandmother, Mrs. Freeman, about the incident, but no one advised her to prosecute the case. She only told her grandmother about the event after Mrs. Freeman inquired why Mary was not going to church. Mary did not tell her father about Turk's advances because of embarrassment.

Church member John Ashcroft then testified that he had asked Reverend Turk if he had hugged Mary. Turk told Ashcroft that he had put his arm around Mary, but did not pull her onto his lap. He claimed that Mary sat on his lap willingly. Ashcroft also asked the preacher if he had attempted to raise Mary's clothes. Turk denied that he had raised Mary's dress, claiming that he had asked Mary why she had not attended church, and the young woman said her shoes were not suitable. Turk then told Ashcroft that he "stooped down and put his hand on her shoes and told her [that her] shoes were good enough."

When Turk was examined by the committee he did not deny putting his arm around Mary's waist, but claimed that she sat on his knee on her own accord. Reverend Turk also stated that he did move to a chair, but Mary again sat on his knee willingly. He then told his account of raising Mary's dress: "I said you will be present next Sabbath and play for the [Sunday] school? She replied, I have no suitable shoes. I put down my hand and raised her dress half way to her knees, and playfully remarked these shoes are good enough to wear anywhere. . . . I had no lewd intentions." Rev. Turk later added that there was windows in the parlor and the organ was by a window, making their activity visible to the outside. The preacher claimed that while Mary was on his lap they talked of her mother's death and he had no "special object in lifting her half way to her knees when I examined her shoes."

The case was then "rested" and left with the committee. On September 18, 1878, Reverend Turk was found guilty of the charges. The committee rendered the following verdict: "We the Committee appointed to try the charge against Reverend Francis S. Turk find that he is guilty as charged and sentence that he must be expelled from the ministry." The verdict was voted on by the committee; six voted to expel Turk from the ministry, while five were against the action. The five dissenting members were in favor of suspending Turk from the ministry for one year.

Reverend Turk immediately filed a motion of appeal after the verdict and was given a new trial. Joseph Tarkington was appointed as president of the new committee. As the trial opened on September 4, 1879, at Lawrenceburg, the counsel for the accused moved that "further prosecution of the case" should cease. The counsel for the church opposed the motion, and Joseph decided that the motion by the defense "could not be entertained" so the case must be tried. The defense then made a compromise proposal: "that the accused be acquitted and located." The church counsel again opposed the proposition, and Joseph again refused the defense's motion.

The following day the "charge and specification" was read and Reverend Turk plead not guilty. Earlier written testimony was then read. The church then called G. W. Winchester as a witness. Winchester testified that he had been pastor of the Palestine Church for nearly a year. Immediately, the defense "objected to the hear say evidence of this witness." However, Joseph allowed the witness to proceed. Winchester declared that Mary Eaton was about twenty-two years of age and was of "very good character." Winchester also claimed that the citizens of Palestine would walk by Mary's house, look in the room where the organ was, and make comments about the events that occurred between Mary and Reverend Turk. The counsel for the accused continued to argue that Turk was innocent. The questions and responses of the 1878 judicial hearing were repeated, and, after a lengthy trial, the committee found that Turk was guilty of "grossly imprudent conduct and that he be suspended from the ministry." The verdict was then voted on, and eleven were in favor of the decision while none were against. Joseph signed the order.[12]

This was not the first time charges had been brought against Methodist preachers in the Southeast Indiana conference for sexual advances. Rev. J. W. Maxwell of Bedford was sanctioned for making advances toward women; Rev. John Royer found himself in trouble for trying to kiss a woman; Rev. William Sheets was charged with seduction; Rev. William B. Clancy was indicted for adultery, as was Rev. A. W. Stout for having sexual intercourse with sixteen-year-old Jennie Anderson; Rev. A. Z. Wade was reprimanded for raping a young girl.[13]

Premarital intercourse was also grounds for suspension. As early as August 2, 1819, Rev. William Hunt of Wayne County was suspended from his official station in the Methodist Episcopal Church after it was discovered that he had premarital intercourse with a woman whom he later married. As a consolation, a child of the union was not declared a bastard after Hunt's wife delivered a baby seven months after their wedding. A doctor certified that he had seen many seven-month babies.[14]

In one case, charges were brought against Rev. John A. Brouse, who had acted as a presiding elder at Jeffersonville, Indiana; at the time charges were brought against him, he was an agent for Indiana Asbury. Brouse was accused of going to the bed of Miss Magdalene Haag, a hired girl residing in his home, in July of 1862 and attempting "immorality." Brouse did not have sexual relations with the young woman, but did lie on the bed with Haag. After a long trial, Joseph, along with his fellow clergymen Bay and Locke, found "in our judgement the charge of immorality is not sustained, but we do from the above finding, adjudge Jno. Brouse guilty of extreme imprudence."[15]

Preachers who "lusted after the flesh" were not immune from having their activities published in local newspapers. In a trial for which Joseph served as a committee member, the *Madison Daily Courier* advertised on January 8, 1877, that "Wesley Chapel holds separate services, as Rev. James S. Reager is not recognized in fellowship by the clergy of the city."[16] Two days later the same newspaper reported, "We are authorized to state that the Rev. S. J. Jones was not present at the meeting of the Ministerial Association at which an agreement was made not to recognize Rev. James S. Reager in fellowship."[17] Shortly before the *Courier* advertisement, the *Greensburg Standard* featured an article on Reager entitled "Sporting Clergyman" with two subtitles: "Secret of a Stateroom Revealed" and "Lively Scandal on the Steamer Ben. Franklin."[18] The newspaper claimed that Reverend Reager, a married man, had been a popular preacher and was presumed to have irreproachable character. However, the impressions were found to be wrong when a steamboat clerk caught the preacher with an attractive widow. A lengthy trial followed the affair.[19]

In addition to his taking on trial duty, Joseph continued to work hard in the church until the late 1880s, when his health began to fail him. Mary Welch, who was living with the Tarkingtons while going to school, reported to her brother Albert on December 8, 1866, about her uncle's work. She also related that Maria had four servants working for her. Mary wrote: "Uncle Tark is not at home more than two nights in a week and hardly ever that long, so Aunt is left alone with the darkies, who are four in number two men, one woman, a big fat girl as lazy as all git out. Aunt is not quite alone either for the boy they took to raise is here yet his name is Bowler, he is about as old as Simpson and I think he is a very good boy."[20]

The Tarkington home was always a welcome place for family and friends. On several occasions family members stayed with Joseph and Maria while attending school or working in the area. Mary Welch moved in with the Tarkingtons in the autumn of 1864. In one letter to her mother, Matilda Welch, she talked of spending Christmas in Greensburg.[21] Matilda returned the letter within a few days, instructing her daughter to stay in Greensburg if the roads were bad.[22] Matilda's other daughter, Emma, lived for several years in Indianapolis with Martha Stewart while attending school. Emma also resided with the Tarkingtons at Greensburg. Augustus Welch sent her money for school when he was fighting in the Civil War.[23] In a letter dated May 27, 1867, Matilda Welch indicated to her son Albert that Emma was still living with the Tarkingtons.[24] The Tarkingtons and Welches remained close and constantly visited each other. On December 4, 1865, Augustus Welch wrote his wife that he had been in Indianapolis for forty days. He said: "I spent last saturday evening with John Tarkington found his wife to be very pleasant and agreeable and John was also but I beat him playing checkers he presses me to call often and spend the evening with him."[25]

Joseph and Maria's son Joseph Asbury Tarkington became a physician during the Civil War and stayed in the pension office in Washington, D.C. He may have been one of the extra doctors on hand who attended Abraham Lincoln when he was assassinated. His granddaughter Louise Tarkington Smith claims that she heard the report that Joseph Asbury assisted Lincoln. Joseph Asbury Tarkington became friends with several presidents, especially Theodore Roosevelt. Joseph's son Joseph Arthur Tarkington went ice-skating with Roosevelt.

Even though he lived in Washington, D.C., Joseph Asbury Tarkington kept in close contact with his family. He wrote Mary Welch from the pension office on February 4, 1867: "Greensburg must be improving very fast for the new church and Hoosier Hall. . . . With love to mother I believe she is the only one of the family at home."[26] The Welch children continued to live with Joseph and Maria intermittently throughout the 1860s and 1870s. Albert Welch,

Maria Tarkington in 1886. From Autobiography of Rev. Joseph Tarkington, One of the Pioneer Methodist Preachers of Indiana, *1899.*

Joseph Tarkington in 1886. From Autobiography of Rev. Joseph Tarkington,
One of the Pioneer Methodist Preachers of Indiana, *1899.*

for instance, was living with the Tarkingtons in 1868. In a brief letter dated
September 8, 1868, he apologized to his parents for not writing them earlier.[27]

In the mid-1860s Matthew Simpson Tarkington was going to school at
Greencastle (Indiana Asbury), but Mary Welch did not think it would do him
much good. Mary added, "I guess fine clothes affect his brain more than study.
So he has the name of going to school, is all he cares for I guess." Joseph and
Maria wanted Matthew to attend school at "Mooreshill," but the rebellious
young man refused. After he started school at Greencastle he was very home-
sick and sorry.[28]

In November of 1871, Emma Welch was still living with the Tarkingtons
at Greensburg.[29] Emma had become the pet of Joseph, and he was afraid that
he would lose her to marriage. Indeed, Joseph's daughter Mary attempted to
match Emma to a man named "Smiley." Mollie Welch described Smiley as a
"kind of old bachelor, worth considerable property." Mollie added that a "high

recommend from Dr. Alexander and wife, who are rather anxious for the match, but I guess Emma is in no hurry to change her way of life."[30] Mollie closed her letter mentioning William S. R. Tarkington's wife, Lena, and stated that Matthew Simpson Tarkington was at home working on the farm. Joseph A. Tarkington was still working as a physician in the pension office, and the young boy, "Bowler," whom the Tarkingtons had raised, "married late in the summer and moved to Kokomo."[31]

The year 1881 was a special one for Joseph and Maria: it was the year of their fiftieth wedding anniversary. A large celebration was planned, and Maria invited all of her relatives from Switzerland County and other areas to celebrate the event.

> The fiftieth anniversary of our marriage occurs on the 21st of September, we will celebrate the event by a family reunion and would like all our Switzerland Co., relatives to be in attendance on that day. Come all that can. Mary Carey is here with our two great grand daughters. Haute and Booth have been with us about three weeks this summer. All are well come if you can.
>
> Maria Tarkington

On September 21, 1881, Joseph and Maria's fiftieth wedding anniversary was featured in the *Greensburg Standard*:

> Just Fifty Years Ago
>
> On Wednesday evening last (21st inst.,) was celebrated at their residence, one mile north-west of this city, the golden wedding of the venerable Father Tarkington and his amiable and devoted wife, which was attended by their children, grandchildren and quite a host of long time friends, and was one of the most enjoyable family reunions ever witnessed in these parts.
>
> For all these long fifty years Father Tarkington has been an industrious laborer in the Lord's Vineyard, most of the time in this immediate section of our State, and though never one of the "bright and shinning lights" of his church, in so far as pulpit oratory went, his labors have been quite as productive, in the ways of good fruits, as those of more brilliant men; and to him are many indebted for a personal knowledge of that Gospel that is the "way of salvation to all that believe."
>
> And not alone to the Father himself, but also to the more venerable wife by whose energy perseverance the then rapidly increasing and growing up family was provided for, are the hundreds who were converted under his ministry indebted

for the measure of grace they have enjoyed. Mother Tarkington is a woman fit to have been a minister's wife and has filled her place as few wives and mothers have.

With a city contemporary, The STANDARD can say, "May this golden reunion of loving hearts be but a type of that which is to come, and will be eternal."[32]

The anniversary party was a festive occasion, as many friends and family members called on Joseph and Maria. Joseph's sister Mary Whaley was present, the descendants that attended were "John S. Tarkington with his wife Elizabeth and their two children Mary B. and Newton B., of Indianapolis, Mrs. Mary Alexander with her husband Dr. John H., and two children John and Joseph of Milford, Indiana, Mrs. Martha A. Stewart, her husband, Daniel Stewart, their children Mary Carey, and her husband John Carey, with two daughters Martha and Eleanore, and Martha Scott, and William Scott, of Indianapolis, Dr. Joseph A. Tarkington, of Washington, D.C., Wm. S. R. Tarkington and Lena, his wife, Matthew S. Tarkington and Clara, his wife."[33] In the evening, by the light of Chinese lanterns decorating the trees and house, the celebration continued as John, representing the children of Joseph and Maria, gave a toast. Matthew Simpson Tarkington and his wife, Clara, prepared a "feast," one of the principal features of the affair.[34]

During the final four years of Joseph's life, he kept a diary of his daily activities. Most of the entries dealt with the weather and with his and Maria's illnesses. On January 1, 1888, he made an entry that referred to a visit by Dr. Bracken.[35] Joseph stated that he had kidney trouble, and the doctor drew a pint of "Blood and water [urine]." The following day the doctor returned and again drained his bladder. The kidney problems did not improve, and the next night Joseph developed a "fever and chill." Maria and Joseph's sister, Mary Whaley, who had traveled from Southport, Indiana, sat up with him over the night.[36]

Dr. Alexander visited Joseph at 7 A.M. on January 11 and returned at 5 P.M. with Mary "to cart wood" that he was using for heating and cooking. On Thursday, January 26, Joseph complained of the temperature—it was zero degrees—and of the fact that he had been confined to the house for twenty-six days because of his illness. He did say that he "got a rabbit" to eat on that day.

The Tarkingtons celebrated Maria's eighty-second birthday on January 22. They had a roast to celebrate the occasion. It was another cold day, with a temperature of fifteen degrees above zero. On February 2, Joseph's son-in-law, Dr. John H. Alexander, bought a horse for $125 and Joseph purchased the horse from Alexander for the same price. Joseph bought a barrel of flour on

Maria with her daughters (left to right) Mary Alexander and Martha Stewart.
Martha's daughter Mary is standing. Courtesy of Jeanette Tarkington Stokely.

February 4, and his daughter Martha Stewart visited on February 8, bringing "several things in the line of eating kind." The weather was extremely cold, right around the zero mark, and Maria, wearing her coat, was confined to bed. Her daughter Mary Alexander arrived two days later with "a basket of eatables." By February 12 Maria was still confined to bed, but Joseph participated in butchering hogs on the following day.

On Saturday, February 18, Joseph took part in cutting wood at the gate. He went to Greensburg and returned with three bushels of timothy seed. He commented that the mare was not well. The next day he began to have trouble with his kidneys again. He made "water every few minutes." Even though Joseph had been violently opposed to the use of spirits during his preaching career, John advised him to drink "Rhine Wine" in his illness.[37]

Joseph's son William visited him on February 25, and the following day John "came in on the afternoon train." John and William looked after the farm for a couple of days, but John returned to Indianapolis on February 28. By March 7, Joseph felt well enough to walk around the house, and the following day he rode a horse one-half mile. While Joseph's health was improving somewhat, his friend and fellow circuit rider, F. C. Holliday, who had written the book *Indiana Methodism,* died on March 18 following a long illness. The next week the weather turned much colder, and the family horse, "Fread," died. Fread was thirty-one years old and had hauled the family to church over two thousand times. Joseph wrote, "Poor Fread is gone where all good horses are gone." The next day, March 24, Greensburg got its largest snowfall of the year. It was six inches deep. However, the large snow did not stop Joseph from buying Maria "two pair of spectacles."

During the last week of March, Joseph began having trouble with his kidneys again. On the night of April 6, he had to get up six times to urinate and passing water was painful by April 9. On April 10, Joseph transferred his position as treasurer and notekeeper of the conference to Reverend Rawls. Joseph had held the position for twenty-one years. Dr. Bracken returned and "drew much bloody water" from his bladder.

The following is a letter of encouragement for Joseph from some of his friends:

Morristown, Indiana

June 5, 1888

Rev Joseph Tarkington

Beloved and venerable Father in the gospel of the grace of God the brethren of the Connersville Dist. send christian greeting, with earnest prayer for God's blessing upon you in your declining physical strength; that you may never lack the support of his grace, the comfort of his peace, the rightness of his hope and the sweet joyfulness of his love. In our hearts we write with you in a hymn of praise to our God for his unfailing goodness and inexhaustible heartfilling, soul satisfying love. Praise the Lord forever more.

John Wellenden

J. B. Lathrup

John G. Chafee[38]

On December 15, 1888, Joseph wrote John and Matthew Simpson that he believed that his and Maria's "separation will be short." He told his sons that he found Maria very "feble" and that she would be hard-pressed to get through the winter. Joseph wrote that he and Maria had "tried to do what we could for our children. . . . I hope I will be able to Say they are trying to do what they can for their Souls. . . . This is my daily prayer." Joseph then asked his sons to come and see him. In the letter he complained of debts that were bothering him.[39] However, his will clearly shows that he died with a sizable estate.

He had some correspondence with his grandson Booth, who had been sent to New Hampshire to attend the Phillips Exeter Academy in the fall of 1887. In Indianapolis, the future two-time Pulitzer Prize winner was in the habit of not going to school, and, after it was discovered that he had managed a two-month truancy from Shortridge High School in 1886, he was sent to the academy.[40] Joseph entered Booth's address in his diary on December 31, 1888, as "Newton Booth Tarkington, Phillips Exeter Academy, Exeter New Hampshire Box 4041."[41]

As a child, Booth Tarkington loved to visit his grandfather's farm at Greensburg. He described the farm as "sweet smelling . . . always heaven to me whenever I got there." After Joseph became superannuated from the Methodists, Booth claimed that his grandfather preached only "upon special occasions, but was unshakable in old convictions that included a necessary modicum of hellfire and brimstone."[42]

Booth Tarkington claimed that his personal religious exposure came from the Tarkingtons' Methodist convictions and from his mother's family's Congregationalism, which had originated in Connecticut. The Booth family had changed its beliefs to Presbyterianism when family members had moved to pioneer Indiana. Booth Tarkington claimed that, in later years, both the Booths' and the Tarkingtons' religious convictions, along with the old orthodoxies, had faded. However, of all his relatives, the only one who had not "lost faith in a personal Satan" was his grandfather, "the Reverend Joseph Tarkington."[43]

Joseph Tarkington was always a superstitious man and believed the devil was always nearby. During the early 1870s some bizarre things seemed to be happening at John Tarkington's home. John wrote Joseph about what was going on at the house, so Joseph drove his buggy forty miles from Greensburg to Indianapolis and "[s]ternly occupied a big chair throughout an hour of afternoon rapping." Booth states that his grandfather "[s]pake not a word till it was over; then said, 'Those sounds are not made by human trickery, but they cannot be from spirits in heaven. There is no countenance for them in the Bible. They are from the Devil.'" Following Joseph's assessment of the situation, Booth claimed that "[o]ne didn't argue with Grandfather Tarkington. This was his say, and having said it, he drove back to the farm with what subsequent thoughts in his mind that we never learned. No one dared speak of raps to him again, nor did he ever utter another word upon the subject he'd so ironly settled."[44] Joseph left quite an impression on Booth. He described the rapping incidents and his grandfather years later in a 1941 article in the *Saturday Evening Post*:

Joseph and John Tarkington with thirteen-year-old Booth, 1882. Courtesy of Patricia Cochran.

The one person who came to see the table's performance and didn't think the dead most probably responsible for it was my Grandfather Tarkington. He didn't think the dead made the raps; he thought something else did. Grandfather was a ruddy, husky voiced, squirely man powerfully agile like my father, and, like all the Tarkingtons, given to cheerfulness and ready laughter; but he could be grim. Neither my father at fifty nor any of my Tarkington aunts and uncles was reckless enough to mention card playing, wine, the theater or dancing in his presence. He thought tobacco abominable, breakfasted at seven, and, in his eighties was on a horse at half past.[45]

On January 1, 1889, Joseph made an entry into his diary that Maria was very sick. The following day he commented that she was "bad with heart." She struggled with her heart problem for most of the year and was confined to the house most of the time. By mid-December her condition was serious. Joseph wrote in his diary on December 15, 1889, that all of his children "are here to see their mother. She can not last long."[46] On her deathbed, Maria asked to see her grandson, Booth. However, young Tarkington remained at school in spite of John and Elizabeth's efforts to make him realize the seriousness of his grandmother's state. Finally, Booth returned, but Maria died before he got home.[47] Maria died a few minutes past ten o'clock on the morning of December 16, 1889, "being 83 years, 10 months and 24 days old."[48] When she died, John said to Joseph "mother is gone." Joseph claimed that Maria died at 10:15 A.M., and "[s]he has been the best of women." Matthew Simpson Tarkington ordered a coffin for his mother that cost ninety-six dollars. On the morning following Maria's death, Joseph claimed that the morning looked lonely without his wife. But he believed "she is in Glory." He added that Maria said "my God is all Mightist." Joseph said his wife looked "so lovely."

Maria's funeral was conducted at the Tarkington house on December 18. The coffin was covered with flowers. E. B. Rawls and E. G. Wood conducted the service, and F. B. Lathrup prayed while Brother "Runnal" read the Twenty-third Psalm and 1 Corinthians 15, a line about the resurrection of the body. Joseph stated that the children were "all here but Ellen. . . . She had gone before." Following the service the family proceeded to the graveyard, where Maria's four sons and two sons-in-law "gave her to the grave."[49] Following Maria's death, Joseph was very depressed. In his diary, he commented on December 19 that it "looks dreary with out Maria today." An unsigned poem was written in an unidentified newspaper in honor of Maria:

Entered Heaven

Mrs. Joseph Tarkington

December 16, 1889 Dear mother—hands so full of loving deeds
    Are softly folded now in endless rest
The fond and tender eyes are closed to earth
    But radiant in God's aidenn of the blest

A precious, faithful child Our Father's called
    To enter full inheritance
With his dead Son; and wear the crown and pale
    He gives their glorious triumph to enhance
How beautiful her meek pure christian life
    O husband God's own minister; thy mate
So long to cheer, to brighten and to aid,
    Now waits with loving watch beside Heaven's gate,
Until the golden hinge shall open swing
To let thy spirit, with triumphant song
Pass with its sheaves unto the Master's feet;
While angels hosts the chorus shall prolong.

Joseph expressed his loneliness in the days following Maria's death. Christmas eve was described as "Warm and Cloudy . . . all seems lonesome," and on Christmas day Joseph made an entry into his diary: "I never had such a lonely Christmas. She who used to cheer me is gone gone." Joseph's grief did not improve. On December 27 he wrote, "Mary and Martha have done all they can to make me comfortable. So had all the children but vacancy remains without my dear Maria." The following day he wrote, "Maria can not come back but I will to her."

During the last year of Joseph's life, he complained that he had suffered financially as well as physically. He looked for various ways to reduce his expenses. One of his expenditures was his projected donation to DePauw University. In the early spring of 1891, Joseph proposed to Newland T. DePauw, the president of the Bank of Commerce in Indianapolis, to substitute fifty-three books to pay for his pledge. On April 8, 1891, Joseph received a letter from John Ray, the bank's vice-president, explaining that he could sympathize with Joseph and was sorry so hear of his "affliction," but would have to consult the board of trustees on the matter. Tarkington would be informed of their decision when the matter was decided.[50]

Martha Stewart and her grandchildren visited Joseph on September 9, 1891. She wrote in Joseph's diary that he would be "91 years old if he should live until Oct. 30. But is now very feeble can not talk much to us." On September 18, Dr. Alexander telephoned Martha that Joseph "was much worse." William Simeon Reeves and Martha arrived at Joseph's home at noon. Martha claimed that Joseph knew them and his oldest daughter, Mary Alexander. When

Joseph and Maria's graves at Greensburg.

the preacher saw his children, he attempted to rise from his bed. He was too weak to accomplish the task. Tarkington did manage to tell them, "Children I am going." This was the last sentence that he ever spoke.[51]

On September 19, 1891, Joseph's second-oldest son, Dr. Joseph A. Tarkington, and his son Joseph Arthur arrived at Greensburg from Washington, D.C. Joseph's sister Mary ("Polly") Whaley and his oldest son, John, arrived in the evening. Martha claimed that Joseph recognized all of his family "when they spoke to him but he is drowsy and will not take any nourishment."[52] She added that her father "has been a great sufferer for years but is insensitive to pain for the first time." Reverend Rawls visited Tarkington during the afternoon and prayed. When Martha asked Joseph if he had heard Rawls he nodded, and then attempted to say good-bye. On September 21, Martha wrote in Joseph's diary: "10 years ago today was the Golden wedding. We thought father would probably pass away. He is growing weaker and there is nothing we can do."[53] The next morning Martha wrote, "Father passed away this morning at seven o'clock. The prayer we so often heard when we were children 'Give us a peaceful hour in which to die,' was answered."[54] Joseph Tarkington died at the age of ninety years, ten months, and twenty-one days. At the time of his death, he was the oldest living Methodist minister in Indiana.

Following Joseph's death, the pastor of Tarkington's church, E. B. Rawls, stated that Joseph suffered many ills during the later years of his life, "[b]ut no word of murmur or complaint passed from his lips."[55] One week prior to Tarkington's death, Rawls had sat at Joseph's bedside and said, "Father Tarkington, I am going to Conference next week." Joseph looked up at Rawls and said, "I am going to Heaven."

The morning Joseph died, he received a telegram from R. A. Kemp of Washington, Indiana, the secretary of the Indiana conference. The message was: "Indiana Conference sends greeting and prays for a glorious sunset."[56] The following day, the *Indianapolis Journal* reported that Joseph had "died of old age."[57] On September 24 his funeral was conducted at 1:30 and then he was buried beside his wife, Maria.

They that be wise shall shine, and they that turn many to righteousness, as the stars for ever and ever.
Daniel 12:3.

Conclusion

Joseph Tarkington and his family personify and provide a window into nineteenth-century Indiana and Methodism. The Tarkingtons are symbolic and representative of a social, cultural, and religious transformation that occurred in only a one-hundred-year span. Following the American Revolution, the Methodists had a small number of church members with only sixty-five churches "scattered throughout the colonies." By the end of the next seven decades, the Methodism was the largest denomination, totaling 2.6 million members.[1] The Methodists were not, as Perry Miller characterizes them, a "banal residue in America of what had been the noble and intellectually rich tradition of Puritanism and Edwardian Calvinism."[2] The Methodists, along with other successful evangelical groups, were able to adapt to a tumultuous and rapidly changing society to become what Jon Butler describes in his classic work, *Awash in a Sea of Faith*, as "the West's most powerful society."[3] The success of Methodism on the Indiana frontier was due to Methodism's simplicity and dynamism. Evangelical churches such as the Methodists rebelled against social hierarchy and formal worship patterns found in highly liturgical churches, rejecting their customs of elaborate dress, behavior, and ornate buildings.

However, by the middle of the nineteenth century, Methodism's plain-style worship, which had been a point of pride for circuit-riding preachers like

Peter Cartwright and Joseph Tarkington, was being "upgraded" from its plainness to a more refined doctrine.

Methodist churches were a mirror of nineteenth-century Indiana, representing a society that had matured. Simple log churches, such as the Bethel Meeting House constructed on the Silver Creek Circuit in 1807, had been replaced by Gothic style churches with steeples and stained-glass windows. A demonstrative religion with ministers preaching in an extemporaneous style had been largely replaced by college-educated pastors delivering refined and more intellectually stimulating sermons. In 1846 Allen Wiley indicated that the revivals had begun to lose much of their flavor and productiveness. He wrote: "When however, we say they were good, I could not be understood to say they would compare with the former meetings. There was much more preaching talent at those meetings than the former; but there was not the same zeal in the preachers or people."[4]

Richard Bushman views the modernizing changes in Methodism as a cultural competition in which the Methodists were only "a step or two behind the Congregationalists and Presbyterians."[5] Some Methodist congregations were resistant to the mid-century changes, as revealed in the 1866 schism at Greensburg over the introduction of a church organ. In spite of some uprisings, the simplicity that had ushered in Methodist society and the influence that preachers such as Joseph Tarkington wielded had waned. Late in the century, Peter Cartwright reflected perhaps nostalgically on times when "Methodists had no pewed churches, no choirs, no organs, in a word, we had no instrumental music in our churches anywhere," just as the people dressed plainly and "Methodist preachers were called by literary gentlemen illiterate, ignorant babblers."[6]

Other schisms in the Methodist church in 1844 over the issue of slavery, along with the similar division among the Presbyterian and Baptist churches, had a national impact, setting the stage for the Civil War. During the nineteenth century, there were few social and cultural issues that Methodism did not influence, including temperance, women's rights, slavery, and many others.

Joseph Tarkington's career as a Methodist preacher is a classic example of Methodists going from rags to riches in one generation. His life story, while interesting and singular in many respects, is not unique. Many preachers replicated his experiences. However, his story has its own special interest. He was driven not to repeat his father's life on the farm at Stanford, Indiana. It was respectability that drove him, and the Methodist Church fostered his upward mobility. Tarkington gained his goals through determination, deprivation, and hard work, remaining focused on his ambition. As a result of Joseph Tarkington's drive and the turbulent nineteenth century, the Tarkingtons became one of Indiana's most noted and esteemed families.

Appendix
Chronology of
Joseph Tarkington's Life

Oct. 30, 1800	Born near Franklin, Tennessee.
1815	Family moves to Indiana.
Aug. 27, 1820	Experiences conversion.
June 10, 1821	Joins Methodist Church.
Sept. 15, 1824	Starts preaching on the Boonville circuit.
1825	Appointed to the Patoka circuit.
1826	Appointed to the Sangamon circuit.
1827	Returns to the Sangamon circuit.
1828	Appointed to the White Lick circuit.
1829	Appointed to the Rushville circuit.
1830	Appointed to the Vevay circuit.
Sept. 21, 1831	Marries Maria Slawson.
1831	Appointed to the Wayne circuit.
June 24, 1832	First son, John Stevenson Tarkington (father of Booth Tarkington), born.

1832	Appointed to the Whitewater circuit.
1833	Appointed to the Greensburg circuit.
Feb. 26, 1834	First daughter, Mary Melissa Tarkington, born.
1834	Appointed to the Charlestown circuit.
1835	Appointed to the Greenville circuit.
Feb. 17, 1836	Second daughter, Martha Ann Tarkington, born.
1836	Appointed to the Vevay circuit.
1837	Superannuated.
Nov. 25, 1837	Second son, Joseph Asbury Tarkington, born.
1838	Appointed to the Lawrenceburg station.
1839	Appointed to the Richmond station.
1840	Returned to the Richmond station.
1841	Appointed to the Liberty circuit.
Nov. 5, 1841	Third son, William Simeon Reeves Tarkington, born.
1842	Appointed to the Centerville circuit.
1843	Appointed to the Centerville district as presiding elder.
Dec. 18, 1843	Third daughter, Ellen Maria Tarkington, born.
1844	Returned to Centerville district.
1845	Appointed to the Brookville circuit.
1846	Returned to the Brookville circuit.
1847	Appointed to the Vincennes district as presiding elder.

1848–51	Appointed to the Putnamville district as presiding elder.
July 16, 1848	Fourth son, Matthew Simpson Tarkington, born.
1851–52	Appointed to the Greensburg district as presiding elder.
1853–54	Agent of Indiana Asbury.
1855	Appointed to the Milroy Church.
1856	Appointed to the St. Omer Church.
1857–58	Superannuated but preaches in the Greensburg Church.
1859	Appointed to the Belleview Church.
1860	Appointed to the Westport Church.
May 2, 1861	Daughter Ellen dies at Greensburg.
1861–62	Superannuated but preaches regularly at St. Omer and other churches around Greensburg.
1863–65	Appointed to the Indianapolis City Mission.
1866–91	Superannuated.
Sept. 21, 1881	Celebrates golden wedding anniversary.
Dec. 16, 1889	Maria dies at Greensburg, Indiana.
Sept. 22, 1891	Dies at Greensburg, Indiana.

Notes

PREFACE

1. Russell E. Richey, *Early American Methodism* (Bloomington: Indiana Univ. Press, 1991), xii.
2. Nathan O. Hatch, *The Democratization of American Christianity* (New Haven and London: Yale Univ. Press, 1989), 16.
3. Nathan O. Hatch, "The Puzzle of American Methodism," Paper presented for the Wesley/Holiness Center Conference, "Methodism and the Shaping of American Culture, 1760–1860," Oct. 7–8, 1994, Asbury Theological Seminary, Wilmore, Kentucky.
4. Donald G. Matthews, "The Methodist Schism of 1844 and the Popularization of Antislavery Sentiment," *Mid-America* 51 (1) (Jan. 1968): 4; Roger Finke and Rodney Stark, *The Churching of America, 1776–1990: Winners and Losers in Our Religious Economy* (New Brunswick, N.J.: Rutgers Univ. Press, 1992), 55.
5. Elizabeth K. Nottingham, *Methodism and the Frontier: Indiana Proving Ground* (New York: Columbia Univ. Press, 1941), 3.
6. William G. McLoughlin, "Pietism and the American Character," *American Quarterly* 17 (Summer 1965): 163.
7. Richard Jensen, "The Religious and Occupational Roots of Party Identification: Illinois and Indiana in the 1870's," *Civil War History* 16 (Dec. 1970): 330.
8. Allen Wiley, "Introduction and Progress of Methodism in Indiana," *Indiana Magazine of History* 23 (4) (Dec. 1927): 398.
9. Douglas Montagna, "The Institutional History of Indiana Methodism, 1801–1860," (Ph.D. diss., Northern Illinois Univ., 1997), 1.

INTRODUCTION

1. Edward Eggleston, *The Circuit Rider: A Tale of the Heroic Age* (New York: J. B. Ford and Company, 1874), 158–59.

2. Nathan O. Hatch, *The Democratization of American Christianity* (New Haven and London: Yale Univ. Press, 1989), 3.

3. Roger Finke and Rodney Stark, "How the Upstart Sects Won America: 1776–1850," *Journal for the Scientific Study of Religion* 28 (1) (1989): 31.

4. Hatch, *The Democratization of American Christianity*, 9–10. Finke and Stark add that churches such as the Anglicans, with their "[h]ighly educated clergy who controlled these denominations disdained the vigorous marketing techniques employed by the upstart evangelicals; they viewed the informal religious practices of the frontier with contempt and distanced themselves from the common folk; the latter responded in kind" (Finke and Stark, "How the Upstart Sects Won America," 29).

5. Hatch, *The Democratization of American Christianity*, 14.

6. R. Carlyle Buley, *The Old Northwest: Pioneer Period, 1815–1840* (Bloomington: Indiana Univ. Press, 1950), 2: 450.

7. A prime example of a preacher rising from the ranks is Benjamin Lakin, one of the first Methodist preachers in Indiana. As a young man, Lakin listened to Richard Whatcoat preach in Redstone County, Pennsylvania, on the subject like "God's free grace provides salvation" and "Christ is the dispenser of the Holy Spirit by whose intervention all the benefits of the atonement are brought into contact with the soul of man." Whatcoat's preaching led Lakin to feel convicted of sin, which was followed by his conversion. This launched Lakin's preaching career. He moved to Kentucky in 1794 and surfaced in Indiana a few years later as an itinerant. Frederick V. Mills, "Mentors of Methodism, 1784–1844," *Methodist History* 12 (1) (Oct. 1973): 43–45.

8. John H. Wigger, "Taking Heaven By Storm: Enthusiasm and Early American Methodism, 1770–1820," *Journal of the Early Republic* 14 (Summer 1994): 181.

9. Roger Finke and Rodney Stark, *The Churching of America, 1776–1990: Winners and Losers in Our Religious Economy* (New Brunswick, N.J.: Rutgers Univ. Press, 1992), 71.

10. Charles C. Cole, *Lion of the Forest: James B. Finley, Frontier Reformer* (Lexington: Univ. Press of Kentucky, 1994), 18.

11. Wigger, "Taking Heaven By Storm," 168.

12. Cole, *Lion of the Forest*, 18.

13. Finke and Stark, *The Churching of America*, 54–108.

14. Buley, *The Old Northwest*, 2: 450.

15. The *Discipline* contained the rules and other aspects of religious life that regulated members' lives. The *Discipline* governed areas such as entertainment, marriage, and dress. The *Indiana Conference Minutes* of 1849 gave the Methodist position on amusements like circuses and dances. Their belief was that these forms of entertainment were "wholly inconsistent with christian character, destructive to vital piety, ruinous to vital religious impressions of the rising generation, and a hindrance to their conversion of irregular neighbors." See *Indiana Conference Minutes* (1849), 18. Archives of DePauw Univ. and Indiana United Methodism.

16. Finke and Stark, *The Churching of America*, 78–79.

17. Ibid., 76.

18. Wesley had insisted that Methodist preachers be well read. When one on his preachers commented, "But I have not taste for reading," Wesley replied, "Contract a taste for it by use or return to your trade." See Robert C. Monk, "Educating

Oneself for Ministry: Francis Asbury's Reading Patterns," *Methodist History* 29 (3) (Apr. 1991): 140–50.

19. Cole, *Lion of the Forest*, 20.

20. Walter Brownlow Posey, "The Development of Methodism in the Old Southwest: 1783–1824" (Ph.D. diss., Vanderbilt Univ., 1933), 24.

21. Finke and Stark, *The Churching of America*, 85.

22. William Warren Sweet, *Circuit-Rider Days in Indiana* (Indianapolis: W. K. Stewart Company, 1916), 2. The early Baptists in Indiana were extreme Antinomians, believing that faith alone was necessary to gain salvation. The Presbyterians were Hopkinsians before 1830; they held that God does all things for His own glory and the happiness of all, that even sin and evil are circumstances of good.

23. L. C. Rudolph, *Hoosier Zion: The Presbyterians in Early Indiana* (New Haven: Yale Univ. Press, 1963), 42.

24. Buley, *The Old Northwest*, 2: 432.

25. Ibid., 417.

26. Ibid., 418.

27. Finke and Stark, *The Churching of America*, 87–94.

28. Sweet, *Circuit-Rider Days in Indiana*, 3.

29. Posey, "The Development of Methodism in the Old Southwest," 19–20.

30. William Frederick Vogel, "Home Life in Early Indiana," *Indiana Magazine of History* 10 (2) (June 1914): 294.

31. Elizabeth K. Nottingham, *Methodism and the Frontier: Indiana Proving Ground* (New York: Columbia Univ. Press, 1941), 63.

32. Peter Cartwright related that there were often five hundred of his congregation "all jerking at once." Cartwright also disclosed an account of a "large drunkard one night get the jerks until between twitching and anger over being unable to hold his flask steady enough to drink the whiskey, he jerked so furiously that he finally broke his neck." See Helen Hardie Grant, *Peter Cartwright: Pioneer* (New York: The Abingdon Press, 1931), 75.

33. James B. Finley, *Autobiography of Rev. James B. Finley: or, Pioneer Life in the West* (Cincinnati: Cranston and Curts, 1853), 165.

34. Maxwell Pierson Gaddis, *Foot-Prints of an Itinerant* (Cincinnati: The Methodist Book Concern, 1856), 71.

35. Two excellent interpretations of the Cane Ridge Revival have recently appeared: Anthony L. Dunnavant, ed., *Cane Ridge in Context: Perspectives on Barton W. Stone and the Revival* (Nashville: Disciples of Christ Historical Society, 1992); and Paul K. Conkin, *Cane Ridge: America's Pentecost* (Madison: Univ. of Wisconsin Press, 1990).

36. Buley, *The Old Northwest*, 2: 422.

37. Finley, *Autobiography*, 166–67.

38. Buley, *The Old Northwest*, 2: 424.

39. Hatch, *The Democratization of American Christianity*, 20.

40. Buley, *The Old Northwest*, 423.

41. Finley, *Autobiography*, 165.

42. Buley, *The Old Northwest*, 460.

43. *Cleaveland Herald*, July 28, Aug. 18, Nov. 6, 1831. The *Advertiser* and other papers attacked St. John vigorously. He retired from his editorship early in 1832. Cited in Buley, *The Old Northwest*, 460.

44. Ibid., 460.
45. Ibid., 423.
46. James B. Finley, *Sketches of Western Methodism: Biographical, Historical, and Miscellaneous, Illustrative of Pioneer Life* (Cincinnati: Methodist Book Concern, 1856), 209.
47. Posey, "The Development of Methodism in the Old Southwest," 21–22.
48. Vogel, "Home Life in Early Indiana," 294.
49. Posey, "The Development of Methodism in the Old Southwest," 22.
50. Ibid., 22–23.
51. Vogel, "Home Life in Early Indiana," 295.
52. Richard J. Carwardine, *Evangelicals and Politics in Antebellum America* (New Haven: Yale Univ. Press, 1993), 44.
53. Patrick B. Mullen, "Ritual and Sacred Narratives in the Blue Ridge Mountains," *Papers in Comparative Studies* (Ohio State Univ.) 2 (1983): 19.
54. David L. Kimbrough, "Solomon and Sarah Saylor: The Emergence of Lay Religion in Eastern Kentucky," *Appalachian Heritage* 21 (3) (Summer 1993): 53.
55. For several humorous conversion tales, see Grant, *Peter Cartwright*, chap. 4, 69–84. See also Donald E. Byrne Jr., *No Foot of Land: Folklore of American Methodist Itinerants* (Metuchen, N.J.: Scarecrow Press, 1975), 105–25.
56. Lewis A Harding, ed., *History of Decatur County Indiana: Its People Industries and Institutions* (Indianapolis: B. F. Bowen and Company, 1915): 521. Incidentally, it is possible that the preacher in the anecdote was Joseph Tarkington. Tarkington was the preacher assigned to the Lawrenceburg circuit at the time.
57. William Warren Sweet, "Early Methodist Circuits in Indiana," *Indiana Magazine of History* 10 (3) (Sept. 1914): 368.
58. Most of the people who attended the camp meetings were also hunters and brought their dogs and guns with them. The dogs often fought with each other, causing quite a stir in the congregations. See F. C. Holliday, *Life and Times of Rev. Allen Wiley, A.M.* (Cincinnati: L. Swormstedt and A. Poe, 1853), 32.
59. George K. Hester Diary, Archives of DePauw Univ. and Indiana United Methodism.
60. Buley, *The Old Northwest*, 451–52.
61. Finke and Stark, *The Churching of America*, 93.
62. Vogel, "Home Life in Early Indiana," 291.
63. Peter Cartwright, *The Backwoods Preacher: Being the Autobiography of Peter Cartwright, an American Methodist Travelling Preacher* (London: Alexander Heylin, 1858), 121–22.
64. Tarkington claims that he made a suit of buckskin to resist being scratched by briars. Joseph Tarkington, *Autobiography of Rev. Joseph Tarkington, One of the Pioneer Methodist Preachers of Indiana* (Cincinnati: Curts and Jennings, 1899), 85.
65. Buley, *The Old Northwest*, 451.
66. Posey, "The Development of Methodism in the Old Southwest," 23–4.
67. Maxwell Pierson Gaddis, ed., *The Ohio Conference Offering: or, Sermons and Sketches of Sermons, on Familiar and Practical Subjects, from The Living and the Dead, In Two Parts* (Cincinnati: The Methodist Book Concern, 1851), 87.
68. Posey, "The Development of Methodism in the Old Southwest," 24.
69. Buley, *The Old Northwest*, 454.
70. Ibid., 453–54.

71. Vogel, "Home Life in Early Indiana," 291.
72. Ibid., 290.
73. Aaron Wood, *Sketches of Things and Peoples in Indiana* (Indianapolis: J. M. Olcott, Publisher, 1883), 24.
74. In 1810, the Vincennes circuit appeared in the annual minutes. William Winans was appointed as the preacher. One of the first services was a night service conducted at the fort. The congregation consisted of some government officers, "a few English and French settlers, and two or three Indians." Only a few tallow candles provided light for the meeting. One of the candles was held by Gov. William Henry Harrison while Winans delivered his text and lined out a hymn. See F. C. Holliday, *Indiana Methodism* (Cincinnati: Hitchcock and Walden, 1873), 27.
75. Wood, *Sketches of Things and Peoples in Indiana*, 24–25.
76. Ibid., 25.
77. Richard McNemar was one of the leading Presbyterian preachers at Cane Ridge in 1801, only to go on to become the leader of the Shaker movement in the West.
78. Wood, *Sketches of Things and Peoples in Indiana*, 25.
79. Ibid., 26–27.
80. Cartwright, *Autobiography*, 19.
81. Ibid., 20.
82. Ibid.
83. Ibid.
84. Sweet, "Early Methodist Circuits in Indiana," 364.
85. Conferences met in the fall of the year, and appointments were for parts of two calendar years; thus, appointments in 1816 extended until the fall of 1817. Ruth Price, "Indiana Methodism," *Indiana Magazine of History* 11 (3) (Sept. 1915): 231.
86. Hugh Cull was an Irishman. His name was originally "O'Cull"; dropping the "O" in a last name was a common practice among the Irish who settled in America. Cull was described as being able to exhort "most feelingly, and weep showers of tears all the time; so that he made powerful impressions on the people in this new country, where they had not much able preaching" (Allen Wiley, "Methodism in Southeastern Indiana," *Indiana Magazine of History* 23 [1] [Mar. 1927]: 38).
87. Holliday, *Indiana Methodism*, 21.
88. Price, "Indiana Methodism," 233–39.
89. Holliday, *Indiana Methodism*, 61.
90. Ibid., 61–62.
91. Ibid., 51–52.

CHAPTER ONE. JOSEPH TARKINGTON'S BIRTH AND EARLY LIFE

1. Joseph Tarkington's parents, Jesse and Mary, were both born in Tyrrell County, North Carolina. Jesse's date of birth was Feb. 21, 1767, and Mary was born Dec. 21, 1773. They were married Aug. 28, 1792. Mary was generally called Polly by her friends and family.
2. Douglass R. Chandler, "Growth and Consolidation," in Gordon Pratt Baker, ed., *Those Incredible Methodists: A History of the Baltimore Conference of the United*

Methodist Church (Baltimore: Baltimore Commission on Archives and History, The Baltimore Conference, 1972), 101.

3. Dickson D. Bruce Jr., *And They All Sang Hallelujah: Plain-Folk Camp Meeting Religion, 1800–1845* (Knoxville: Univ. of Tennessee Press, 1974), 34.

4. Ibid. 15–22.

5. Warren R. Hofstra and Robert D. Mitchell, "Town and Country in Backcountry Virginia: Winchester and the Shenandoah Valley, 1730–1800," *Journal of Southern History* 59 (4) (Nov. 1993): 635.

6. Ibid., 23.

7. John Tarkington Collection, Indiana Historical Society.

8. William L. Saunders, ed., *The Colonial Records of North Carolina* (Raleigh: The State of North Carolina, 1886), 1: 453.

9. Tarkington, *Autobiography*, 65.

10. Holliday, *Indiana Methodism*, 251.

11. Sydney E. Ahlstrom, *A Religious History of the American People* (New Haven: Yale Univ. Press, 1972), 623.

12. Finke and Stark, *The Churching of America*, 79.

13. Ahlstrom, *A Religious History*, 624.

14. William W. Sweet, "The Churches as Moral Courts of the Frontier," *Church History* 2 (Jan. 1933): 3.

15. Tarkington, *Autobiography*, 65.

16. Ibid., 67–68.

17. Ibid., 68–69.

18. Samuel W. Watkins, "The Causes and Cure of Earthquakes: Methodists and the New Madrid Earthquakes, 1811–1812," *Methodist History* 30 (4) (July 1992): 242.

19. The Great Revival did not originate in Tennessee and Kentucky. The revivals have a heritage that can be traced back to Scotland. See Leigh Eric Schmidt, *Holy Fairs: Scottish Communions and American Revivals in the Early Modern Period* (Princeton: Princeton Univ. Press, 1989).

20. Jeremy Rifkin with Ted Howard, *The Emerging Order: God in the Age of Scarcity* (New York: G. P. Putnam's Sons, 1979): 140.

21. Catherine L. Albanese, "Savage Sinner, and Saved: Davy Crockett, Camp Meetings, and the Wild Frontier," *American Quarterly* 33 (1981): 487.

22. John Hoyt Williams, *Sam Houston: A Biography of the Father of Texas* (New York: Simon and Schuster, 1993), 31.

23. W. D. Snively and Louanna Furbee, *Satan's Ferryman: A True Tale of the Old Frontier* (New York: Frederick Ungar Publishing Company, 1968), 46–56.

24. Otto A. Rothert, "The Harpes, Two Outlaws of Pioneer Times," *The History Quarterly* (Filson) 4 (1) (July 1927): 155.

25. Ibid., 159. Itinerant Jacob Young related that Micajah Harpe's brother-in-law visited one of his meetings. Young said the man's appearance was frightening, but as he preached he saw tears roll down the man's cheeks. The man later joined the church and "became a Christian." See Jacob Young, *Autobiography of a Pioneer* (Cincinnati: Cranston and Curts, 1857), 95–96.

26. Bertram Wyatt-Brown, *Southern Honor: Ethics and Behavior in the Old South* (New York: Oxford Univ. Press, 1982), 295.

27. Ibid.

28. Elmer T. Clark, J. Manning Potts, and Jacob S. Payton, eds., *The Journal and Letters of Francis Asbury* (Nashville: Abingdon Press, 1958), 2: 83.

29. Tarkington, *Autobiography*, 72–73.

30. Marshall Scott Legan, "Popular Reactions to the New Madrid Earthquakes, 1811–1812." *Filson Club Historical Quarterly* 50 (1) (Jan. 1976): 60.

31. Between Dec. 16, 1811, and Mar. 15, 1812, over eighteen hundred tremors were felt in the lower Mississippi Valley. See Wayne Viitanen, "The Winter the Mississippi Ran Backwards: Early Kentuckians Report the New Madrid, Missouri, Earthquake of 1811–12," *Register of the Kentucky Historical Society* 71 (1) (Jan. 1973): 51.

32. Holliday, *Indiana Methodism*, 251.

33. Samuel W. Watkins, "The Causes and Cure of Earthquakes: Methodists and the New Madrid Earthquakes, 1811–1812." *Methodist History* 30 (4) (July 1992): 243.

34. Tarkington, *Autobiography*, 73.

35. Watkins, "Causes and Cure of Earthquakes," 246.

36. Legan, "Popular Reactions to the New Madrid Earthquakes," 60.

37. Holliday, *Indiana Methodism*, 251–52. Margaret Bolling states in the "Hamline Historical Highlights" that the prayer book Tarkington describes was an Episcopal prayer book. See Margaret Bolling, "Hamline Historical Highlights," Hamline Chapel United Methodism, Lawrenceburg, Indiana, Sept. 20, 1981, 5.

38. Other "cosmic omens" caused early Americans to regard them as some sort of "providential interposition." Unusual snowfalls in the cold summer of 1816, meteor showers, comets, and other solar phenomena, such as an eclipse, caused many to become converted. See Byrne, *No Foot of Land*, 69–72. Generally, religious enthusiasms declined after these "cosmic omens" ceased. See Watkins, "The Causes and Cure of Earthquakes," 250.

39. Watkins, "The Causes and Cure of Earthquakes," 248–49.

40. Viitanen, "The Winter the Mississippi Ran Backwards," 65.

41. Carwardine, *Evangelicals and Politics in Antebellum America*, 44.

42. Mary Tarkington's conversion was influenced by the Methodists. Their position was post-millennialist in that they believed that there would be a thousand years of peace before Christ's second coming. After conversion a individual was expected to continually grow in grace. It was believed that absolute sinless perfection could be attained before death. It was a person's duty to work toward sanctification or holiness, paving the way for the thousand years of peace and then Christ's return. See Carwardine, *Evangelicals and Politics in Antebellum America*, 3. Some evangelists were pre-millennialist, believing that Christ would shortly return to earth and "restore the Davidic monarchy of Israel and rule for a thousand years." See Ahlstrom, *A Religious History*, 810.

43. *South-East Indiana Conference Minutes*, 400.

44. Bill Cecil-Fronsman, *Common Whites: Class and Culture in Antebellum North Carolina* (Lexington: Univ. Press of Kentucky, 1992), 183.

45. Watkins, "The Causes And Cure Of Earthquakes," 250.

46. Newton Townsend, "His Spirit Was Willing," *Tennessee Historical Quarterly* 21 (1962): 276–77.

47. Tarkington, *Autobiography*, 70.

48. Tarkington, *Autobiography*, 73–74. In both the North and South, black and whites

worshipped together in the same congregation in the period following the American Revolution. In 1786 at St. George's church in Philadelphia a special gallery was erected to house black members. As a result, the black members left the church. In 1794, one of the blacks, Richard Allen, purchased a blacksmith shop and converted it into a church. Bishop Asbury dedicated the building on June 29, 1794. They gave their reason for establishing a separate church: "Wheras, from time to time many inconveniences have arisen from white people and people of color mixing together in public assemblies,—more particularly in places of public worship,—we have thought it necessary to provide for ourselves a convenient house to assemble in separate from our white brethren." The African Methodist church was formed in the North during April 1816, when an invitation was sent out to various localities, which banned together and formed the organization. See Matthew Simpson, *Cyclopaedia of Methodism* (Philadelphia: Evarts and Stewart, 1878), 14–15.

49. Larry M. James, "Biracial Fellowship in Antebellum Baptist Churches," In John Boles, ed., *Masters and Slaves in the House of the Lord: Race and Religion in the American South, 1740–1870* (Lexington: Univ. Press of Kentucky, 1988), 37.

50. Clark, Potts, and Payton, *Journal and Letters of Francis Asbury*, 298.

51. Lacy K. Ford, Jr., *Origins of Southern Radicalism: The South Carolina Upcountry, 1800–1860* (New York: Oxford Univ. Press, 1988), 24.

52. Tarkington, *Autobiography*, 71–72. Joseph claimed that Adkins, "Like most old soldiers, drank hard." When he was too drunk to find his way home, Joseph would assist him. Joseph claimed that he never saw Amos mistreated and was impressed with his wife. When Mrs. Atkins would find her husband drunk, she would say, "Now Amos you have been at it again. Why do you do so, Amos?" Mrs. Adkins left a lifelong impact on Joseph. In his *Autobiography* he claimed that he could not forget "that good woman and her song." The first thing he ever heard her sing was:

> If I met one by the way,
> I always had something to say
> About that heavenly union.
> O, backslider, come away,
> And learn to do, as well as say,
> And then you will feel this heavenly union.
>   (Tarkington, *Autobiography*, 72)

53. Ibid., 75.

54. Ibid., 75–76.

55. Harry L. Watson, *Liberty and Power: The Politics of Jacksonian America* (New York: Oxford Univ. Press, 1990), 23.

56. Ibid., 23.

57. Hubert H. Hawkins, *Indiana's Road to Statehood* (Indianapolis: Indiana Historical Bureau, 1969), 23. The Northwest Territory consisted of areas known today as Indiana, Illinois, Wisconsin, Michigan, Ohio, and Minnesota.

58. Emma Lou Thornbrough, *The Negro in Indiana Before 1900: A Study of a Minority*, Indiana Historical Society Publications no. 37, Indianapolis, 1957, 1–4.

59. Thornbrough, *The Negro in Indiana*, 1–7.

60. Rolla M. Hogue, "Life in Indiana, 1800–1820," *Indiana Magazine of History* 9 (1913): 83.

CHAPTER TWO. RELIGION IN EARLY INDIANA

1. Roscoe R. Leak, "Salem Methodist Church," *Indiana Magazine of History* 29 (1) (Mar. 1933): 17. The area of Clark County where these churches were built was located in Clark's Grant, the one hundred and fifty thousand acres of land in the Northwest Territory awarded by Congress to George Rogers Clark and his men for their service at Kaskaskia and Vincennes.
2. Eva Elizabeth Luke, "Our Contributors: The Centennial of Indiana Methodism," *Western Christian Advocate*, Sept. 17, 1902, 9.
3. Sweet, "Early Methodist Circuits in Indiana," 361.
4. William McKendree is regarded as the father of western Methodism. He was born in King William County, Virginia, on July 6, 1757. During the American Revolution he served as a private, but was advanced to the rank of adjutant in the commissary department. McKendree was present when General Cornwallis surrendered at Yorktown. In 1787 he was converted and a year later was received by the Methodists. In the early 1790s he began traveling with Francis Asbury, and in 1796 he was appointed presiding elder. McKendree was sent to the West in 1801 to supervise the societies in Ohio, Kentucky, western Virginia, and Illinois, while also being appointed as presiding elder of the Cumberland district. He became widely known and highly esteemed for his work and in 1808 was elected to the office of bishop after delivering a sermon to the General Conference. After 1816 he was senior bishop for nineteen years. He died Mar. 5, 1835, near Nashville, Tennessee, at his brother's home. See Simpson, *Cyclopaedia of Methodism*, 577–78.
5. From a letter of I. N. Britton, a lifelong friend of Andrew Mitchell. The letter is among the records of the Methodist Church at Charlestown, Indiana. Sweet, "Early Methodist Circuits in Indiana," 361.
6. Sweet, "Early Methodist Circuits in Indiana," 361.
7. Luke, "Our Contributors," 9.
8. Holliday, *Indiana Methodism*, 23.
9. Cartwright, *Autobiography*, 77.
10. Luke, "Our Contributors," 9.
11. Sweet, "Early Methodist Circuits in Indiana," 361.
12. Benjamin Lankford died of cholera at Charlestown, Indiana, in 1833. Luke, "Our Contributors," 11.
13. Silver Creek Quarterly Conference Minutes. Archives of DePauw Univ. and Indiana United Methodism.
14. Sweet, *Circuit-Rider Days in Indiana*, 3.
15. Holliday, *Indiana Methodism*, 26.
16. Luke, "Our Contributors," 10.
17. Holliday, *Indiana Methodism*, 26.
18. Sweet, "Early Methodist Circuits in Indiana," 367.
19. Leak, "Salem Methodist Church," 19.
20. Luke, "Our Contributors," 9.
21. Sweet, "Early Methodist Circuits in Indiana," 366.

22. Luke, "Our Contributors," 9.
23. Leak, "Salem Methodist Church," 19. In 1864 the building was torn down and a new church, known as the Salem Methodist Church, was built. The logs from the old church were used as a stable. Two early church members, Eliza and Hanna Robinett, are buried where the old church stood. It was their request that they be buried where the pulpit had been located.
24. Luke, "Our Contributors," 10.
25. Vogel, "Home Life in Early Indiana," 291.
26. Ibid., 291–92.
27. Ashworth was described as "[t]he apostle of Methodism in southern Indiana." He began his ministry work about 1805. Ashworth was appointed to the Salt River and Shelby circuits in the Kentucky conference. In 1806 he was assigned to the Wayne circuit, located in the Cumberland district, and in 1807 the Silver Creek circuit. See John E. Iglehart, "The Life and Times of John Shrader," *Indiana Magazine of History* 17 (1) (Mar. 1921): 16–17.
28. Holliday, *Indiana Methodism*, 27.
29. Sweet, "Early Methodist Circuits in Indiana," 362.
30. Holliday, *Indiana Methodism*, 30.
31. Ibid., 27.
32. Hester Diary, 155.
33. Pigeon Roost had acquired its name from the many flocks of pigeons that were common to the area. Many trees had broken limbs due to the accumulated weight of the many birds that roosted on the branches. "The stench arising from the deposits of large portions of manure was perceivable for more than a mile distant." However, as a result, the land was fertile and was not "surpassed even in the richest lands of Kentucky" (ibid., 147). As a result many families were moving to the area to start farms.
34. Luke, "Our Contributors," 10.
35. Hester Diary, 154.

CHAPTER THREE. THE TARKINGTON FAMILY MOVES TO INDIANA

1. Tarkington, *Autobiography*, 76–77.
2. Allen Wiley, "Methodism in Southeastern Indiana," *Indiana Magazine of History* 23 (1) (Mar. 1927): 35.
3. Tarkington, *Autobiography*, 77.
4. Ibid., 77.
5. Ibid., 78.
6. Ibid.
7. The early settlers remained afraid of the Indians. Even after Indiana became a state, Indian agents were employed to protect the Indians "in order to keep them peaceful." In 1824–25 Indians were brought in from all over the state to watch the executions of white men who had killed innocent Indians. This was done to assure them that the "Great White Father punished their enemies." See Helen Thurman, "The Fall Creek Tragedy," *Indiana Magazine of History* 27 (3) (Sept. 1931): 230–35.

8. R. David Edmunds, *Tecumseh and the Quest for Indian Leadership* (Boston: Little, Brown, and Company, 1984), 212.

9. Bill Whorrall, with contributions by Stephen Harold Riggins and Thomas E. Rodgers, *A Photographic History of Martin County: Indiana Album* (Shoals, 1993), 25.

10. E. Y. Guernsey, "Indian Depredations," *Indiana History Bulletin*, July 1, 1924, 17–18.

11. Ibid., 18–19.

12. James Albert Woodburn, "Local Life and Color in the New Purchase," *Indiana Magazine of History* 9 (4) (Dec. 1913): 215. Woodburn states: "This 'New Purchase' was a tract of land bounded on the north and west by the Wabash river; on the southwest by what is known as the 'eleven o'clock line,' a line going in the direction of a shadow would fall at eleven o'clock forenoon, and running from the center of Jackson county to a point on the Wabash near Clinton."

13. Woodburn comments that the "men of the New Purchase attributed the scarcity of cash to the non-existence of banks, while in the Old Purchase that scarcity was attributed to their existence" (ibid., 228).

14. Tarkington, *Autobiography*, 65. To protect settlers against Indians, blockhouses were occupied by rangers employed by the United States "at the Wabash Rapids at Fort Knox, at Busroan, at Fort Harrison, at Stafford's, at Bono, at Vallonia, at Napolean, at Bryson's, at Garretson's and Whitewater, near Milton. These posts continued to be occupied by soldiers until 1815." See Wood, *Sketches of Things*, 14.

15. Tarkington, *Autobiography*, 80. Joseph adds that Jesse's grave "is under the hotel at Edwardsport."

16. Tarkington, *Autobiography*, 80. The author currently owns and resides on this property in Monroe County. The original records list Tarkington's property as being located at NE S31. After 1820, the government reduced the price of land to $1.25 per acre, which encouraged settlement. Jesse Tarkington purchased the land on Sept. 23, 1816. See Margaret R. Waters, *Indiana Land Entries Vincennes District, 1807–1877*, vol. 2 (Knightstown, Ind., 1980): 198.

17. Benjamin S. Parker, "Pioneer Life," *Indiana Magazine of History* 3 (1) (Mar. 1907): 125.

18. Vogel, "Home Life in Early Indiana," 26.

19. Ibid.

20. Ibid.

21. Thomas D. Clark, *Pills, Petticoats, and Plows: The Southern Country Store* (Norman: Univ. of Oklahoma Press, 1944), 15.

22. Tarkington, *Autobiography*, 87.

23. Ibid.

24. A pirogue was made by splitting a canoe and then inserting broad boards lengthwise through the middle of the craft. This process greatly increased the volume of the boat.

25. Ibid., 87–88.

26. Ibid., 88.

27. Ibid.

28. Ibid., 88–89.

29. Ibid., 90.
30. Ibid., 90–91.
31. William A. Cockrum, A *Pioneer History of Indiana*, 161. Cited in Vogel, "Home Life in Early Indiana," 2.
32. Joseph Wheeler Walker, "Hoosier Pioneers," *Indiana Magazine of History* 20 (1) (Mar. 1924): 62–63.
33. Tarkington, *Autobiography*, 81. Saddler's property was located at W-SE-S31. He purchased his property on Sept. 23, 1816. See Waters, *Indiana Land Entries*, 198.
34. Abraham Lincoln's first home in Spencer County was one of these half-faced camps. See Vogel, "Home Life in Early Indiana," 2.
35. Ibid., 1–3.
36. Tarkington, *Autobiography*, 81–82.
37. L. C. Rudolph, *Hoosier Zion: The Presbyterians in Early Indiana* (New Haven: Yale Univ. Press, 1963), 6.
38. Tarkington, *Autobiography*, 82.
39. Ibid., 82.
40. Rev. T. M. Hopkins, "Reminiscences of Col. John Ketcham of Monroe County, Indiana," in *The Garland Library of Narratives of North American Indiana*, ed. Wilcomb E. Washburn (New York: Farland Publishing Company, 1977), 19.
41. Tarkington, *Autobiography*, 82.
42. Vogel, "Home Life in Early Indiana," 10.
43. Holliday, *Indiana Methodism*, 253.
44. Ibid.
45. The Hamilton grist mill was built by Robert Hamilton in the early 1820s. Monroe County historian Weston A. Goodspeed comments that it was an "extremely rude affair," but received "liberal patronage." Orion Crocker was the first miller. The mill was operated until late in the nineteenth century. Sawmills were often operated in conjunction with the grist mills. See Weston A. Goodspeed, "History of Monroe County," in *Counties of Morgan, Monroe, and Brown, Indiana: Historical and Biographical*, ed. Charles Blanchard (Chicago: F. A. Battery and Co., Publishers, 1884), 509.
46. Tarkington, *Autobiography*, 83.
47. Ibid. Campbell Berry lived in an area known as the Blue Springs Community. Berry's family founded the community in 1826. Dissension arose in the group in 1827, when the women began quarreling over what color men's homespun jeans should be dyed.
48. Benjamin S. Parker, "Pioneer Life," *Indiana Magazine of History* 3 (1) (Mar. 1907): 1–2.
49. Ibid., 4.
50. Ibid., 7.
51. Emil Pocock, "Reverend James Welsh on Three Frontiers, 1790–1825," *Indiana Magazine of History* 86 (4) (Dec. 1990): 347.
52. Members of the Cross Roads Church worshiped in the log church until 1847. See Gary R. Shiplett, ed., "The History of Cross Roads Methodist Church, 1821–1971": Sesquicentennial edition (pamphlet), 4.
53. Sweet, *Circuit-Rider Days in Indiana*, 22.
54. Holliday, *Indiana Methodism*, 253.
55. Ibid., 254.

56. In 1873 the orchard that Joseph planted was still bearing apples. I have been unable to locate the site of the trees. Joseph claimed that they were located near the graves of his parents. Ibid., 254.

57. Tarkington, *Autobiography*, 84–85.

58. Ibid., 85. Joseph claims that Anderson arrived in 1820. However, he confuses the date. Anderson was appointed to the Bloomington circuit in 1818. William Chamberlain was appointed to the Bloomington circuit in 1820.

59. Sweet, *Circuit-Rider Days in Indiana*, 23.

60. The first quarterly meeting for the Bloomington circuit was held at the home of Stephen Grimes four miles west of Bloomington on Jan. 22, 1820. Samuel Hamilton was the presiding elder.

61. Daniel Anderson formed a class at the crossroads in 1818. The members worshipped at private homes until 1826, when a "very respectable log church was built twenty-five feet wide, thirty-five feet long, with twelve foot ceilings, plastered, five double windows, sash and glass." The first members were Daniel Rawlins, Rebecca Rawlins, John Sedwick and his wife, John C. Smith, Stephen Grimes and wife, and Edward Archer and his wife. I apologize for listing the women as "wife," but names were not provided in the church records.

62. James A. Woodburn, "Local Life and Color in the New Purchase," *Indiana Magazine of History* 9 (4) (Dec. 1913): 230.

63. Baynard Rush Hall, *The New Purchase* (New Albany: J. R. Nunemacher, 1855), 344–45.

64. Tarkington, *Autobiography*, 83

65. Ibid., 84

66. Ibid., 93–94.

67. Holliday, *Indiana Methodism*, 254–55.

68. The early churches in Indiana were not static in their denominational beliefs. It was common for an entire church to change faiths. A good example was the Friendship Church located in Washington County. In 1821 the church was established as a Baptist church with eleven members. By 1833, when the membership reached thirty-seven, the organization changed into a Church of Christ. See Lennie Martin Berkey, "Friendship Church," *Indiana Magazine of History* 30 (3) (Sept. 1934): 238.

69. Tarkington, *Autobiography*, 91.

70. Ibid., 7.

71. Records of Vernal Baptist Church, Jan. 1819–July 7, 1855, 7–15. Monroe County Historical Collection, Lilly Library, Indiana Univ., Bloomington, Indiana.

72. *History of Lawrence and Monroe County Indiana: Their People Industries and Institutions* (Indianapolis: B. F. Bowen, 1914), 309.

73. Ibid., 309–10. During early years Bloomington was visited by both Barton W. Stone and Alexander Campbell. Stone visited Bloomington in 1826, 1835, 1838, and 1843. Campbell stopped in Bloomington in 1850 and again in 1861. I wish to thank F. G. Summitt of Bloomington for pointing this out to me. Aaron Wallace (sometimes spelled "Willis") was the black preacher's full name.

74. Goodspeed, "History of Monroe County," 479.

75. Isaac Reed, "The Christian Traveler, 1828," in *Indiana As Seen By Early Travelers: A Collection of Reprints from Books of Travel, Letters and Diaries Prior to 1830*, ed. Harlow Lindley (Indianapolis: Indiana Historical Commission, 1916), 479.

76. Goodspeed, "History of Monroe County," 479.

77. Ibid., 480.

78. Tarkington spelled Daniel Rawlins name "Rollins." Daniel Anderson formed a class in Bloomington in 1818. Member were Nelson Moore, Lucinda Moore, Sarah Dorsey, George Anderson (Daniel's brother), Mrs. Lee, and Lucinda Howe. Shiplett, "The History of Cross Roads United Methodist Church," 4.

79. Parker, "Pioneer Life," 1.

CHAPTER FOUR. HEARING THE CALLING

1. Holliday, *Indiana Methodism*, 256.

2. The Methodists were selling various books throughout the county. In the notebook of Monroe Countian Henry Batterson, dated Dec. 20, 1825, he received 204 spelling books from James Armstrong. They were to be sold for twelve and one-half cents a piece. Batterson claimed that he would "return or account for to him or order on or before the first of Sept. next." Notebook located in Archives of DePauw Univ. and Indiana United Methodism.

3. James Armstrong (1787–1834) was a native of Ireland. He entered the ministry in 1821. See William Warren Sweet, *Religion on the American Frontier: The Methodists* (New York: Cooper Square 1964), 4: 472.

4. Cole, *Lion of the Forest*, 18.

5. Hoosier Lloyd Milner Graves comments seventy years after the first churches surfaced in Indiana that the "folkways were not yet entirely uprooted. The center of communal life was still the church . . . the church was the main vehicle of a social as well as religious life." Lloyd Milner Graves, "My Indiana Homestead: Symbol of an Epoch That Was," *Indiana Magazine of History* 36 (2) (June 1940): 102.

6. Tarkington, *Autobiography*, 91–94.

7. Ibid., 92.

8. Ibid., 95.

9. Holliday, *Indiana Methodism*, 256.

10. The school was actually Indiana Seminary, which later became Indiana University.

11. Tarkington, *Autobiography*, 95–96.

12. Holliday, *Indiana Methodism*, 256–57.

13. Tarkington, *Autobiography*, 96.

14. Holliday, *Indiana Methodism*, 257.

15. Tarkington, *Autobiography*, 96–97.

16. Ibid., 97

17. Edward Eggleston, *The Circuit Rider: A Tale of the Heroic Age* (New York: J. B. Ford and Company, 1874), 127.

18. Tarkington, *Autobiography*, 98.

19. Pocock, "Reverend James Welsh," 348–57. Songbooks that became common in early Indiana were the *Missouri Harmony* and the *Christian Psalmist*, along with the *Sacred Melodeon*. Lowell Mason and A. D. Filmore's songbooks were also standard.

20. Tarkington, *Autobiography*, 98–99. John Shrader was born in 1792 at Baltimore, Maryland. In 1795 he moved with his parents to Knoxville, Tennessee. He was

converted and joined the Methodist Church in 1810. He was licensed to preach in 1812 and was admitted to the Tennessee Conference in 1814. According to Iglehart, "He was ordained deacon by Bishop Asbury at Lebanon, Tennessee in 1814, and ordained elder by Bishop Roberts in 1818 at Olwells camp ground near Alton, Illinois. In 1814 he served the Green River circuit in Kentucky under Peter Cartwright as presiding elder, with ten appointments four hundred miles around." In 1815 he was sent to the Vincennes circuit, which was in the Tennessee conference, which had twenty appointments and was three hundred miles around. He spent his life traveling as a circuit rider, preaching throughout Indiana and adjoining states. John E. Iglehart, "The Life and Times of John Shrader: Including the Introduction and Problems of Methodism in Southwestern Indiana," *Indiana Magazine of History* 17 (1) (Mar. 1921): 10.

21. Tarkington, *Autobiography*, 99.
22. Ibid., 99.
23. Hugh McGary's father was also named Hugh McGary. He was responsible for leading Kentuckians into the bloody Battle of the Blue Licks in 1782, where at least sixty of his fellow warriors were killed by Indians under British command. Among the dead was Daniel Boone's son, Israel. McGary was later castigated for the fiasco "in that he was accused of spurring his fellow soldiers into the attack against the better judgement of his superior officers." See Thomas D. Clark, *A History of Kentucky* (Lexington: The John Bradford Press, 1960): 57–58.
24. John E. Iglehart, "The Life and Times of John Shrader," *Indiana Magazine of History* 17 (1) (Mar. 1921): 3–4.
25. Robert Parrett has always been known as the "father of Methodism" in Evansville. However, Parrett did not arrive in Evansville until 1825 when a class had already been established. Methodist preachers such as Parrett and the Wheeler's took turns preaching on alternate Sundays. They worked under the direction of the circuit rider.
26. For a full description of the English Settlement, which at this date, or soon afterwards, represented about one-half of the leading citizens of Vanderburgh County, see Iglehart, "The Life and Times of John Shrader," 4.
27. Iglehart, "The Life and Times of John Shrader," 5–6.
28. Ibid., 9.
29. Orceneth Fisher was born Nov. 5, 1803, in Vermont. Fisher began breaching with the Methodists in 1824. In 1841 he moved to Texas and continued his circuit-riding career until 1855, when Fisher transferred to the Pacific conference of the Methodist Episcopal Church South. Fisher returned to Texas in 1870 and continued to preach until his death on August 28, 1880. See Sweet, *Religion on the American Frontier*, 469. For a complete study of Fisher's life see Robert E. Ledbetter Jr., "Orceneth Fisher: Pioneer Methodist Preacher of Texas and the Pacific Coast," (M.A. thesis, Univ. of Texas, 1938).
30. Tarkington, *Autobiography*, 100.
31. Ibid.
32. Ibid.
33. Ibid., 102.
34. Ruth Price, "Indiana Methodism," *Indiana Magazine of History* 11 (3) (Sept. 1915): 239.
35. Sweet, "Early Methodist Circuits in Indiana," 359–60.

36. Price, "Indiana Methodism," 231.
37. Sweet, "Early Methodist Circuits in Indiana," 360.
38. Robert H. Williams, "Methodist Church Trials in Illinois," *Methodist History* 1 (1) (Oct. 1962): 16.
39. Ibid., 16–21.
40. William W. Sweet, "The Churches as Moral Courts of the Frontier," *Church History* 2 (Jan. 1933): 17–21.
41. Ibid., 18.
42. Ibid., 10–19.
43. Eli P. Farmer was a preacher who never received pay for his ministerial duties. He was a self-supporting farmer. Like Peter Cartwright, Farmer often left his pulpit and delivered "personal chastisement" to rowdies who disrupted his meetings. See Sweet, *Religion on the American Frontier*, 285.
44. Illinois Conference Minutes. Archives of DePauw Univ. and Indiana United Methodism.
45. Tarkington, *Autobiography*, 103–16.
46. Ibid., 104. Tarkington mistakenly thought that Robert Dale Owen "bought out" Father Rapp and established New Harmony. Robert Dale Owen's father, Robert Owen, made the purchase. See William E. Wilson, *The Angel and the Serpent: The Story of New Harmony* (Bloomington: Indiana Univ. Press, 1964). Robert Dale Owen was a two-term U.S. congressman from Indiana. He wrote an introduced a bill that established the Smithsonian Institution and was a fighter for women's rights.
47. Ibid., 105.
48. "Richard Posey Early Pastor in Bruceville: History Places Methodists at Bruceville in 1820," *Vincennes Sun-Commercial*, Aug. 1, 1954.
49. "Trinity Methodist Church Born in Log Cabin Called Simply, 'The Meetin' House'" *Vincennes Sun-Commercial*, Aug. 1, 1954.
50. Marie Wittenmeyer McCormick, "The History of Asbury Chapel Methodist Church." Brief history MS in the DePauw Univ. Archives.
51. Illinois Conference Minutes. Archives of DePauw Univ. and Indiana United Methodism.
52. Tarkington, *Autobiography*, 106. The preachers at the conference were John Strange, James Armstrong, Charles Holiday, Peter Cartwright, William Shanks, George Locke, Clavin Ruter, Edwin Ray, Nehemiah B. Griffith, Stephen R. Beggs, and Thomas Hewsom. See Illinois Conference Minutes, 17.
53. Document obtained from Mrs. Glen Whaley of Bloomington, Indiana.
54. Tarkington, *Autobiography*, 106–7.
55. Ibid., 107.
56. Samuel Henderson's rates. *Indiana Journal*, Dec. 3, 1829.
57. For insight on the first roads in Indiana, see George Amick, "Post Roads in Southern Indiana," *Indiana Magazine of History* 30 (4) (Dec. 1934).
58. Walker, "Hoosier Pioneers," 71.
59. Ibid., 71–72.
60. Ibid., 72–73. Postage was expensive during the early years in Indiana. An individual receiving a one-page letter was charged six cents for a distance of thirty miles. Postage stamps were not used until 1847, and it was not until 1857 that the sender paid the postage.

61. Tarkington, *Autobiography*, 108.
62. Ibid.
63. Ibid.
64. Ibid., 109.
65. Illinois Conference Minutes, 29.
66. William Evans was married by Joseph Tarkington. Evans lived in a log cabin at the corner of Franklin and Central Avenues. Joseph preached his first sermon in the "grand jury room of the court house-southwest upper room." This room was also used by Presbyterians and Baptists before they built churches. Around thirty persons attended Joseph's meeting. See Harding, *History of Decatur County*, 211–12.
67. Rev. John Tinsley of Greensburg claimed that the first Methodist sermon preached in the town was heard by John Robbins in September 1822. It was delivered by Rev. James Murray of the Connersville circuit which was still part of the Ohio conference. The meeting was held at the double log cabin of Col. Thomas Hendricks. After Murray's sermon, Robbins formed a class at his home. See ibid., 211.
68. George L. Curtiss, *A Monograph of Methodism in Shelbyville* (Shelbyville: n.p., 1878): 6–8.
69. John Mack Faragher, *Sugar Creek: Life on the Illinois Prairie* (New Haven and London: Yale Univ. Press, 1986), 165.
70. Ibid., 166.
71. Ruth Price, "Indiana Methodism," *Indiana Magazine of History* 11 (3) (Sept. 1915): 235.
72. Tarkington, *Autobiography*, 118–19.
73. For an excellent account of life in the rural Madison area, see Harrison Burns, *Personal Recollections of Harrison Burns as written in 1907* (Indianapolis: Indiana Historical Society, 1975). The first Methodist preaching was initiated by Walter Griffin in 1811, when a class of six persons was organized. The class met at the house of George Burton around a year before Griffin arrived. The first Methodist church was built in 1815. See Simpson, *Cyclopaedia of Methodism*.

CHAPTER FIVE. A YOUNG PREACHER WEDS

1. Allen Wiley, "Introduction and Progress of Methodism in Southeastern Indiana," *Indiana Magazine of History* 23 (4) (Dec. 1927): 407–8.
2. Holliday, *Indiana Methodism*, 120.
3. Buley, *The Old Northwest: Pioneer Period*, 452.
4. Tarkington, *Autobiography*, 28–29.
5. Ibid., 29–30.
6. Ibid., 30.
7. Elnathan C. Gavitt, *Crumbs from My Saddle bags*, 172–73, in Buley, *The Old Northwest*, 452–53.
8. Tarkington, *Autobiography*, 118.
9. Bishops generally did not receive much of a salary either. Between 1802 and 1810 the Western conference paid Francis Asbury an average of twenty-five dollars per annum. It was not until 1789 that the *Discipline* listed a salary for bishops. In 1816

they received one hundred dollars. They received no living expenses. They were forced to pay for expensive ferries, corn for the horses, clothing, and numerous other expenses. See Edwin A. Schell, "Support of the Bishops in Early American Methodism," *Methodist History* 4 (3) (Apr. 1966): 42–50.

10. Tarkington, *Autobiography*, 118.

11. Ibid., 31–32.

12. Leonard I. Sweet, *The Minister's Wife: Her Role in Nineteenth-Century American Evangelicalism* (Philadelphia: Temple Univ. Press, 1983), 3.

13. Richard Shiels, "The Feminization of American Congregationalism," *American Quarterly* 33 (Spring 1981): 46.

14. Nancy F. Cott, "Passionless: An Interpretation of Victorian Sexual Ideology, 1790–1850," *Signs* 4 (Winter 1978): 225.

15. Lori D. Ginzberg, citing Shiels, in "Women in an Evangelical Community: Oberlin 1835–1850," *Ohio History* 89 (1980): 81.

16. Ibid., 79.

17. Sweet, *The Minister's Wife*, 60.

18. Maria was born in Orange County, New York, on Jan. 22, 1806. Simeon Slawson was born Jan. 19, 1776, at Stamford, Connecticut, to Jonathan and Lydia Lockwood Slawson. He was the fourth son and sixth child of the family. Around 1800 the Slawsons moved to Orange County, New York. On Apr. 6, 1805, Simeon married Martha Wood, who was born Feb. 5, 1786, near Saratoga Springs, New York. Simeon died Jan. 22, 1858, and Martha died July 7, 1866. One of Simeon's brothers was killed when a barge of lumber crushed him at a wharf in New York City. Letter from John S. Tarkington to Emma Welch, Mar. 11, 1914.

According to Maria, "Slauson" was the proper spelling of the family's surname. After the family moved to Indiana and Simeon purchased his land, patents from the government giving him ownership spelled the name "Slawson." Simeon Slawson's neighbors also spelled his name that way, so Simeon got into the habit of writing a "w" instead of a "u" in his name. See Tarkington, *Autobiography*, 152.

19. Tarkington, *Autobiography*, 159. As the area around Maria's home was settled, the Methodists included it in the Cincinnati circuit, which was part of the Miami district. As early as 1802 camp meetings were conducted on William Cotton's land grant on Indian Creek, and Peter Cartwright preached there in 1804. In 1806 the area became part of the Enon circuit. It was not until 1810 that regular preachers were making frequent trips to the region. Allen Wiley preached the first funeral service in Vevay at the funeral service of Mrs. Cole. The Enon circuit was changed to the Lawrenceburg circuit, Ohio conference, in 1811. In 1814, Lorenzo Dow, called the "evangelist of the woods," preached on Vevay street corners in "buckskin, unshaved and unshorn." A Frenchman named Dufour translated the sermon into French in order that the French settlers in the area could understand it. In 1816, Allen Wiley and Russell Bigelow were appointed to the Lawrenceburg circuit, which was extended to Madison and Versailles. Within the circuit they preached at Lawrenceburg, Aurora, Rising Sun, Vevay, Madison, Canaan, Versailles, Moorefield, Mt. Sterling, Wesport, Patriot, Wilmington, Manchester, and Guilford. It took the men four weeks to complete the circuit, preaching every day of the week and twice on Sunday. Frederick Waldo was the first-class leader of the Vevay church. Simeon Slawson's home became a popular place for camp meet-

ings. They were also conducted at other sites in the area, such as at David Lees's home and near Quercus Grove. See Vevay Methodist Church records, Archives of DePauw Univ. and Indiana United Methodism.

20. The children were Maria (b. Jan. 22, 1806), Malissa (b. July 1, 1807), Delanson (b. Jan. 8, 1810), Josephus (b. July 21, 1812), Mahala (b. Sept. 18, 1815), and Simeon (b. May 23, 1818). After arriving in Indiana, four additional children were born to the Slawsons: Matilda (b. June 8, 1820), Maluda (May 19, 1822), Daniel W. (May 15, 1825), and John Wright (May 17, 1827). All of the children except the youngest two had nicknames: Ri, Lis, Lant, Eph, Hale, Bub, Til, and Lude, respectively. See Bro. Harris "Reminiscences," *Vevay Reveille*, May 27, 1897. Maluda also married a Methodist itinerant, Rev. John J. Winchester, on Dec. 14, 1844. She moved to an elegant home in Greensburg after her husband retired from the circuit. Matilda was known as the peacemaker of the family. Delanson was described as a "very intelligent, upright, worthy man of considerable culture." Simeon Jr. was much like his father "intemperment, industry, frugality, and moral worth." See Harris, "Reminiscences."

21. Tarkington, *Autobiography*, 157.

22. Letter from Martha Slawson to her unnamed nephew, Nov. 16, 1834, Slawson-Tarkington Collection, Indiana Historical Society.

23. The Slawsons later purchased 480 additional acres in other areas of Indiana. See ibid.

24. Tarkington, *Autobiography*, 158. The Slawson's neighbor, William Cotton, lived in a large, hollow sycamore tree until he built his cabin. Cotton had arrived in Switzerland County in 1798. In 1816 Cotton was a delegate to the constitutional convention which formed the constitution of Indiana. See Julia Leclerc Knox, "Vevay and Switzerland County," *Indiana Magazine of History* 11 (3) (Sept. 1915): 230.

25. Daniel died on Dec. 27, 1830, Josephus on Feb. 17, 1831, Malissa on Mar. 13, Mahala on Mar. 17, and John on Jan. 30, 1832.

26. Slawson-Tarkington Collection, Indiana Historical Society.

27. R. Laurence Moore, "Religion, Secularization, and the Shaping of the Culture Industry in Antebellum America," *American Quarterly* 41 (June 1989): 221.

28. Simeon Slawson to an unnamed nephew, Nov. 16, 1834, Slawson-Tarkington Papers, Indiana Historical Society.

29. Tarkington, *Autobiography*, 160.

30. Ibid.

31. Ibid., 34–35.

32. Ibid., 35–36.

33. Ibid., 160–61.

34. Ibid., 161–62.

35. Ibid., 36–37.

36. Ibid., 121.

37. Holliday, *Indiana Methodism*, 260.

38. Tarkington, *Autobiography*, 121.

39. Ibid., 122–23.

40. Ibid., 123–24.

CHAPTER SIX. JOSEPH AND MARIA BEGIN
THEIR LONG LIFE TOGETHER

1. Tarkington, *Autobiography*, 124.
2. Chelsea L. Lawlis, "Prosperity and Hard Times in the Whitewater Valley, 1830–1840," *Indiana Magazine of History* 43 (1) (Mar. 1947): 374.
3. Charles B. Strozier, *Lincoln's Quest for Union: Public and Private Meanings* (New York: Basic Books, Inc., 1982), 40.
4. Sweet, *The Minister's Wife*, 44.
5. Ibid., 60.
6. Tarkington, *Autobiography*, 124.
7. Ibid., 125. John Tarkington became the father of famous Hoosier novelist Newton Booth Tarkington. John Tarkington received his A.B. in 1852 from Indiana Asbury (DePauw). In 1855 he received his A.M. Following his graduation he became secretary to Governor Wright, later entering the law office of Governor Porter. From 1858 to 1862, John Tarkington was a trustee at Indiana University. In 1863, he was a member of the Indiana legislature. During the Civil War, Tarkington was a captain and provost marshall in the 132nd Indiana Volunteer Infantry in 1864. He was a judge of the Marion County Circuit Court from 1871 to 1872. John Tarkington was an author in his own right: he wrote two novels, *Hermit of Capri* and *The Auto-Orphan*. He died at his home, 3219 N. New Jersey Street, in Indianapolis on January 30, 1923.
8. Glenda Riley, *The Female Frontier: A Comparative View of Women on the Prairie and the Plains* (Lawrence: Univ. Press of Kansas, 1988), 49.
9. Ibid.
10. Letter from Simeon Slawson to Augustus Welch, May 22, 1842, James Welch Collection. Augustus Welch married Simeon's daughter Matilda on Nov. 21, 1841. Augustus Welch was born in Ontario County, New York, Jan. 25, 1811. His mother died when he was three years old. His father, William, brought him to Indiana when he was eight years of age. When Augustus was twelve his father took him to Bowling Green, Kentucky, to live with relatives. Augustus remained with the family until he was eighteen years old. He then moved to Louisville, Kentucky, to learn the carpenter's trade. After serving his apprenticeship, he went to Cincinnati and built houses. Later he moved south and worked in Natchez and New Orleans. Augustus spent three years and three months in the 50th Regiment of the Indiana Infantry during the Civil War and was later elected to the state legislature for two years. The final thirty-two years of his life were spent on his farm in Switzerland County. Matilda went to Covington, Kentucky, to live with her husband for a brief time after their marriage, but she returned to Switzerland County, where she remained until she died in 1903. The couple had eight children.

The Slawsons were fond of their son-in-law and joked with him constantly. In one letter that Matilda cut short, Maluda wrote a sentence at the bottom of the page stating "You must excuse your *old* lady for mother has just started to meeting and Matilda is going to run after her" (letter from Maluda Slawson to Augustus Welch, May 22, 1842). Similar to newlyweds of today. the Welches borrowed from the Slawsons on occasion. In 1843 while Augustus was working at Natchez, he told his wife to borrow from her father and he would settle the account later.

See letter from Augustus Welch to Matilda Slawson Welch, Mar. 16, 1843, James Welch Collection.

Simeon Slawson wrote his son-in-law Augustus Welch on Jan. 21, 1846, informing Augustus that he was the father of a new child. He stated that Martha was so pleased with the child that she tried to show it "her pappy in the picture book." Conditions were horrible for women bearing children. In this case, it was extremely cold and there was five inches of snow on the ground. With regard to Matilda, Simeon reported, "The doctor says if she takes no cold she will soon be up again. Wm is gone to get a girl to nurse her" (letter from Simeon Slawson to Augustus Welch, Jan. 21, 1846). Approximately one month later Matilda wrote her husband stating "I feel thankful for a merciful provider that has brought me through so much affliction" (letter from Matilda Slawson Welch to Augustus Welch, Feb. 14, 1846).

11. T. A. Goodwin, "The Heroic Women of Early Indiana Methodism," T. A. Goodwin file, Archives of DePauw Univ. and Indiana United Methodism.

12. Tarkington, *Autobiography*, 125.

13. Charles E. Rosenberg, *The Cholera Years: The United States in 1832, 1849, and 1866* (Chicago: Univ. of Chicago Press, 1962), 36–37.

14. Yellow fever did strike colder climates in cities such as Philadelphia. In 1793, almost 10 percent of the city's population died from the disease. For an analysis of the yellow fever epidemic, see J. H. Powell, *Bring Out Your Dead: The Great Plague of Yellow Fever in Philadelphia in 1793* (Philadelphia: Univ. of Pennsylvania Press, 1949).

15. Rosenberg, *The Cholera Years*, 40–44.

16. Ibid., 40–42.

17. The doctors' assumptions were only partly right. The disease was usually found in the lower classes, but it was not a result of "sin." The disease flourished as a consequence of insanitary conditions found where the poor resided. In the larger cities, overcrowding was common and people ingested contaminated foods along with drinking water that had been drawn from bacteria-infested rivers. Garbage and human waste were simply thrown into the streets, while hogs were allowed to wander throughout the cities, eating the matter.

18. *Western Christian Advocate*, June 26, 1835.

19. Tarkington, *Autobiography*, 125–26.

20. Albert Fletcher Bridges, "Early Methodism in Clay County," *Indiana Magazine of History* 20 (2) (June 1924): 160.

21. Memo from Welch family notes.

22. Tarkington, *Autobiography*, 127.

23. Diary of Alfred Berry Nisbit, Archives of DePauw Univ. and Indiana United Methodism.

24. Tarkington, *Autobiography*, 126.

25. Alfred Berry Nisbit claimed in his diary that services were conducted in private homes until 1835, when a one-room brick church was erected at 320–324 North Franklin Street. Nisbit stated that the property was purchased on Feb. 23, 1834, and the church was erected one year later. Greensburg became a station with a resident pastor in 1839. In 1849 a two-story church was built on West Washington Street for twelve hundred. Diary of Alfred Berry Nisbit.

26. Tarkington, *Autobiography*, 127–28.

27. Ibid., 128–29.

28. *Western Christian Advocate*, Nov. 7, 1834.

29. Tarkington, *Autobiography*, 129–30.

30. Ibid., 130

31. Ibid.

32. Ibid., 130–31.

33. Ibid., 131.

34. Ibid.

35. Frank W. Stephenson, "The Development of the Methodist Church Particularly in the Midwest," *Methodist History* 3 (1) (Oct. 1964): 37.

36. Tarkington, *Autobiography*, 131.

37. Robert D. Clark, "Matthew Simpson, the Methodists, and the Defeat of Governor Samuel Bigger, 1843," *Indiana Magazine of History* 50 (1) (1954): 23.

38. Tarkington, *Autobiography*, 132.

39. Clark, "Matthew Simpson," 23.

40. Ibid., 24.

41. Simpson, *Cyclopaedia of Methodism*, 475.

42. Clark, "Matthew Simpson," 24. The depression lingered until 1843. It was the worse in United States history. The economic collapse set off a tidal wave of bankruptcies. Under the Bankruptcy Act of 1841 nearly twenty-eight thousand debtors were freed of almost a half-billion dollars of debt. Rural areas such as Indiana were the hardest hit by the economic catastrophe, but they were self-sustaining, which helped in relief. Mobs in cities such as New York looted, while violence exploded in other eastern areas, resulting in the phrase that was coined by Horace Greeley: "Go to the Great West, anything rather than to remain here."

43. Ibid., 24.

44. Tarkington, *Autobiography*, 133.

45. Ella Porter Griffith, "Joshua Griffith: Pioneer Preacher," *Indiana Magazine of History* 36 (1) (Mar. 1940): 38.

46. Edward Eggleston, *The Hoosier Schoolmaster: An Engaging Story of Life in a Backwoods Village of Indiana in the 1850's* (New York: Orange Judd, 1871).

47. James Albert Woodburn, "James Woodburn: Hoosier Schoolmaster," *Indiana Magazine of History* 32 (3) (Sept. 1936): 242.

48. John Tarkington recalled the event many years later. John Stevenson Tarkington to Simeon Slawson, Nov. 2, 1855, Firestone Library, Princeton Univ.

49. From the family notes of Emma Welch. Rufus Welch became famous. At the age of fifteen, young Rufus joined the circus and became a clown. He later became manager of a small circus around 1818. Later, Welch toured great seaport cities as well as the West Indies with his shows. In October 1836 he brought his show back to Switzerland County and exhibited lions, tigers, and other exotic animals. Methodist preachers such as Joseph Tarkington thought it was sinful even to look at a circus tent. The Methodists preached against the evils of the circus and most other forms of amusement. Most newspapers would not advertise a circus. Promotion of the event was done by handbills. See Benj. C. Waldenmaier, "The Welch Family," *The Vevay Reveille-Enterprise*, Dec. 14, 1934.

50. Notes of Emma Welch.

51. Perret Dufour, *The Swiss Settlement of Switzerland County Indiana* (Indianapolis: Indiana Historical Commission, 1925), 120.

52. John Steventon, *The Auto-Orphan* (Boston: The Gorham Press, 1913): 16. Patricia Cochran, Joseph Tarkington's great-great-granddaughter, informed me that John Stevenson Tarkington wrote this book under the pseudonym of John Steventon. She added that the book was based on John's childhood experiences at the Slawson farm.

53. Ibid., 30–31.

54. Ibid., 47–48.

55. In 1802, one year before Lawrenceburg was founded, it was included in the Miami circuit. Elisha W. Bowman was the circuit rider and William Burk was presiding elder for a period of four years. In 1803 when the city was being planned, John Sales and Joseph Oglesby were appointed to the circuit and were succeeded in 1805 by Benjamin Lakin and Joshua Riggin. In 1806 the name of this circuit was changed from Miami to Whitewater. In 1811 the name of the circuit was changed to Lawrenceburg. In 1938 the Lawrenceburg station was founded with Joseph Tarkington as its first pastor. See Lawrenceburg M.E. Church records.

56. Steventon, *The Auto-Orphan*, 48.

57. Ibid., 49.

58. Ibid., 49–50.

59. John Tarkington Collection, Indiana Historical Society.

60. Tarkington, *Autobiography*, 135. Several German-speaking Methodist churches surfaced in southern Indiana. At Shelbyville in the Southeast Indiana conference was a German-speaking church led by Levi Heiss. Most of the German-speaking churches disbanded a few years after their founding. Most German youths were converted to English-speaking church, and many other members moved away. Finally, the German-speaking churches merged with English-speaking churches.

61. Nottingham, *Methodism and the Frontier*, 35.

62. W. J. Rorabaugh, *The Alcoholic Republic: An American Tradition* (New York 1979): 25. Cited in Williams, *Sam Houston*, 61.

63. Williams, *Sam Houston*, 61.

64. Ibid.

65. Ibid.

66. Nottingham, *Methodism and the Frontier*, 35.

67. Dufour, *The Swiss Settlement of Switzerland County*, 208.

68. Posey, "The Development of Methodism in the Old Southwest," 109.

69. Ivan Burnett Jr., "Methodist Origins: John Wesley and Alcohol," *Methodist History* 13 (4) (July 1975): 12.

70. Ibid., 4–13.

71. Sweet, *Methodism in American History*, 172.

72. Wood, *Sketches of Things and Peoples in Indiana*, 47.

73. Ibid., 48. Aaron Wood was one of whiskey's most savage enemies. He simply hated the effects that it had on society. His final words in his autobiography were "I say to young and old men, KEEP SOBER" (ibid.).

74. Wiley, "Methodism in Southeastern Indiana," 2.

75. Vevay Methodist Church records. Archives of DePauw Univ. and Indiana United Methodism.

76. Posey, "The Development of Methodism in the Old Southwest," 109.
77. Ibid., 110.
78. Ibid.
79. Iglehart, "Life and Times of John Shrader," 35.
80. Curtiss, *Methodism in Shelbyville*, 19.
81. Ibid., 26.

CHAPTER SEVEN. FROM PREACHER TO PRESIDING ELDER

1. Steventon, *The Auto-Orphan*, 50–51.
2. Tarkington, *Autobiography*, 12.
3. Sweet, *Circuit-Rider Days in Indiana*, 74–75.
4. Tarkington, *Autobiography*, 18–19.
5. Margaret Bolling, "Hamline Historical Highlights, September 20, 1985," 5. Located in Hamline Chapel United Methodist Church Records, Lawrenceburg, Indiana. Archives of DePauw Univ. and Indiana United Methodism.
6. Ibid., 135.
7. Diary of Alfred Berry Nisbit.
8. Tarkington, *Autobiography*, 135–36.
9. Ibid., 136.
10. Lawlis, "Prosperity and Hard Times," 373.
11. Tarkington, *Autobiography*, 46–47.
12. Ibid., 136.
13. Steventon, *The Auto-Orphan*, 59–60.
14. John does not mention in his work *The Auto-Orphan* that three physicians, Dr. Vail, Dr. Salter, and Dr. Palmer actually attended the preacher. Tarkington, *Autobiography*, 137.
15. Steventon, *The Auto-Orphan*, 63.
16. Rosenberg, *The Cholera Years*, 5.
17. Diary of Reverend Alexander Douglass, Archives of DePauw Univ. and Indiana United Methodism.
18. Tarkington, *Autobiography*, 137.
19. Ibid.
20. Letter from Matilda Slawson Welch to Augustus Welch, July 17, 1842.
21. Tarkington, *Autobiography*, 139.
22. Ibid., 140.
23. Letter from Maria Tarkington to Joseph Tarkington, Oct. 23, 1843.
24. Tarkington, *Autobiography*, 144–45.
25. Ibid., 145.
26. Ibid.
27. Ibid., 146.
28. Ibid.
29. Ibid., 147.
30. Ibid.
31. John L. Smith, *Indiana Methodism: A Series of Sketches and Incidents, Grave and Humorous Concerning Preachers and People of the West* (Valparaiso: n.p., 1892), 156.

32. Ibid., 156–57.
33. Ibid., 157.
34. Ibid.
35. John Steventon, *The Auto-Orphan*, 46.
36. Ibid., 46–47.
37. Tarkington, *Autobiography*, 150.
38. In 1850 and 1851 the area that Joseph was working was called the Putnam district.
39. Curtiss, *Methodism in Shelbyville*, 24.

CHAPTER EIGHT. FROM CIRCUIT RIDER
TO ESTABLISHED MINISTER

1. Tarkington, *Autobiography*, 150–51.
2. Harding, *History of Decatur County*, 928.
3. Tarkington, *Autobiography*, 151.
4. Rhys Isaac, "Evangelical Revolt: The Nature of the Baptists' Challenge to the Traditional Order of Virginia, 1765 to 1775," *William and Mary Quarterly* 3d Ser. 31 (July 1974): 345–68.
5. Joseph Asbury Tarkington later became a prominent physician in Washington, D.C. He was a member of the American Medical Association and the District of Columbia Medical Association. During the Civil War, Joseph enlisted in the Seventh Indiana Regiment and served throughout the war of rebellion. After the war he moved to Washington, D.C., and worked for the Interior Department. While he was working he began his medical studies. Joseph later graduated from both Georgetown and Columbia Medical Institutes. He married Elva Meredith Yeatman of Washington, D.C., on Jan. 14, 1885. Elva died on Jan. 8, 1891, leaving two children, Arthur Joseph Tarkington and Elvin Yeatman Tarkington. Dr. Tarkington continued to practice medicine in Washington after the death of his wife, but left Washington and moved back to the Tarkington farm in Greensburg in 1900 after he became ill. He died on May 1, 1902. "Dr. J. A. Tarkington Dead," *Indianapolis Journal*, May 2, 1902.
6. Larrabie School Records, Archives of DePauw Univ. and Indiana United Methodism.
7. Harding, *History of Decatur County*, 182.
8. Ibid., 183.
9. Ibid., 183–88.
10. Ibid., 188.
11. Charles Sellers, *The Market Revolution: Jacksonian America, 1815–1846* (New York: Oxford Univ. Press, 1991).
12. Joseph could not resist adding that "[i]t would take a whole week for the trip. Now some people would smoke out in tobacco the worth of that load on the trip. But these folks made the trip with no cover on the wagon. The energy of those times has been rewarded with the now fine farms in Randolph, Jay, Adams, and Wells Counties" (Tarkington, *Autobiography*, 143).
13. Nottingham, *Methodism and the Frontier*, 171.
14. Wiley, "Methodism in Southeastern Indiana," 208.

15. Matilda Welch to Augustus Welch, Sept. 3, 184?. The camp meetings and protracted meetings were beginning to wane during this period. In a letter from a Welch family member to Martha Slawson dated Mar. 15, 1861, the writer complained that at a protracted meeting "only four or five gained." James Welch Collection.

16. Bruce, *And They All Sang Hallelujah*, 56.

17. Randy J. Sparks, *On Jordan's Stormy Banks: Evangelicalism in Mississippi, 1773–1876* (Athens: Univ. of Georgia Press, 1994), 97.

18. Indiana Conference Minutes, Archives of DePauw Univ. and Indiana United Methodism.

19. Sparks, *On Jordan's Stormy Banks*, 97–104.

20. Gayle Thornbrough and Paula Corpus, eds., *The Diary of Calvin Fletcher: Including Letters to and from Calvin Fletcher, 1865–1866*, vol. 9 (Indianapolis: Indiana Historical Society, 1983), 132.

21. Christopher H. Owen, "By Design: The Social Meaning of Methodist Church Architecture in Nineteenth-Century Georgia," *Georgia Historical Quarterly* 75 (Summer 1991): 231.

22. Tarkington, *Autobiography*, 141.

23. Ibid.

24. Ibid. By 1852 most churches in the North allowed the sexes to sit together in services whereas they had been segregated in earlier meetings. See Owen, "By Design: The Social Meaning of Methodist Church Architecture," 230.

25. Southeast Indiana Minutes, 1852–1865, Archives of DePauw Univ. and Indiana United Methodism.

26. Ahlstrom, *A Religious History*, 637.

27. For the definitive work on spiritualism, see Ann Braude, *Radical Spirits: Spiritualism and Women's Rights in Nineteenth-Century America* (Boston: Beacon Press, 1989).

28. For an excellent source on Mormonism, see Jan Shipps, *Mormonism: The Story of a New Religious Tradition* (Urbana and Chicago: Univ. of Illinois Press, 1985). Ruth Alden Doan, *The Miller Heresy, Millennialism, and American Culture* (Philadelphia: Temple Univ. Press, 1987), is the best work on Millerism.

29. Jay Monaghan, "Was Abraham Lincoln Really a Spiritualist?" *Journal of the Illinois State Historical Society* 34 (June 1941): 222.

30. Leigh Eric Schmidt, "A Church-going People Are a Dress loving-People: Clothes, Communication, and Religious Culture in Early America," *Church History* 58 (Mar. 1989): 50.

31. Tarkington, *Autobiography*, 17.

32. Sellers, *The Market Revolution*, 155.

33. Owen, "By Design: The Social Meaning of Methodist Church Architecture," 225–37.

34. Richard L. Bushman, *The Refinement of America: Persons, Houses, Cities* (New York: Alfred A Knopf, 1992), 346.

35. Harding, *History of Decatur County*, 212.

36. *Homecoming 1988: Greensburg United Methodist Church, One Hundred Sixty-Five Years of Methodism in Greensburg, 1823 to 1988* (pamphlet), Aug. 27–28, 1988, 2–3.

37. Letter from Mason and Hamlin Organ Company to J. S. Winchester, Feb. 2, 1870, John S. Winchester Correspondence, Indiana Historical Library.

38. Sparks, *On Jordan's Stormy Banks*, 103.

39. Timothy S. Huebner, "Joseph Henry Lumpkin and Evangelical Reform in Georgia: Temperance, Education, and Industrialization, 1830–1860," *Georgia Historical Quarterly* 75 (Summer 1991): 271.

40. Sparks, *On Jordan's Stormy Banks*, 110.

41. In 1872 Switzerland County Commissioner Bela Herrick wrote Augustus Welch a letter claiming it "soures up the old blood in his veins" to witness the fall of the old Federal party for its opposition to the War of 1812. Herrick added that he felt that the Democratic party was so "completely inoculated with treason that it could not survive much longer." He felt that "Greely, Trumbull, Sumner and Co could save the country." Bela Herrick to Augustus Welch, Apr. 2, 1872, James Welch Collection.

42. Dufour, *The Swiss Settlement of Switzerland County*, 163.

43. Harry L. Watson, *Liberty and Power: The Politics of Jacksonian America* (New York: Oxford Univ. Press, 1990), 25.

44. The Whig Party collapsed in 1852 after Gen. Winfield Scott lost the presidential election to Franklin Pierce. The founding of the Republican Party had little to do with moral issues of slavery, but instead with the action of the 1854 Democratic Congress, which let Kansas and Nebraska determine their own status in regard to slavery.

45. These political rallies filled the void that the camp meetings left.

46. Edward Eggleston, *Roxy* (New York: C. Scribner's Sons, 1878), 3.

47. Ibid.

48. William E. Wilson, *Indiana: A History* (Bloomington: Indiana Univ. Press, 1966), 171–72.

49. Watson, *Liberty and Power*, 27.

50. R. Laurence Moore, "Religion, Secularization, and the Shaping of the Culture Industry in Antebellum America," *American Quarterly* 41 (June 1989): 226–27.

51. Ibid., 227.

52. Ibid., 220.

53. Ibid., 221.

CHAPTER NINE. A PREACHER FACES SLAVERY
AND THE CIVIL WAR

1. The Booths had come to Indiana from Connecticut and were originally Congregationalists who were direct descendants of the famous preacher, Thomas Hooker. The Booths departed their faith and joined the Presbyterians after moving to Indiana. Bebee Booth, John Tarkington's father-in-law, had fought in the War of 1812, and John's brother-in-law, Newton Booth, was an attorney in Terre Haute, but left Indiana for California and was elected governor of the state in 1871. In 1875, Newton Booth was elected United States senator.

   Bebee Booth came to Indiana in 1818 at the age of twenty-five, walking from Woodbridge, Connecticut, to Salem, Indiana. His father, Walter Booth, had been an affluent man and gave his son one hundred dollars and his "blessing." Young Booth came to Indiana with a soldering iron and some implements that he used to mend pots and pans. When Booth arrived in Salem, he found friends and work quickly. On May 11, 1818, he married Hannah Pitts, who had come to Salem with her parents from Chatham County, North Carolina. In 1819 the Booths had their first child, Mary. Five additional children were born to the family: Walter (b. 1832), Newton (b. 1825), Lyman (b. 1830), Elizabeth (b. 1833), and Lucius (b. 1838).

Between the years 1818 and 1838, Booth became a prosperous man by building mills and by merchandising items such as clothing and shoes. With the assistance of a friend who was the editor of a local newspaper, he published the first book to be published in Indiana, *The Life of Napoleon*. Booth was also president of the first peace society in the area surrounding Salem, due to the inspiration of some Quaker friends that had moved there because of their anti-slavery beliefs. Around 1850 Booth moved to Terre Haute, Indiana. The National Road that was being built passed through the city. Booth strategically placed stores along the new road and installed his sons as store managers. Booth's chain-store operation was one of the first in history.

John Tarkington and Elizabeth had two children. Mary Booth "Hautie" was born Nov. 11, 1861, and Newton Booth was born July 29, 1869. Newton Booth Tarkington was named in honor of Elizabeth's brother Newton Booth. Booth Tarkington's first novel, *The Gentleman from Indiana* (1899) received moderate attention. His second major work, *Monsieur Beaucaire* (1900), established him as a best-selling novelist. *The Magnificent Ambersons* (1918) and *Alice Adams* (1921) were both Pulitzer Prize winners. However, Tarkington is best remembered for his adolescent novels based on the lives of his sister's sons. *Penrod* (1914), *Seventeen* (1916), *Penrod and Sam* (1916), and *Penrod Jashber* (1929), proved popular with both teenagers and adults.

2. Elmer Croy to Augustus Welch, Aug. 30, 1857, James Welch Collection.

3. Letter from Rose Rankin, Greensburg Public Library, to Dr. W. S. Hendricks of Bristol, Virginia. Daniel Stewart's distant cousin, Thomas A. Hendricks, was "one of the framers of the state convention of 1852." He served two terms in congress 1851–55, and then was appointed commissioner of the U.S. general land office. In 1863 he was elected to the U.S. Senate and in 1872 was elected Governor of Indiana, serving four years. In 1876 he was nominated by Democrats as candidate for vice-president with Tilden but lost when the famous electoral commission ruled for the Republicans "after a number of states were contested." In 1884 Hendricks was again nominated for vice-president on the ticket with Grover Cleveland and was elected, but died after serving six months. See "Colonel Hendricks: Founder of Greensburg Buried in Old Grounds," *Greensburg Daily News*, June 8 1959.

The Hendrickses and Stewarts were Democrats and Presbyterians, as opposed to the Tarkingtons, who were Methodists and have always been staunch Republicans. Daniel Stewart's mother, Mary, named him Daniel in honor of her brother, who had drowned in the Ohio River as the Hendricks family was moving to Indiana in 1821.

4. Daniel and Martha Stewart's daughter Mary became one of the largest contributors to the state of Indiana. She was born March 5, 1859, and lived the first three years of her life in Greensburg. After her parents moved to Indianapolis she grew up in the city. She entered Mount Vernon Seminary in Washington, D.C., in 1875. In 1879, Mary wed John Newman Carey. Because of her stubbornness,

Mary's parents told Carey, "She will have her way." The Careys later named their farm north of Indianapolis "Haverway" as a result of the statement. Mary was a patron of the arts and inspired many Hoosier artists by purchasing their paintings. Some of the better-known artists were Clifton Wheeler, T. C. Steele, William Forsyth, and Wayman Adams ("Museum Gets Carey Paintings," *Indianapolis Star*, 1938). Mary was also a supporter of the Jon Herron Art Institute, giving it twelve paintings from her private collection.

At the end of the nineteenth century, Mary visited Berlin and was impressed with the Germans' rounded street corners. She returned to Indianapolis and persuaded the city officials to utilize the practice in the city (Anton Scherrer, "Memories of the Old Carey Home Which Became the Children's Museum," *Indianapolis News*, Sept. 27, 1948). As a member of the Cornelia Cole Fairbanks chapter of the D.A.R., Mary influenced the state legislature to approve the official state flag of Indiana. She contributed the one-hundred-dollar first prize to Paul Hadley, the designer. Perhaps Mary Carey's greatest contribution was the founding of the Indianapolis Children's Museum.

5. William Simeon Reaves Tarkington married Helena ("Lena"), the daughter of Joseph's brother William Claiborn Tarkington. William Claiborn Tarkington was a prominent Bloomington businessman and was also a member of the state legislature. Matthew Simpson Tarkington married Clare Baker of Greensburg. She was the daughter of a large landholder in Decatur County.

6. Tarkington, *Autobiography*, 140.

7. Curtiss, *Methodism in Shelbyville*, 36.

8. Sweet, *Circuit-Rider Days in Indiana*, 71–72.

9. Ibid., 36–37.

10. Holliday, *Indiana Methodism*, 55.

11. Ibid., 55–59.

12. Sweet, *Circuit Rider Days in Indiana*, 324–25.

13. Bruce, *And They All Sang Hallelujah*, 57.

14. Williams, "Methodist Church Trials in Illinois," 22.

15. Ronald A. Bruger, "Elijah Holmes Pilcher: Methodist Preacher Extraordinary," *Methodist History* 2 (3) (Apr. 1964): 10.

16. Sweet, *Methodism in American History*, 229.

17. Mitchell Snay, *Gospel of Disunion: Religion and Separatism in the Antebellum South* (Cambridge: Cambridge Univ. Press, 1993).

18. Ibid., 30–49.

19. Nottingham, *Methodism and the Frontier*, 139.

20. Homer L. Calkin, "The Slavery Struggle, 1780–1865," in *Those Incredible Methodists: A History of the Baltimore Conference of the United Methodist Church*, ed. Gordon Pratt Baker (Baltimore: Baltimore Commission on Archives and History, The Baltimore Conference, 1972), 193.

21. Matthews, "The Methodist Schism of 1844," 14.

22. Simpson, *Cyclopaedia of Methodism*, 803.

23. Ibid., 803–4.

24. Ibid., 804.

25. Ibid.

26. Ibid.

27. Calkin, "The Slavery Struggle," 194.

28. Clark, Potts, and Payton, *Journal and Letters of Francis Asbury*, 1: 489.
29. Simpson, *Cyclopaedia of Methodism*, 807.
30. Calkin, "The Slavery Struggle," 194–95.
31. Lewis Purifoy, "The Methodist Anti-Slavery Tradition, 1784–1844," *Methodist History* 4 (4) (July 1966): 3.
32. Clark, *History of Kentucky*, 204.
33. Calkin, "The Slavery Struggle," 199.
34. Marie S. White, "The Methodist Antislavery Struggle in the Land of Lincoln," *Methodist History* 10 (4) (July 1972): 35.
35. Tarkington, *Autobiography*, 160–61.
36. Charles Zimmerman, "The Origin and Rise of the Republican Party in Indiana from 1854 to 1860," *Indiana Magazine of History* 13 (3) (Sept. 1917): 251.
37. C. C. Goen, *Broken Churches, Broken Nation: Denomination Schisms and the Coming of the Civil War* (Macon, Ga.: Mercer Univ. Press, 1985), 82.
38. Matthews, "The Methodist Schism of 1844," 16. The principal antagonist in the Andrew controversy was James B. Finley. For a good coverage of Finley's role, see Charles C. Cole Jr., *Lion of the Forrest: James B. Finley, Frontier Reformer* (Lexington: Univ. Press of Kentucky, 1994), 129–61.
39. Goen, *Broken Churches, Broken Nation*, 83.
40. Matthews, "The Methodist Schism of 1844," 16.
41. Simpson, *Cyclopaedia of Methodism*, 600.
42. Diane Winston, "The Southern Baptist Story," in *Southern Baptists Observed: Multiple Perspectives on a Changing Denomination*, ed. Nancy Tatom Ammerman, (Knoxville: Univ. of Tennessee Press, 1993), 12.
43. However, southerners also used the Bible to condone their stand on slavery. See Snay, *Gospel of Disunion*, 54–59.
44. Letter from Stephen Greenleaf to Augustus Welch, Jan. 4, 1861. James Welch Collection.
45. Letter from Stephen Greenleaf to Runy Welch, Nov. 4, 1860. James Welch Collection.
46. Harding, *History of Decatur County, Indiana*, 528–29.
47. Ibid., 420.
48. Ibid., 425–28. It was found that bands were not as essential to the army as supposed. Most of the members of the Greensburg band were sent home in 1862.
49. Letter from John Tarkington to Joseph Tarkington, Apr. 20, 1861, Slawson-Tarkington Papers, Indiana Historical Society.
50. Letter from John Tarkington to William Simeon Reeves Tarkington and Joseph Asbury Tarkington, Sept. 16, 1861, Slawson-Tarkington Papers, Indiana Historical Society.
51. Letter from Daniel Stewart to Joseph Asbury Tarkington, Dec. 19, 1861, Slawson-Tarkington Papers, Indiana Historical Society.
52. Letter from Martha Tarkington Stewart to Joseph Asbury Tarkington, Dec. 15, 1861, Slawson-Tarkington Papers, Indiana Historical Society.
53. Letter from Daniel Stewart to Joseph Asbury Tarkington, Dec. 19, 1861, Slawson-Tarkington Papers, Indiana Historical Society.
54. Hauty, later spelled Hautie, was John and Elizabeth's first child. She was born Nov. 11, 1861. Her actual name was Mary Booth Tarkington.

55. Letter from John Tarkington to Joseph Asbury Tarkington, Jan. 20, 1862, Slawson-Tarkington Papers, Indiana Historical Society.

56. Harding, *History of Decatur County, Indiana*, 430–31.

57. Ibid., 633. After the close of the Civil War, Dr. Alexander returned to Greensburg and practiced medicine. He served fourteen years as secretary of the board of pension examiners. He also functioned as secretary of the county board of health for ten years. John and Mary had two children, John T. and Joseph H., who later became traveling drug salesmen in Indiana and Illinois.

58. Letter from Joseph Tarkington to Martha Slawson, Dec. 23, 1861, Slawson-Tarkington Papers, Indiana Historical Society.

59. Letter from Martha Stewart to William Simeon Reeves Tarkington, Apr. 15, 1862, Slawson-Tarkington Papers, Indiana Historical Society.

60. Ibid.

61. Ibid.

62. Letter from Martha Stewart to Joseph Asbury Tarkington, Mar. 9, 1862, Slawson-Tarkington Papers, Indiana Historical Society.

63. Clark, "Matthew Simpson," 23–33.

64. Clarence True Wilson, "Bishop Matthew Simpson, the Man Who Inspired the Emancipation Proclamation," *Current History* 31 (Oct. 1929–Mar. 1930): 104.

65. Ibid.

66. Ibid.

67. Agreement between David Shaddy and Matilda Welch, Aug. 11, 1863, James Welch Collection.

68. Curtiss, *Methodism in Shelbyville*, 32

69. George Johnson, "Rev. S. B. Chamberlain," *Indiana Weekly Visitor*, Sept. 12, 1863.

70. *South-East Indiana Conference Church Trials, 1859–1937*, Feb. 1, 1864. Archives of DePauw Univ. and Indiana United Methodism.

71. Steventon, *The Auto-Orphan*, 120.

CHAPTER TEN. FINAL YEARS

1. Newspaper clipping, the Slawson-Tarkington Papers, 1804–1911, Indiana Historical Society.

2. Ibid.

3. Letter from Mary Welch to Albert Welch, Sept. 12, 1864, James Welch Collection.

4. M. S. Mahan, "Mrs. Martha Slawson," *Western Christian Advocate*, Oct. 3, 1866.

5. Letter from Mary Welch to Albert Welch, Sept. 12, 1864.

6. Letter from Augustus Welch to Matilda Welch, Jan. 8, 1865. After suffering her injuries, Martha had health problems for the remainder of her life. Arthritis became the main difficulty. Emma Welch visited Martha during the 1920s and reported that she could not address Christmas cards "because of her hands."

7. "Pioneer Minister Passes Away, Death of Rev. Joseph Tarkington, the Oldest Methodist Preacher in Indiana," *Indianapolis Journal* September 23, 1891: n.p.

8. John Tarkington Collection, Indiana Historical Society.

9. Indiana Conference Minutes, 1857, Archives of DePauw Univ. and Indiana United Methodism.

10. South-East Indiana Conference Minutes, Archives of DePauw Univ. and Indiana United Methodism.

11. Letter from F. C. Holliday to T. A. Morris, Feb. 23, 1872, Indiana State Library.

12. South-East Indiana Conference Church Trials. Archives of DePauw Univ. and Indiana United Methodism.

13. Ibid.

14. William Hunt trial, Aug. 2, 1819, Methodist Episcopal Church, Wayne County, Indiana, Lilly Library, Indiana Univ., Bloomington, Indiana.

15. South-East Indiana Conference Trials.

16. "The Week of Prayer," *Madison Daily Courier*, Jan. 8, 1877.

17. *Madison Daily Courier*, Jan. 10, 1877.

18. "Sporting Clergyman," *Greensburg Standard*, n.d.

19. South-East Indiana Conference Trials.

20. Letter from Mary Welch to Albert Welch, Dec. 8, 1866, James Welch Collection.

21. Letter from Mary Welch to Matilda Welch, Nov. 20, 1864, James Welch Collection.

22. Letter from Matilda Welch to Mary Welch, Nov. 28, 1864, James Welch Collection.

23. Letter from Augustus Welch to Matilda Welch, Nov. 30, 1865, James Welch Collection.

24. Letter from Matilda Welch to Albert Welch, May 27, 1867, James Welch Collection.

25. Letter from Augustus Welch to Matilda Welch, Dec. 4, 1865, James Welch Collection.

26. Letter from Joseph A. Tarkington to Mary Welch, Feb. 4, 1867, James Welch Collection.

27. Letter from Albert Welch to Augustus and Matilda Welch, Sept. 8, 1868, James Welch Collection.

28. Letter from Mary Welch to Albert Welch, Dec. 8, 1866, James Welch Collection.

29. Early in the 1870s citizens of Greensburg began to notice that a tree was growing out of the roof of their courthouse. As time passed the tree continued to grow and reached a height of fifteen feet. In 1888 the tree was trimmed out of fear that the tree would damage the tower roof. A sprout of the original tree continues to grow and can be seen at a great distance from the city. The tree is of the large tooth aspen variety, and people have traveled to Greensburg from virtually every state in the Union and many foreign countries to see it. Greensburg occupies a unique place in the cities of the world with its famous and uncommon tower tree.

30. Letter from Mollie Welch to Albert Welch, Nov. 19, 1871. Emma Welch returned to Switzerland County to the Welch homestead and never married. Ninety-year-old Dorothy Slawson Manuel told me that Emma was "set in her way" and would never have married. In her later years Emma became very heavyset and used a tobacco stick as a cane. Interview with Dorothy Slawson Manuel, May 16, 1995, Lawrenceville, Illinois.

31. Letter from Mollie Welch to Albert Welch, Nov. 19, 1871.

32. "Just Fifty Years Ago," *Greensburg Standard*, Sept. 21, 1881.

33. *Saturday Review*, Sept. 24, 1881.

34. Ibid., n.p.

35. Dr. William Bracken was a respected doctor in Decatur County. He first lived and

practiced medicine in Milroy, but moved to Greensburg in 1863. He served the community until he reached the age of eighty.

36. Joseph Tarkington Diary, Jan. 1–3, 1888.
37. Letter from John Tarkington to Joseph Tarkington, n.d.
38. Letter from Wellenden, Lathrup, and Chafee to Joseph Tarkington, Morristown, Indiana, June 5, 1888, Slawson-Tarkington Papers, Indiana Historical Society. I may have misspelled the names of the authors because of the difficulty in reading their signatures.
39. Letter from Joseph Tarkington to John and Matthew Tarkington, Dec. 15, 1888, Slawson-Tarkington Papers, Indiana Historical Society.
40. Susanah Mayberry, My Amiable Uncle: Recollections about Booth Tarkington (West Lafayette: Purdue Univ. Press, 1983), 18.
41. According to Booth Tarkington's niece, Patricia Cochran of Indianapolis, he had been placed in the academy by his father for disciplinary reasons. While living in Indianapolis, Tarkington attended Shortridge High School but was bored with his teachers. He felt that he was superior to his instructors and started "playing hookey." As a result, John Tarkington sent him to the Phillips Exeter Academy.
42. Booth Tarkington, "As I Seem to Me," Saturday Evening Post, Aug. 9, 1941, 51.
43. Ibid., 61.
44. Ibid., 51.
45. Ibid., 50–51.
46. Joseph Tarkington Diary, Dec. 15, 1889.
47. Mayberry, My Amiable Uncle, 19.
48. Minutes of the South-East Indiana Conference, 275.
49. Joseph Tarkington Diary, Dec. 18, 1889.
50. Letter from John Ray to Joseph Tarkington, Apr. 8, 1891.
51. Joseph Tarkington Diary (entered by Tarkington's daughter Martha Stewart), Sept. 18, 1891.
52. Ibid., Sept. 19, 1891.
53. Ibid., Sept. 21, 1891.
54. Ibid., Sept. 22, 1891.
55. Minutes of the South East Indiana Conference, 402.
56. Telegram from R. A. Kemp to Joseph Tarkington, Sept. 21, 1891.
57. "Pioneer Minister Passes Away: Death of Reverend Joseph Tarkington, the Oldest Methodist Preacher in Indiana," Indianapolis Journal, Sept. 23, 1891.

CONCLUSION

1. Finke and Stark, "How the Upstart Sects Won America," 31.
2. Hatch, "The Puzzle of American Methodism," 3.
3. Jon Butler, Awash in a Sea of Faith: Christianizing the American People (Cambridge, Mass.: Harvard Univ. Press, 1990), 291.
4. Wiley, "Methodism in Southeastern Indiana," 208
5. Bushman, The Refinement of America, 346.
6. Ibid., 348.

Selected Bibliography

Ahlstrom, Sydney E. *A Religious History of the American People*. New Haven: Yale Univ. Press, 1972.

Albanese, Catherine. "Savage Sinner, and Saved: Davy Crockett, Camp Meetings, and the Wild Frontier." *American Quarterly* 33 (1981): 482–501.

Amick, George. "Post Roads in Southern Indiana." *Indiana Magazine of History* 30 (4) (Dec. 1934): 331–34.

Batterson, Henry. Notebook. 1825. Archives of DePauw Univ. and Indiana United Methodism.

Berkey, Lennie Martin. "Friendship Church." *Indiana Magazine of History* 30 (3) (Sept. 1934): 238–41.

Bolling, Margaret. "Hamline Historical Highlights" (pamphlet). Hamline Chapel United Methodism, Lawrenceburg, Indiana, Sept. 20, 1981.

Braude, Ann. *Radical Spirits: Spiritualism and Women's Rights in Nineteenth-Century America*. Boston: Beacon Press, 1989.

Brauer, Jerald C. "Conversion from Puritanism to Revivalism." *The Journal of Religion* 58 (3) (1978): 227–43.

Bridges, Albert Fletcher. "Early Methodism in Clay County." *Indiana Magazine of History* 20 (2) (June 1924): 160–73.

Bruce, Dickson D. *And They All Sang Hallelujah: Plain-Folk Camp Meeting Religion, 1800–1845*. Knoxville: Univ. of Tennessee Press, 1974.

Bruger, Ronald A. "Elijah Holmes Pilcher: Methodist Preacher Extraordinary." *Methodist History* 2 (3) (Apr. 1964): 10–23.

Buley, F. Carlyle. *The Old Northwest: Pioneer Period, 1815–1840*, 2 vols. Bloomington: Indiana Univ. Press, 1950.

Burnett, Ivan Jr. "Methodist Origins: John Wesley and Alcohol." *Methodist History* 13 (4) (July 1975): 3–17.

Burns, Harrison. *Personal Recollections of Harrison Burns as written in 1907*. Indianapolis: Indiana Historical Society, 1975.

Bushman, Richard L. *The Refinement of America: Persons, Houses, Cities*. New York: Alfred A Knopf, 1992.

Butler, Jon. *Awash in a Sea of Faith: Christianizing the American People*. Cambridge: Harvard Univ. Press, 1990.

Byrne, Donald E. *No Foot Of Land: Folklore of American Methodist Itinerants*. Metuchen, N.J.: Scarecrow Press, 1975.

Calkin, Homer L. "The Slavery Struggle, 1780–1865." In *Those Incredible Methodists: A History of the Baltimore Conference of the United Methodist Church*, edited by Gordon Pratt Baker, 192–228. Baltimore: Baltimore Commission on Archives and History, The Baltimore Conference, 1972.

Cartwright, Peter. *The Backwoods Preacher: Being the Autobiography of Peter Cartwright, an American Travelling Preacher*. London: Alexander Heylin, 1858.

Carwardine, Richard J. *Evangelicals and Politics in Antebellum America*. New Haven: Yale Univ. Press, 1993.

Cecil-Fronsman, Bill. *Common Whites: Class and Culture in Antebellum North Carolina*. Lexington: Univ. Press of Kentucky, 1992.

Chandler, Douglass R. "Growth and Consolidation." In *Those Incredible Methodists: A History of the Baltimore Conference of the United Methodist Church*, edited by Gordon Pratt Baker, 83–120. Baltimore: Baltimore Commission on Archives and History, The Baltimore Conference, 1972.

Clark, Elmer T., J. Manning Potts, and Jacob S. Payton, eds. *The Journal and Letters of Francis Asbury*, 3 vols. Nashville: Abingdon Press, 1958.

Clark, Robert D. "Matthew Simpson, the Methodists, and the Defeat of Governor Samuel Bigger, 1843." *Indiana Magazine of History* 50 (1) (1954): 23–33.

Clark, Thomas D. *A History of Kentucky*. Lexington: The John Bradford Press, 1960.

———. *Pills, Petticoats, and Plows: The Southern Country Store*. Norman, Oklahoma: Univ. of Oklahoma Press, 1944.

Cole, Charles C. *Lion of the Forest: James B. Finley, Frontier Reformer*. Lexington: Univ. Press of Kentucky, 1994.

"Colonel Hendricks Founder of Greensburg Buried in Old Grounds." *Greensburg Daily News*, June 8, 1959, 2.

Conkin, Paul. *Cane Ridge: America's Pentecost*. Madison: Univ. of Wisconsin Press, 1990.

Cott, Nancy F. "Passionlessness: An Interpretation of Victorian Sexual Ideology, 1790–1850." *Signs* 4 (Winter 1978): 219–36.

Croy, Elmer. Letter to Augustus Welch, Aug. 30, 1857, James Welch Collection.

Curtiss, George L. *A Monograph of Methodism in Shelbyville*. Shelbyville, Indiana: n.p., 1878.

Doan, Ruth Alden. *The Miller Heresy: Millennialism and American Culture*. Philadelphia: Temple Univ. Press, 1987.

Douglass, Alexander. Diary. Archives of DePauw Univ. and Indiana United Methodism.

Dufour, Perret. *The Swiss Settlement of Switzerland County Indiana*. Indianapolis: Indiana Historical Commission, 1925.

Dunnavant, Anthony L., editor. *Cane Ridge in Context: Perspectives on Barton W. Stone and the Revival*. Nashville: Disciples of Christ Historical Society, 1992.

Edmunds, R. David. *Tecumseh and the Quest for Indian Leadership*. Boston: Little, Brown, and Company, 1984.

Eggleston, Edward. *The Circuit Rider: A Tale of the Heroic Age*. New York: J. B. Ford and Company, 1874.

————. *The Hoosier Schoolmaster: An Engaging Story of Life in a Backwoods Village of Indiana in the 1850's*. New York: Orange Judd, 1871.

————. *Roxy*. New York: C. Scribner's Sons, 1878.

Faragher, John Mack. *Sugar Creek: Life on the Illinois Prairie*. New Haven and London: Yale Univ. Press, 1986.

Finke, Roger, and Rodney Stark. *The Churching of America, 1776–1990: Winner and Losers in Our Religious Economy*. New Brunswick, N.J.: Rutgers Univ. Press, 1992.

————. "How the Upstart Sects Won America: 1776–1850." *Journal for the Scientific Study of Religion* 28 (1) (Mar. 1989): 27–44.

Finley, James B. *Autobiography of Rev. James B. Finley: or, Pioneer Life in the West*. Cincinnati: Cranston and Curts, 1853.

————. *Sketches of Western Methodism: Biographical, Historical, and Miscellaneous, Illustrative of Pioneer Life*. Cincinnati: Methodist Book Concern, 1856.

Ford, Lacy. *Origins of Southern Radicalism: The South Carolina Upcountry, 1800–1860*. New York: Oxford Univ. Press, 1988.

Gaddis, Maxwell Pierson. *Footprints of an Itinerant*. Cincinnati: Methodist Book Concern, 1856.

Gaddis, Maxwell Pierson, editor, *The Ohio Conference Offering: or Sermons and Sketches of Sermons, on Familiar and Practical Subjects, from the Living and the Dead, in Two Parts*. Cincinnati: Methodist Book Concern, 1851.

Ginzberg, Lori D. "Women in an Evangelical Community: Oberlin 1835– 1850." *Ohio History* 89 (1980): 78–88.

Goodspeed, Weston A. "History of Monroe County." In *Counties of Morgan, Monroe, and Brown, Indiana: Historical and Biographical*, edited by Charles Blanchard. Chicago: F. A. Battery and Co., Publishers, 1884.

Grant, Helen Hardie. *Peter Cartwright: Pioneer*. New York: Abingdon Press, 1931.

Graves, Lloyd Milner. "My Indiana Homestead: Symbol of an Epoch That Was." *Indiana Magazine of History* 36 (2) (June 1940): 95–109.

Greenleaf, Stephen. Letter to Augustus Welch, Jan. 4, 1861, James Welch Collection.

————. Letter to Runy Welch, Nov. 4, 1860, James Welch Collection.

Griffith, Ella Porter. "Joshua Griffith: Pioneer Preacher." *Indiana Magazine of History* 36 (1) (Mar. 1940): 34–42.

Guernsey, E. Y. "Indian Depredations." *Indiana History Bulletin* July 1, 1924, 17–18.

Hall, Baynard Rush. *The New Purchase*. New Albany, Ind.: J. R. Nunemacher, 1855.

Harding, Lewis A., editor, *History of Decatur County Indiana: Its People, Industries and Institutions*. Indianapolis: B. F. Bowen and Company, 1915.

Harris, Bro. "Reminiscences." *VeVay Reveille*, May 27, 1897.

Hatch, Nathan O. *The Democratization of American Christianity.* New Haven and London: Yale Univ. Press, 1989.

———. "The Puzzle of American Methodism," Paper presented for the Wesley/Holiness Center, "Methodism and the Shaping of American Culture, 1760–1860," Oct. 7–8, 1994, Asbury Theological Seminary, Wilmore, Kentucky.

Hawkins, Hubert H. *Indiana's Road to Statehood.* Indianapolis: Indiana Historical Bureau, 1969.

Herrick, Bela. Letter to Augustus Welch, Apr. 2, 1872, James Welch Collection.

Hester, George K. Diary. Archives of DePauw Univ. and Indiana United Methodism.

Hofstra, Warren R. and Robert D. Mitchell. "Town and Country in Backcountry Virginia: Winchester and the Shenandoah Valley, 1730–1800." *Journal of Southern History* 59 (4) (Nov. 1993): 619–46.

Hogue, Rolla M. "Life in Indiana, 1800–1820." *Indiana Magazine of History* 9 (1913): 83–92.

Holliday, F. C. *Indiana Methodism: Being an Account of the Introduction, Progress, and Present Position of Methodism in the State; and also a History of the Literary Institutions Under the Care of the Church, with Sketches of the Principal Methodist Educators in the State, Down to 1872.* Cincinnati: Hitchcock and Walden, 1873.

———. *Life and Times of Rev. Allen Wiley, A.M. containing Sketches of Early Methodist Preachers in Indiana, and Notices of the Introduction and Progress of Methodism in the State; also including his Original Letters, Entitled, "A Help to the Performance of Ministerial Duties."* Cincinnati: L. Swormstedt and A. Poe, 1853.

———. Letter to T. A. Morris, Feb. 23, 1872, Indiana State Library.

Homecoming 1988: Greensburg United Methodist Church, One Hundred Sixty-Five Years of Methodism in Greensburg, 1823 to 1988 (pamphlet). Aug. 27–28, 1988.

Hopkins, T. M. "Reminiscences of Colonel John Ketcham of Monroe County, Indiana." In *The Garland Library of Narratives of North American Indiana Captivities*, edited by Wilcomb E. Washburn. New York: Garland Publishing Company, 1977.

Huebner, Timothy S. "Joseph Henry Lumpkin and Evangelical Reform in Georgia: Temperance, Education, and Industrialization, 1830–1860." *Georgia Historical Quarterly* 75 (Summer 1991): 254–74.

Hunt, William. Trial transcript, Aug. 2, 1891, Methodist Episcopal Church, Wayne County, Indiana, Lilly Library, Indiana Univ., Bloomington, Indiana.

Iglehart, John E. "The Life and Times of John Shrader." *Indiana Magazine of History* 17 (1) (Mar. 1921): 3–49.

Illinois Conference Minutes, 1824–1835. Archives of DePauw Univ. and Indiana United Methodism.

Indiana Conference Minutes. Archives of DePauw Univ. and Indiana United Methodism.

Indiana Conference Trials. Archives of DePauw Univ. and Indiana United Methodism.

Isaac, Rhys. "Evangelical Revolt: The Nature of the Baptists' Challenge to the Traditional Order of Virginia, 1765 to 1775." *William and Mary Quarterly* 3d ser., 31 (July 1974): 345–68.

James, Larry M. "Biracial Fellowship in Antebellum Baptist Churches." In *Masters and Slaves in the House of the Lord: Race and Religion in the American South, 1740–1870*, edited by John Boles, 37–57. Lexington: Univ. Press of Kentucky, 1988.

Jameson, Margaret Booth. Jameson Family Notes. Private collection of Patricia Cochran.

Jensen, Richard. "The Religious and Occupational Roots of Party Identification: Illinois and Indiana in the 1870's." *Civil War History* 16 (4) (Dec. 1970): 325–43.

Johnson, George. "Rev. S. B. Chamberlain." *Indiana Weekly Visitor*, Sept. 12, 1863.

"Just Fifty Years Ago." *Greensbury Standard*, Sept. 21, 1881.

Kemp, R. A. Telegram to Joseph Tarkington. Sept. 21, 1891, Slawson-Tarkington Papers, Indiana Historical Society.

Kimbrough, David L. "Solomon and Sarah Saylor: The Emergence of Lay Religion in Eastern Kentucky." *Appalachian Heritage* 21 (3) (Summer 1993): 49–57.

Knox, Julia Leclerc. "Vevay and Switzerland County." *Indiana Magazine of History* 11 (3) (Sept. 1915): 216–30.

Larrabie School Records. Archives of DePauw Univ. and Indiana United Methodism.

Lawlis, Chelsea L. "Prosperity and Hard Times in the Whitewater Valley, 1830–1840." *Indiana Magazine of History* 43 (1) (Mar. 1947): 23–40.

Lawrenceburg Methodist Episcopal Church Records. Archives of DePauw Univ. and Indiana United Methodism.

Leak, Roscoe R. "Salem Methodist Church." *Indiana Magazine of History* 29 (1) (Mar. 1933): 17–21.

Ledbetter, Robert E., Jr. "Orceneth Fisher: Pioneer Methodist Preacher of Texas and the Pacific Coast." M.A. thesis, Univ. of Texas, 1938.

Legan, Marshall Scott. "Popular Reactions to the New Madrid Earthquakes, 1811–1812." *The Filson Club Historical Quarterly* 50 (1) (Jan. 1976): 60–71.

Luke, Eva Elizabeth. "Our Contributors: The Centennial of Indiana Methodism." *Western Christian Advocate*, Sept. 17, 1902.

Madison Daily Courier, Jan. 10, 1877.

Mahan, W. S. "Mrs. Martha Slawson." *Western Christian Advocate*, Oct. 3, 1866.

Mason and Hamlin Organ Company. Letter to J. S. Winchester, Feb. 2, 1870. John S. Winchester Correspondence, Indiana Historical Library.

Matthews, Donald G. "The Methodist Schism of 1844 and the Popularization of Antislavery Sentiment." *Mid America* 51 (1) (Jan. 1968): 3–23.

Mayberry, Susanah. *My Amiable Uncle: Recollections about Booth Tarkington*. West Lafayette, Ind.: Purdue Univ. Press, 1983.

McCormick, Marie Wittenmeyer. "The History of Asbury Chapel Methodist Church." Archives of DePauw Univ. and Indiana United Methodism.

McLoughlin, William G. "Pietism and the American Character." *American Quarterly* 17 (2) pt. 1 (Summer 1965): 163–86.

Mills, Frederick V. "Mentors of Methodism, 1784–1844." *Methodist History* 12 (1) (Oct. 1973): 43–57.

Monaghan, Jay. "Was Abraham Lincoln Really a Spiritualist?" *Journal of the Illinois State Historical Society* 34 (June 1941): 207–32.

Monk, Robert C. "Educating Oneself for Ministry: Francis Asbury's Reading Patterns." *Methodist History* 29 (3) (Apr. 1991): 140–54.

Montagna, Douglass. Ph.D. diss., Northern Illinois Univ., 1996.

Moore, R. Laurence. "Religion, Secularization, and the Shaping of the Culture Industry in Antebellum American." *American Quarterly* 41 (June 1989): 216–42.

Mullen, Patrick B. "Ritual and Sacred Narratives in the Blue Ridge Mountains." *Papers in Comparative Studies* (Ohio State Univ.), 2 (1983): 17–38.

"Museum Gets Carey Paintings." *Indianapolis News*, Sept. 27, 1948.

Nisbit, Alfred Berry. Diary. Archives of DePauw Univ. and Indiana United Methodism.

North Indiana Conference. Archives of DePauw Univ. and Indiana United Methodism.

Nottingham, Elizabeth K. *Methodism and the Frontier: Indiana Proving Ground.* New York: Columbia Univ. Press, 1941.

Owen, Christopher H. "By Design: The Social Meaning of Methodist Church Architecture in Nineteenth Century Georgia." *Georgia Historical Quarterly* 75 (Summer 1991): 221–53.

Parker, Benjamin S. "Pioneer Life." *Indiana Magazine of History* 3 (1) (Mar. 1907): 1–11.

———. "Pioneer Life." *Indiana Magazine of History* 3 (2) (Mar. 1907): 51–57.

———. "Pioneer Life." *Indiana Magazine of History* 3 (3) (Mar. 1907): 125–32.

"Pioneer Minister Passes Away, Death of Rev. Joseph Tarkington, the Oldest Methodist Preacher in Indiana." *Indianapolis Journal*, Sept. 23, 1891.

Pocock, Emil. "Reverend James Welsh on Three Frontiers, 1790–1825." *Indiana Magazine of History* 86 (4) (Dec. 1990): 347–73.

Posey, Walter Brownlow. *The Development of Methodism in the Old Southwest: 1783–1824.* Ph.D. diss., Vanderbilt Univ., 1933.

Price, Ruth. "Indiana Methodism." *Indiana Magazine of History* 11 (3) (Sept. 1915): 231–47.

Purifoy, Lewis M. "The Methodist Anti-Slavery Tradition, 1784–1844." *Methodist History* 4 (4) (July 1966): 3–16.

Rankin, Rose. Letter to Dr. W. S. Hendricks, n.d.

Ray, John. Letter to Joseph Tarkington, Apr. 8, 1891. Slawson-Tarkington Papers, Indiana Historical Society.

Reed, Isaac. "The Christian Traveler, 1828." In *Indiana As Seen by Early Travelers: A Collection of Reprints from Books of Travel, Letters and Diaries Prior to 1830*, edited by Harlow Lindley, 463–505. Indianapolis: Indiana Historical Commission, 1916.

"Richard Posey Early Pastor in Bruceville: History Places Methodists at Bruceville in 1820." *Vincennes Sun Commercial*, Aug. 1, 1954.

Richey, Russell E. *Early American Methodism.* Bloomington: Indiana Univ. Press, 1991.

Rifkin, Jeremy, with Ted Howard. *The Emerging Order: God in the Age of Scarcity.* New York: G. P. Putnam's Sons, 1979.

Riley, Glenda. *The Female Frontier: A Comparative View of Women on the Prairie and the Plains.* Lawrence: Univ. Press of Kansas, 1988.

Rosenberg, Charles E. *The Cholera Years: The United States in 1832, 1849, and 1866.* Chicago: Univ. of Chicago Press, 1962.

Rothert, Otto A. "The Harpes, Two Outlaws of Pioneer Times." *The (Filson) History Quarterly* 4 (1) (July 1927): 155–63.

Rudolph, L. C. *Hoosier Zion: The Presbyterians in Early Indiana.* New Haven: Yale Univ. Press, 1963.

Saturday Review, Sept. 24, 1881.

Saunders, William L., editor. *The Colonial Records of North Carolina.* Raleigh: The State of North Carolina, 1886.

Schell, Edwin A. "Support of the Bishops in Early American Methodism." *Methodist History* 4 (3) (Apr. 1966): 42–50.

Scherrer, Anton. "Memories of the Old Carey Home which Became the Children's Museum." *Indianapolis News*, Sept. 27, 1948.

Schmidt, Leigh Eric. "A Church-going People Are a Dress-loving People: Clothes, Communication, and Religious Culture in Early America." *Church History* 58 (Mar. 1989): 36–51.

———. *Holy Fairs: Scottish Communions and American Revivals in the Early Modern Period.* Princeton: Princeton Univ. Press, 1989.

Schneider, A Gregory. *The Way of the Cross Leads Home: The Domestication of American Methodism.* Bloomington: Indiana Univ. Press, 1993.

Sellers, Charles. *The Market Revolution: Jacksonian America, 1815–1846.* New York: Oxford Univ. Press, 1991.

Shaddy, David. Written agreement with Matilda Welch, Aug. 11, 1863. James Welch Collection.

Shiels, Richard. "The Feminization of American Congregationalism." *American Quarterly* 33 (Spring 1981): 46–62.

Shiplett, Gary R., editor. "The History of Cross Roads Methodist Church, 1821–1971." Sesquicentennial edition (pamphlet).

Shipps, Jan. *Mormonism: The Story of a Religious Tradition.* Urbana and Chicago: Univ. of Illinois Press, 1985.

Silver Creek Quarterly Conference Minutes, Archives of DePauw Univ. and Indiana United Methodism.

Simpson, Matthew. *Cyclopaedia of Methodism.* Philadelphia: Evarts and Stewart, 1878.

Slawson, Maluda. Letter to Augustus Welch, May 22, 1842. James Welch Collection.

Slawson, Martha. Letter to an unnamed nephew, Nov. 16, 1834. Indiana Historical Society. James Welch Collection.

Slawson, Simeon. Letter to an unnamed nephew, November 16, 1834. Indiana Historical Society.

———. Letter to Augustus Welch, May 22, 1842. James Welch Collection.

———. Letter to Augustus Welch, Jan. 21, 1846. James Welch Collection.

Smith, J. C. *Reminiscences of Early Methodism in Indiana.* Indianapolis: J. M. Olcott, 1879.

Smith, John L. *Indiana Methodism: A Series of Sketches and Incidents, Grave and Humorous Concerning Preachers and People of the West.* Valparaiso: n.p., 1892.

Snay, Mitchell. *Gospel of Disunion: Religion and Separatism in the Antebellum South*. Cambridge: Cambridge Univ. Press, 1993.

Snively, W. D., and Louanna Furbee. *Satan's Ferryman: A True Tale Of The Old Frontier*. New York: Frederick Ungar Publishing Company, 1968.

Southeast Indiana Minutes, 1852–1865. Archives of DePauw Univ. and Indiana United Methodism.

Sparks, Randy J. *On Jordan's Stormy Banks: Evangelicalism in Mississippi, 1773–1876*. Athens and London: Univ. of Georgia Press, 1994.

"Sporting Clergyman." *Greensbury Standard*, n.d.

Stephenson, Frank W. "The Development of the Methodist Church Particularly in the Midwest." *Methodist History* 3 (1) (Oct. 1964): 33–42.

Stewart, Daniel. Letter to Joseph Asbury Tarkington, Dec. 18, 1861. Indiana Historical Society.

Stewart, Martha Tarkington. Letter to Joseph Asbury Tarkington, Dec. 15, 1861. Indiana Historical Society.

———. Letter to Joseph Asbury Tarkington, Mar. 9, 1862. Indiana Historical Society.

———. Letter to William Simeon Reeves Tarkington, Apr. 15, 1862. Indiana Historical Society.

Strozier, Charles B. *Lincoln's Quest for Union: Public and Private Meanings*. New York: Basic Books, 1982.

Sweet, Leonard I. *The Minister's Wife: Her Role in Nineteenth-Century American Evangelicalism*. Philadelphia: Temple Univ. Press, 1983.

Sweet, William Warren. "The Churches As Moral Courts of the Frontier." *Church History* 2 (Jan. 1933): 3–21.

———. *Circuit-Rider Days in Indiana*. Indianapolis: W. K. Stewart Company, 1916.

———. "Early Methodist Circuits in Indiana." *Indiana Magazine of History* 10 (3) (Sept. 1914): 359–68.

———. *Methodism in American History*. New York: Methodist Book Concern, 1933.

———. *Religion on the American Frontier, 1783–1840*, vol. 4, *The Methodists*. New York: Cooper Square, 1964.

Tarkington, Maria Slawson. Letter to Joseph Tarkington, October 23, 1843. Indiana Historical Society.

Tarkington, John S. (pseudonym John Steventon). *The Auto-Orphan*. Boston: Gorham Press, 1913.

———. Collection. Indiana Historical Society.

———. Letter to Emma Welch. Mar. 11, 1914. Welch Family Collection. Vevay, Indiana. Contributed by James Welch.

———. Letter to Joseph Asbury Tarkington, Jan. 20, 1862. Slawson-Tarkington Papers, Indiana Historical Society.

———. Letter to Joseph Tarkington, Apr. 20, 1861. Slawson-Tarkington Papers, Indiana Historical Society.

———. Letter to Joseph Tarkington, n.d. Slawson-Tarkington Papers, Indiana Historical Society.

———. Letter to Simeon Slawson. Nov. 2, 1855. Firestone Library, Princeton Univ.

—————. Letter to William Simeon Reeves Tarkington and Joseph Asbury Tarkington, Sept. 16, 1861. Indiana Historical Society.

Tarkington, Joseph. *Autobiography of Rev. Joseph Tarkington, One of the Pioneer Methodist Preachers of Indiana*. Cincinnati: Curts and Jennings, 1899.

—————. Diary, 3 vols., 1888–1891. Indiana Historical Society.

—————. Letter to John and Matthew Simpson Tarkington, Dec. 15, 1888. Indiana Historical Society.

—————. Letter to Martha Slawson, Dec. 23, 1861. Indiana Historical Society.

Tarkington, Joseph A. Letter to Mary Welch, Feb. 4, 1867. James Welch Collection.

Tarkington, Newton Booth. "As I Seem to Me." *Saturday Evening Post*, Aug. 9, 1941, 47–54.

Thornbrough, Emma Lou. *The Negro in Indiana Before 1900: A Study of a Minority*. Indianapolis: Indiana Historical Society Publications, vol. 37, 1957.

Thornbrough, Gayle, and Paula Corpus, eds., *The Diary of Calvin Fletcher: Including Letters to and from Calvin Fletcher, 1865–1866*. Indianapolis: Indiana Historical Society, vol. 9, 1983.

Thurman, Helen. "The Fall Creek Tragedy." *Indiana Magazine of History* 27 (3) (Sept. 1931): 230–35.

Townsend, Newton. "His Spirit Was Willing." *Tennessee Historical Quarterly* 21 (1962): 275–86.

"Trinity Methodist Church Born in Log Cabin Called Simply, 'The Meetin' House.'" *Vincennes Sun Commercial*, Aug. 1, 1954.

Vernal Baptist Church Records, Jan. 1819–July 7, 1855. Lilly Library, Indiana Univ., Bloomington, Indiana.

Vevay Methodist Church Records. Archives of DePauw Univ. and Indiana United Methodism.

Viitanen, Wayne. "The Winter the Mississippi Ran Backwards: Early Kentuckians Report the New Madrid, Missouri, Earthquake of 1811–12." *Register of the Kentucky Historical Society* 71 (1) (Jan. 1973): 51–68.

Vogel, William Frederick. "Home Life in Early Indiana." *Indiana Magazine of History* 10 (2) (June 1914): 1–29.

—————. "Home Life in Early Indiana." *Indiana Magazine of History* 10 (3) (Sept. 1914): 284–320.

Waldenmaier, Benj. C. "The Welch Family." *Vevay Reveille-Enterprise*, Dec. 14, 1934.

Walker, Joseph Wheeler. "Hoosier Pioneers." *Indiana Magazine of History* 20 (1) (Mar. 1924): 62–91.

Waters, Margaret R. *Indiana Land Entries Vincennes District, 1807–1877*, 3d Printing. Knightstown, Ind.: The Bookmark 1980.

Watkins, Samuel W. "The Causes and Cure of Earthquakes: Methodists and the New Madrid Earthquakes, 1811–1812." *Methodist History* 30 (4) (July 1992): 242–50.

Watson, Harry L. *Liberty and Power: The Politics of Jacksonian America*. New York: Oxford Univ. Press, 1990.

"The Week of Prayer." *Madison Daily Courier*, Jan. 8, 1877.

Welch, Albert. Letter to Augustus and Matilda Slawson Welch, September 8, 1868.

Welch, Augustus. Letter to Matilda Slawson Welch, Mar. 16, 1843. James Welch Collection.

———. Letter to Matilda Slawson Welch, Jan. 8, 1865.

———. Letter to Matilda Slawson Welch, Dec. 4, 1865

Welch, Emma. "Welch Family Notes." James Welch Collection.

Welch Family Member (Unknown). Letter to Martha Slawson, March 15, 1861. James Welch Collection.

Welch, Mary. Letter to Albert Welch, Sept. 12, 1864. James Welch Collection.

———. Letter to Albert Welch, Dec. 8, 1866. James Welch Collection.

———. Letter to Matilda Welch, Nov. 20, 1864. James Welch Collection.

Welch, Matilda Slawson. Letter to Albert Welch, May 27, 1867. James Welch Collection.

———. Letter to Augustus Welch, July 17, 1842. James Welch Collection.

———. Letter to Augustus Welch, Feb. 14, 1846. James Welch Collection.

———. Letter to Augustus Welch, Sept. 3, 184?. James Welch Collection.

Welch, Mollie. Letter to Albert Welch, Nov. 19, 1871. James Welch Collection.

Wellenden, Lathrup, and Chafee. Letter to Joseph Tarkington, June 5, 1888. Slawson-Tarkington Papers, Indiana Historical Society.

Western Christian Advocate, Nov. 7, 1834.

———. June 26, 1835.

White, Marie. "The Methodist Antislavery Struggle in the Land of Lincoln." *Methodist History* 10 (4) (July 1972): 33–52.

Whorrall, Bill, with contributions by Stephen Harold Riggins and Thomas E. Rodgers. *A Photographic History of Martin County: Indiana Album*. Shoals: published by the author, 1993.

Wigger, John. "Taking Heaven By Storm." *Journal of the Early Republic* 14 (Summer 1994): 167–94.

Wiley, Allen. "Introduction and Progress of Methodism in Southeastern Indiana." *Indiana Magazine of History* 23 (3) (Sept. 1927): 239–332.

———. "Introduction and Progress of Methodism in Southeastern Indiana." *Indiana Magazine of History* 23 (4) (Dec. 1927): 393–466.

———. "Methodism in Southeastern Indiana." *Indiana Magazine of History* 23 (1) (Mar. 1927): 3–64.

———. "Methodism in Southeastern Indiana." *Indiana Magazine of History* 23 (2) (June 1927): 130–216.

Williams, John Hoyt. *Sam Houston: A Biography of the Father of Texas*. New York: Simon and Schuster, 1993.

Williams, Robert H. "Methodist Church Trials in Illinois." *Methodist History* 1 (1) (Oct. 1962): 14–32.

Wilson, Clarence True. "Bishop Matthew Simpson, the Man Who Inspired the Emancipation Proclamation." *Current History* 31 (Oct. 1929–Mar. 1930): 99–106.

Wilson, William E. *The Angel and the Serpent: The Story of New Harmony*. Bloomington: Indiana Univ. Press, 1964

———. *Indiana: A History*. Bloomington: Indiana Univ. Press, 1966.

Winston, Diane. "The Southern Baptist Story." In *Southern Baptists Observed: Multiple Perspectives on a Changing Denomination*, edited by Nancy Tatom Ammerman, 12–29. Knoxville: Univ. of Tennessee Press, 1993.

Wood, Aaron. *Sketches of Things and Peoples in Indiana*. Indianapolis: J. M. Olcott, Publisher, 1883.

Woodburn, James A. "James Woodburn: Hoosier Schoolmaster." *Indiana Magazine of History* 32 (3) (Sept. 1936): 231–47.

———. "Local Life and Color in the New Purchase." *Indiana Magazine of History* 9 (4) (Dec. 1913): 215–33.

Wyatt-Brown, Bertram. *Southern Honor: Ethics and Behavior in the Old South*. New York: Oxford Univ. Press, 1982.

Young, Jacob. *Autobiography of a Pioneer: Or the Nativity, Experiences, Travels, and Ministerial Labors of Rev. Jacob Young, with Incidents, Observations, and Reflections*. Cincinnati: Cranston and Curts, 1857.

Zimmerman, Charles. "The Origin and Rise of the Republican Party in Indiana from 1854 to 1860." *Indiana Magazine of History* 13 (3) (Sept. 1917): 211–69, 349–412.

Index

Individuals' roles and/or their relationship to Rev. Tarkington are noted parenthetically.

Anglican Church, 1, 164n4. *See also* Episcopal church

Anthony, Susan B., 133

Arminianism, 6, 11, 54. *See also* Grace; Pietism

Asbury, Bp. Francis, 12, 19, 22, 23–24, 68, 114, 127, 179–80n9. *See also* Bishops, Methodist; Methodist; Methodist church

Ashworth, Rev. Moses, 32, 35, 172n27. *See also* Methodism, "fathers" of

Attire. *See* Dress

Awash in a Sea of Faith (by Jon Butler), 156

Banking/banks, 41. *See also* Currency; Economy

Bankruptcy Act of 1841, 184n42

Baptism: immersion vs. sprinkling, 1; and Ohio River tragedy, 96–97. *See also* Conversion; Religious experience; Salvation

Baptist church/Baptists, 4, 21, 22, 29, 48, 79, 129, 165n22. *See also* Calvinism

Barter system, 40; *See also* Currency, alternate forms of; Economy

Beecher, Rev. Lyman, 6

Behavior, problematic. *See* Alcohol; Immorality, Preachers, misconduct of; Sociocultural issues

Bethel Meeting House [Indiana], 33, 34. *See also* Churches; Circuit riders; Worship services

Bible, 8, 26, 35, 46, 74, 108, 118. *See also* Parables; Scriptures

Bishops, Methodist, 3, 95, 101, 102, 105, 128, 129, 179n9. *See also* Asbury, Francis; Roberts, Robert Richford

Blacks. *See* African Americans

Books, xvi, 72, 73, 84, 108, 112. *See also* Bible; Catechism; *The Methodist Discipline*; Novels; Poetry

Boone, Daniel, 177n23

Booth, Elizabeth, 199

Booth family, background of, 189–90n1

Booth Tarkington Collection, xvi. *See also* Tarkington, Newton Booth

Brook Farm commune, 112. *See also* Communes

Burial. *See* Funerals

Busroe [Bushrun] settlement, 13, 14, 39. *See also* Shakers

Calling, divine, 3, 12. *See also* Ch. 4, 51–65; Conversion; Religious experience; Salvation

Calvinism/Calvinists, 6, 11, 22, 48. *See also* Baptist church/Baptists

Camp meetings, xv–xvi, 4, 7, 37, 46, 65, 103, 166n58; "birth" of, at Cane Ridge, Kentucky, 5, 165n35; as central to social life, 7; decline of, 110, 188n15; interdenominational, 5, 47; opposition to, 6–7. *See also* Circuit riders; Preaching; Religious experience; Sermons; Worship services

Cane Ridge revival, 5–6, 165n35. *See also* Revivalism

Capitalism, 116. *See also* Economy, free market

Carey, Mary Stewart (granddaughter, Indiana philanthropist), 190–91n4

Cartwright, Rev. Peter (lifelong friend), 3, 11, 14, 16, 30, 127, 128, 165n32

Catechism, 36. *See also* Sabbath school; Sunday school

Celibacy, 68. *See also* Courtship; Marriage, delayed; Sex/sexuality

Checks on Calvinism, 48

Children: and absent fathers, 80–81; intoxicated, 27; as preachers, 103–4

Cholera, 71, 82–83, 98, 99–100. *See also* Disease; Home remedies; Sanitation

Christ, second coming of, 14, 26

Christian Advocate and Journal, 117

Churches: construction and design of,

32, 97, 33–34, 114, 115, 157;
multidenominational, 34–35. *See also*
names of individual denominations
*Circuit Rider, The: A Tale of the Heroic
Age*, 1
Circuit riders, xii, xiv, xv; decline of,
117; and delayed marriage, 66–68;
dress of, 11–12; education and
training of, 3; hardships, 9, 17, 59,
61–62, 79; and Methodist hierarchy,
3; mocking of, 49; on "preacher's
day," 10; salesmanship of, 2. *See also*
Ch. 2, 7, and 8, 29–37, 95–118;
Camp meetings; Circuits; Preachers;
Sermons; Worship services
Circuits: first in Indiana, 32, 35; listed,
16–17, 35, 159–61; scope of, 9, 17,
64, 102, 110. *See also* Circuit riders;
Methodism; Methodist church
Circus, Methodist opposition to, 87–88,
184n49. *See also* Amusements
Civil War, 130, 157. *See also* Ch. 9, 119–
35; Abolition; Lincoln, Abraham;
Slavery
Class meetings, 51, 111. *See also* Circuit
riders; Worship services, in homes
Clay, Henry, 127
Clergy. *See* Bishops; Methodist church,
hierarchy of; Ministers; Preachers
Clinton, De Witt, 116
Clothing. *See* Dress
Colleges and universities, 86–87, 125.
See also Education; names of
individual institutions; Religious
education; Seminaries
Colonists, 28, 121, 127. *See also*
Abolition; Slavery
Communes, 59, 112, 178n46
*Confession of Faith of the Presbyterian
Church*, 48
Congregationalism, 2, 150
Congregations, Methodist: described,
11–12; female, 69; members expelled,
31, 49, 134. *See also* Laity, Methodist;

Methodism; Methodist church;
Worship services
Continental Congress, 28
Conversion, 4, 6, 47, 103; forced, 8–9;
See also Religious experience;
Revivalism; Salvation
Courtship, 66, 68, 70, 74. *See also*
Celibacy; Marriage, delayed; Sex/
sexuality
Credit, 41. *See also* Banking; Currency;
Economy
Creek Indians, 24
Crime, 23, 64. *See also* Sex/sexuality, and
sexual offenses; Violence
Crockett, David, 23
Currency: alternate forms of, 40, 59, 64;
shortage of, 12, 40, 64. *See also*
Banking; Credit; Economy

Dancing, 45. *See also* Amusements
Deism, 54
Delaware Indians, 39
Democratic Party, 132
DePauw, Newland T., 153
DePauw University, xvi, 182n7
Devil, belief in, 6, 114, 150. *See also* Evil
Disease, 82, 131, 183n17; as punishment
for sin, 82, 83. *See also* Cholera;
Home remedies; Sanitation; Typhoid;
Whooping cough; Yellow fever
Doctors. *See* Physicians
Doctrine, Methodist. *See* Methodism;
Methodist church; *The Methodist
Discipline*; Wesley, John
Dred Scott Decision, 124, 128. *See also*
Abolition; Emancipation; Slavery
Dress, 45, 96, 113–14. *See also* Circuit
riders, dress of; Preachers, dress of;
Pioneers, typical
Dualism, 8

Earthquakes: described, 25–26; New
Madrid, 24; and religious revivals, 25.
See also Natural disasters; Revivalism

Methodist church in, 33; frontier, xv, 4; population, 17, 28, 65; in "state of war," 39; statehood, xi–xiii; and slavery, 28. *See also* Ch. 2, 29–37
Indiana Asbury University, xiii, 67, 86, 96, 132. *See also* Simpson, Matthew
Indiana College, 86
Indiana Historical Society, xv
Indiana Methodism, 149
Indiana Weekly Visitor, 134
Indianapolis Journal, 138, 155
Indians: attacks on pioneers, xi, xvi, 36, 39–40; battle U.S. Army, 27; Creek, 24; Delaware, 39; horse stealing, 21, 24; Miami, 39; Shawnee, 36, 39; treaties with, 40; U.S. protection of, 172n7. *See also* Frontier life; Pioneers
Itinerants, xiv–xv. *See also* Circuit riders

Jackson, Andrew, 166
Jefferson, Thomas, 54
Jeffersonians, 2

Kansas-Nebraska Act of 1854, 116, 124, 128
Kentucky, 5. *See also* Cane Ridge revival
Kentucky in Liberia Society, 127

Laity, Methodist, 3, 109. *See also* Congregations, Methodist
Lakin, Rev. Benjamin, 29, 30, 164n7
Land: clearing of, 43–44; disputes, 24; Louisiana Purchase, 124; "New Purchase," 28, 173n13, 14; "school," 39. *See also* Farmers/farming; Frontier life
Language, immoral, 31, 44–45. *See also* Immorality; Preachers, misconduct of
Lees, Ann, 14. *See also* Shakers
Lincoln, Abraham, 113, 128, 130, 133, 135, 144. *See also* Abolition; Civil War; Emancipation; Slavery

Mail service, 63, 178n60

Marriage: complex system of, 112; delayed, 66; as a sin, 14. *See also* Frontier life; Sex/sexuality; Tarkington, Rev. Joseph, Marriage and family life; Tarkington, Maria, Marriage and family life
Maryland, xi, 20
Mather, Cotton, 69
McKendree, William ("father" of western Methodism), 171n4
Media, 117–18. *See also* Newspapers
Meeting houses. *See* Camp meetings; Churches; Class meetings
Men: and male/female spheres, 70. *See also* Courtship; Farmers/farming; Marriage; Sex/sexuality
Methodism: "curing" of, 26; "fathers" of, 171n4, 177n25; "oldstyle," 27; and pietism, xiv–xv; and post-millennialism, 169n42; from sect to denomination, xiii, xiv, xvi, 1. *See also* Bishops; Circuit riders; Methodist church; *Methodist Discipline; Wesley, John; Western Christian Advocate*
Methodist church/Methodists, xi–xiv, 21; as church for "plain folks," 2, 19–20, 26; and criticism of the war effort, 134; and dispute over organ purchase, 114–15; growth of, xiv, 2, 4, 7, 19, 26, 31, 36, 65, 86, 88, 102, 156; hierarchy of, xiv, 3, 16, 31, 57, 84; in Indiana, xv–xvi, 4, 29, 31, 32, 33; North-South split within, 120, 125, 128–29; and "radical secession," 66; and rival denominations, 13, 14, 79, 98; and slavery issue, 88, 120–25; in Tennessee, xvi, 5, 23, 177n20. *See also* Congregations, Methodist; Indiana Asbury University; Methodism; *Methodist Discipline; Wesley, John; Western Christian Advocate*
Methodist Discipline, The, 12, 36, 48, 57, 74, 126–27, 164n15

Slawson, Simeon (brother-in-law), 181n20

Slawson family: as antislavery views of, 135; background of, 180n18; children's names listed, 181n20; "cultured" family, 82; on Indiana farm, 70–71, 72, 82, 88–89; in New York, 70. *See also* Slawson, Simeon; Tarkington, Maria Slawson (wife of Rev. Joseph Tarkington)

Smith, David Tarkington, xxi

Social classes, xv, 109. *See also* Egalitarianism; Immigrants; Sociocultural issues

Sociocultural issues, 12, 90, 157. *See also* Alcohol; Crime; Disease; Education; Immorality; Slavery/slaves; Social classes

Spiritualism, 112–13. *See also* Religious experience

Stanton, Elizabeth Cady, 133

Steventon, John (pseudonym of John S. Tarkington), 182n7, 185n52

Stewart, Daniel (son-in-law), 119, 131

Stone, Barton W. (leader of Cane Ridge revival), 5, 49

Stowe, Harriet Beecher, 112

Sunday school, 111, 115. *See also* Children, education of; Class meetings; Education, religious; Sabbath school

Superstition, 150

Tallmadge Amendment, 124

Tarkington, Booth. *See* Tarkington, Newton Booth

Tarkington, Bowler (foster son), 131, 146

Tarkington, Burton (brother), 27

Tarkington, Clare Williams Baker (daughter-in-law), 120

Tarkington, Elizabeth Booth (daughter-in-law), 119

Tarkington, Ellen Maria (daughter), 101, 136–37, 161

Tarkington, Elva Meridith Yeatman (daughter-in-law), 119

Tarkington, George (brother), 44

Tarkington, Hardin (brother), 64

Tarkington, Jesse (brother), 41

Tarkington, Jesse (father), 21, 22, 24, 39, 41, 60–61, 137. *See also* Tarkington, Mary ("Polly")

Tarkington, John (great-great-grandfather), xx, 20

Tarkington, John Stevenson (son), 81, 89, 95, 98, 99, 102, 104, 119, 131, 182n7, 185n52

Tarkington, Rev. Joseph

— Ancestors, xi, xx, 20, 82, 167n1. *See also* Tarkington, Jesse (father); Tarkington, Mary ("Polly") (mother)

—Attitudes: toward abolition, 121, 128, 129; toward African Americans, 19, 27; toward alcohol, xvi, 19, 49, 91; toward amusements, xvi, 87–88, 151; women, 85, 111

—Autobiography, xii, xv, 48; diaries/journals, 147, 152

—Bachelorhood, xii, xv, xvi, 65, 70, 72–75; proposes to Maria Slawson, 74

—Birth and early life: birth of, 19; childhood Baptism of, 22; describes moves to new homes, 38, 41–43. *See also* Ch. 1, 19–28

—Chronology of life, 159–61

—Death and burial, 154–55

—Health/illnesses, 83, 87, 98–99, 143, 147–49

—Marriage and family life: as absentee father, 70; anecdotes about children, 88, 89, 90; children's names and birthdates listed, 160, 161; children's spouses, 119; daughter Ellen's death, 136; daughter Martha's crippling injury; 137; as demanding father, xvi; describes wedding trip, 77; family relations, xviii; fiftieth wedding anniversary, 146–47; foster son,